THE GLOBAL
ACTIVIST'S MANUAL

THE GLOBAL
ACTIVIST'S MANUAL
Local Ways to Change the World

Mike Prokosch and Laura Raymond
(United for a Fair Economy)

Thunder's Mouth Press/Nation Books
New York

THE GLOBAL ACTIVIST'S MANUAL: *Local Ways to Change the World*

Published by
Thunder's Mouth Press/Nation Books
161 William St., 16th Floor
New York, NY 10038

Nation Books is a co-publishing venture of the Nation Institute and Avalon Publishing Group Incorporated.

Library of Congress Cataloging-in-Publication Data is available for this title.

ISBN 1-56025-401-7

9 8 7 6 5 4 3 2

Book design by Michael Walters
Printed in the United States of America
Distributed by Publishers Group West

Contents

THE GLOBAL
ACTIVIST'S MANUAL

What is This Movement?

Introduction

Naomi Klein

This movement began five hundred years ago or on November 30, 1999, depending on who you ask. I prefer the idea that it ebbs and flows, lies dormant for years, then rushes back onto the scene in a brand new outfit and under an assumed name.

Many of the campaigns and organizations featured in this book trace their beginnings back to the early nineties fight against the North American Free Trade Agreement. It was during this massive lobbying effort that the Minnesota Fair Trade Campaign got started, as well as the Citizen's Trade Campaign. It was then that the first signs of a coalition emerged among organized labor, environmentalists, farmers and consumer groups. And it was on January 1, 1995, the day NAFTA became law, that the Zapatistas fatefully said the words that ended the era of polite lobbying and ushered in the new era of direct action: "Ya Basta!"

But the fight against free trade looked different during the NAFTA years. Most of us thought these were battles distinct to our nations. In the United States, workers worried that Mexicans would steal away jobs and drive down environmental standards. In Canada, we worried that closer ties with the United States would Americanize us. And all the while, the voices of Mexicans opposed to the deal were off the public radar.

Only a few years later, the debate over trade, and over our economic destiny in general, has been transformed. The fight against globalization has morphed into a struggle against corporatization and, for some, against capitalism itself, certainly in its current unregulated form. Maude Barlow, director of the Council of Canadians, spearheaded the free-trade fight twelve years ago. Since then, she's been working with organizers from other countries and with anarchists suspicious of nationalism in her own country. Her post-NAFTA experience has had

> **Global democratic deficit**
>
> We have to acknowledge that there are issues here. There is a global democratic deficit which now manifests itself in various forms through environmental, economic, and social protest and we have to face that fact. . . . These protesters have unwittingly hit upon something which has become one of the major questions of our time: How do large institutions such as the World Trade Organization, the International Monetary Organization [sic], and the World Bank deal with global issues which effect [sic] our world today? Some of the people at the top of such organizations wield great power but nobody knows who they are. Who elects them? And they are unaccountable to us.
>
> —*Don Cruickshank, chairman of the London Stock Exchange and of SMG (owners of the* Herald, Sunday Herald, *Scottish Television, and Grampian), quoted in Kenny Kemp,* "London Stock Exchange Chief Backs Anti-Capitalists," Sunday Herald UK, *May 7, 2000.*

a profound effect. "I've changed," she told me. "I used to see this fight as saving a nation. Now I see it as saving democracy." And that is a fight that transcends nationhood.

At the WTO protests in Seattle, it was the Teamsters and turtles who got most of the attention, but there were many equally remarkable coalitions. Mexican textile workers and U.S. steelworkers were marching together; so were Indian farmers and Filipino peasants and French cheese makers. And all over, there were young people from across Europe and North American declaring that they too were Zapatistas. It's a favorite tactic of the Right to paint the protesters as "protectionists"—selfish Westerners wanting to hoard the goodies of free trade for themselves. But the real news out of Seattle was that organizers around the world were beginning to see their local and national struggles—for better funded public schools, against union-busting and casualization, for family farms, and against the widening gap between rich and poor—through a new global lens.

So how did we get here? Who or what convened this new international people's movement? Who sent out the memos? Who built these complex coalitions? The short answer is that a handful of multinationals did it, albeit by accident. Thanks to the sheer imperialist ambition of the corporate project at this moment in history—the boundless drive for profit, liberated by trade deregulation, and the wave of mergers and buy-outs, liberated by weakened antitrust laws—corporations have grown so blindingly rich, so diverse in their holdings, so transnational in their reach, that they have created our coalitions for us.

Around the world, activists are piggybacking on the ready-made infrastructure of global corporations. This can mean cross-border unionizing (page 54), but also cross-sector organizing—among workers, environmentalists, consumers, even prisoners. Thanks to Monsanto, farmers in India are working with environmentalists in Britain and consumers around the world to develop direct-action strategies that cut off genetically modified foods in the fields and in the supermarkets. Thanks to Shell Oil and Chevron, human rights activists in Nigeria, artists in Europe, and environmentalists in North America have united in a fight against the unsustainability of the oil industry. And thanks to catering giant Sodexho-Marriott Services' decision to invest in the Corrections Corporation of America, university students are able to protest America's exploding for-profit prison industry simply by boycotting the food in their campus cafeteria (page 68).

It is Nike, however, that has done the most to pioneer this new brand of activist synergy: Students facing the corporate takeover of their campuses by the swoosh have linked up with workers making their branded campus apparel, as well as with parents concerned about the commercialization of youth, with unions and with church groups campaigning against child labor—all united by their different relationships to a common brand. Exposing the underbelly of high-gloss consumer brands has provided the early narratives of this movement, a call-and-response to the very different narratives these companies tell about themselves through advertising and public relations every day.

The ins and outs of several of these investigative, name-naming campaigns are discussed in this handbook, as are many others: Rio

Tinto, Kaiser Aluminum, Fidelity Investment, British Petroleum, General Electric. Some campaigns don't target a logo but x-ray an industry, such as coffee (page 216). A new coalition, meanwhile, has decided to piggyback on the Citigroup/Citibank brand, precisely because, as North America's largest financial institution, it does business with some of the worst corporate renegades around (page 169). If this initiative takes off, it will handily knit together dozens of issues—from clearcut logging in California to an oil and pipeline project in Chad and Cameroon—into one meta-campaign.

The value of focusing on corporations, as opposed to the more traditional activist route of focusing on pieces of legislation, is that through this tactic, organizers are able to graphically show how so many issues of social, ecological, and economic justice are interconnected. From there, it's only a few short steps to the doorsteps of the World Bank and World Trade Organization—and who knows where after that. These campaigns are only a start, and no activist I've met believes that the world economy can be changed one corporation at a time, but the campaigns have opened a door into the arcane world of international trade and finance. "It's a gateway drug," Oregon student activist Sarah Jacobson told me.

But if anti-corporate campaigns are the doorways, it is the human connections made along the way that have kept those doors open. Through the Shell campaign, the world met Ken Saro-Wiwa, one of the men who was murdered by the Nigerian military dictatorship in 1995 because he dared to protest Shell Oil's ravaging of the Niger Delta. Through the Nike campaign, thousands met Cicih Sukaesih, who lost her job for organizing a wildcat strike at a Nike factory, and took her story on the road, telling it in schools and meeting halls across North America and Europe. We hear similar stories of human connections over and over again in this handbook. About how it was only when JoAnn Greene, a U.S. factory worker, traveled to Mexico to meet fellow workers that she began to look past protectionist rage at "those damn Mexicans" to see a common struggle against corporate greed (page 000). And it was not until antisweatshop activist Marion Traub-Werner left her U.S. campus to live in Guatemala that she realized maquila workers were much more than victims in need of good-hearted charity (page 194). "As our grassroots campaigns continue," she writes, "we need to focus on the diversity of maquila women's and girls' experiences and exchange images of helpless victims with solid partnerships."

Hundreds of human connections like these paved the way to Seattle, connections that showed that "The New Economy" is not abstract; it is a collection of stories about people's real lives. It was this process that made globalization real to tens of thousands of people, kidnapping it from the wonkish domain of Washington think tanks and turning it into a street movement.

But in part because of the movement's momentum since Seattle—barreling on towards one mass mobilization after another, in Washington, Philadelphia, Los Angeles, Prague—the discussions have lost some of their early humanity. We see ourselves too often as masses of people and lose sight of those individual stories and personal connections that make up a mass. We are "activists," not organizers, neighbors, students, workers. The people involved in this movement tend to understand the connections binding together their various causes intuitively. To outsiders, however, the mere scope of modern protests can be a little bit mystifying. Eavesdropping on this movement from the outside—which is what most people do—one often hears a cacophony of seemingly disjointed slogans, a laundry list of grievances without clear goals.

It doesn't help that the decentralized, nonhierarchical structure of this movement makes it extremely unfriendly to traditional media. There are no tightly organized press conferences, no single charismatic leadership, and protests tend to pile on top of each other. Rather than looking like a pyramid, with leaders up on top and followers down below, it looks more like an elaborate web.

In part, this web-like structure is the result of Internet-based organizing. But it is also a response to the very political realities that sparked the protests in the first place: the total failure of traditional party politics. As Patrick Bond points out, all over the world citizens have

maquila (mah kee' lah, fr. Sp. "maquiladora"): a light assembly factory, usu. for apparel or electronic products. Syn: sweatshop.

worked to elect social democratic and workers parties, only to watch them plead helplessness in the face of market forces and IMF dictates. Modern activists lack the political naïveté necessary to believe that change will come through electoral politics, which is why most are more interested in challenging the structures that make democracy toothless—the IMF's structural adjustment policies, the WTO's ability to override national and state laws, corrupt campaign financing—than in sweating to get their guy into the White House.

But the questions remain: Does this movement have a positive vision of what it is *for* as well as agreement about what it is *against*?

The failure of traditional politics

Many leaders and political parties of Second and Third World societies who at one point (at least momentarily) had carried the aspirations of a mass-popular electorate, confronted globalization during the 1980s–90s, rapidly reversed allegiance, and imposed ineffectual and terribly unpopular structural adjustment programmes. Very different circumstances prevailed, amidst very different ideologies, but this fate befell, amongst others, Aquino (Philippines), Arafat (Palestine), Aristide (Haiti), Bhutto (Pakistan), Chiluba (Zambia), Dae Jung (South Korea), Havel (Czech Republic), Manley (Jamaica), Megawati (Indonesia), Musoveni (Uganda), Mugabe (Zimbabwe), Nujoma (Namibia), Ortega (Nicaragua), Perez (Venezuela), Rawlings (Ghana), Walesa (Poland), and Yeltsin (Russia). The trend was just as pronounced in labour and social democratic parties in Western Europe, Canada, and Australia, and even where once-revolutionary parties remained in control of the nation-state—China, Vietnam, Angola, and Mozambique, for instance—ideologies wandered over to hard, raw capitalism.
—*Patrick Bond, "Can Thabo Mbeki change the world?" Frantz Fanon Inaugural Memorial Lecture, University of Durban-Westville School of Governance, August 17, 2000, p. 4.*

How can it move from symbolic victories to deeper, more lasting structural change? Perhaps as well as continuing to organize "The Next Seattle," we should pause to ask these soul-searching questions. In fact many already are. And it's not outside intellectuals who are being commissioned to do the work—no one is being locked up in a library like Karl Marx and given a deadline to write the movement manifesto. Rather, it's the activists themselves—on college campuses, in union locals, in independent media centers, in this very book—that are turning their attention to this tremendously exciting intellectual project.

This is a movement that has declared that it has "no followers, only leaders." We have seen what thousands of leaders can achieve on the streets, from Seattle to Prague. Now we are about to see if we are equally capable of inventing new democratic mechanisms for developing a true agenda and vision for this movement, while still respecting the principles of decentralization and radical democracy that have formed its foundations.

What is there to report so far? This process looks like nothing we've seen before. Rather than handing down manifestos from on high, the task has become a process of identifying the key ideological threads—the shared principles—that bind together this web of activism. Self-determination is clearly one. Democracy another. So is freedom and, more specifically, the right to plan and manage our own communities based on human needs as part of a larger global community: globalism and localism in balance.

The seeds of an agenda for this movement lie in these very old ideas and the imperative to rescue them from their status as empty political platitudes and advertising slogans. All around the world, citizens are watching power and control shift to points further and further away from their communities; we are all losing the power to plan our economies. We are all dealing with unwanted directives to slash taxes, privatize, deregulate—whether these are overt quid pro quos coming from the IMF, or the more underhanded threats to richer countries coming from the bond market, and the OECD (see Glossary, page 309). On smaller scales, these are the same fights for self-determination and sustainability against World Bank dams, clearcut logging, and resource extraction on contested native lands, and of families and co-ops losing their farms to Monsanto and Cargill.

If the crisis of democracy and erosion of self-determination is what unites the movement in protest, then there is also a common element to the spirit of many of those protests. More and more, activists are reclaiming privatized resources for the public good, sometimes by force. Students are kicking ads out of the classrooms. European ravers are throwing "Reclaim the Streets" parties in the middle of intersections. Landless Thai peasants are planting vegetables on golf courses. Bolivian citizens are overturning the privatization of their water system. British environmentalists are uprooting genetically modified test crops. Kids are trading art and music with each other on the Internet. All are reclaiming a few saved spaces—pieces of our ecology, social fabric, and culture that are outside the reach of commercialism, that are not building blocks for multinationals to play with.

In other words, the news is good. The vision for this movement we are all looking for is already here, under the surface. It lies in universal human values that reach across industries, sectors, and across national borders. Our task is not to invent a movement from scratch; it is simply to learn to better recognize the one we already have, to strengthen the threads of connection.

A movement based on clearly articulated principles of self-determination and democracy will not be all things to all people. For instance, such a movement would never see a union leader in the United States sharing a stage with Republican politicians railing against Chinese workers stealing "our" jobs—even if such a short-term coalition could block an unwanted trade bill. Instead, as Angela Sanbrano argues, it would become a fiercely pro-immigration movement, fighting for the rights of workers to cross borders freely and without criminalization (page 58).

As the threads connecting this movement are strengthened with sharper arguments and clearer analysis, organizers will still face criticism from those waiting for a single political party along with a single manifesto and a cabinet of charismatic leaders. They will be faced with tens of thousands of leaders telling their own stories of globalization, as well as a man in the mountains of Chiapas who never takes off his ski mask. Instead of one vision in the form of a manifesto, there will be a kind of vision-jam, a layering of voices and ideas, tangents that veer off in unexpected directions, and an ever-widening web.

It may be a little messier than the movements of the past, but it's going to make for a much more interesting ride.

Naomi Klein is the author of No Logo: Taking Aim at the Brand Bullies *(Picador).*

Localizing the Globalization Movement

Mike Prokosch

Many of us in the U.S. globalization movement support sweatshop workers and labor rights, indigenous peasants and environmental justice—in the developing world. In the United States, those are "domestic issues" and those people belong to different movements.

Global apartheid explains where this peculiar idea came from and shows us a way through it.

In "Global Apartheid" (*The Nation,* July 9, 2001) Salih Booker and William Minter named the global economy as a new system of apartheid by race, gender, class, and place. Apartheid by place enriches nations like the United States, but nationhood is superficial. Look deeper and you see the other apartheids running through us.

Who should lead the U.S. globalization movement? Should its public face be white, young, middle-class, or should those most affected represent the movement?

> *African-Americans didn't have to go to Seattle to fight globalization. If you go to Mossville, Louisiana, globalization is literally ten to fifteen feet outside of your front door, where a multinational petrochemical industrial complex is spewing industrial pollution on you and your children.*
> —Kim Freeman

Before September 11, 2001 these questions were urgent. Now they're inescapable. Our time frame now is of years, not months. We must build a far broader movement with leadership from the people who need change most.

For more articles and thoughts on this subject, visit www.globalroots.net.

-Mike Prokosch coordinates the globalization program at United for a Fair Economy.

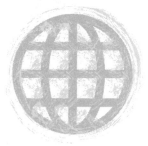

Crossing Borders

The articles in this section show the transforming power of cross-border work.

Crossing borders transforms individuals. It creates people who are willing to stand up for people of other races and places.

Crossing borders transforms organizations. It inoculates them against xenophobia and protectionism.

It transforms movements. In Seattle, thousands of Teamsters, Turtles, and youth crossed the social borders that isolated them. The movement is still running on the energy they released by breaking through class and cultural taboos.

Border-crossing organizations cleared the way for the globalization movement. Some, like the Coalition for Justice in the Maquiladoras, inspired new waves of labor and women's solidarity in the Southwest. Meanwhile, the Central America movement helped create the anti-sweatshop movement (p. 197), SOA Watch (p. 48), and many faith-based projects (p. 44, 215).

We have plenty of borders to cross at home. Crossing them will strengthen us as it strengthened the civil rights warriors of the 1960s. But we need to go abroad too, because we are trying to build a global movement. The sooner we start meeting our partners, the sooner we will learn how much we need their clarity and determination.

—Mike Prokosch

Building a Movement on Both Sides of the Border

Tennessee Workers Organize for Fair Trade
Kristi Disney

From 1985 to 1989, the state of Tennessee lost over two hundred thousand manufacturing jobs due to automation, corporate mergers, and capital flight to the south of the U.S. border. Many displaced manufacturing workers moved into the service sector where there are fewer unions, lower wages, fewer benefits, and low job security.

The Tennessee Industrial Renewal Network (TIRN) was launched to respond to these trends. Workers, labor unions, community groups, religious leaders, and public officials studied ways to keep decent jobs in their communities at a June 1989 conference. One of their first programs was worker-to-worker exchanges.

Following the money

There was much talk, anger, and misunderstanding among workers whose jobs were moving to Mexico. Workers wanted to see the factories that had moved from Tennessee to Mexico and to meet with the workers who were "taking their jobs." In July of 1991, nine women from TIRN made a six-day trip to the cities of Matamoros and Reynosa. The delegation was hosted by the Coalition for Justice in the Maquiladoras and the Comite Fronterizo de Obreras (Border Committee of Women Workers or CFO). It made sense

TIRN works on issues of fair trade and economic justice. It includes nearly forty labor, community, religious, environmental, student, and other organizations. Since 1994 it has organized work in geographically based membership clusters while maintaining statewide committees for joint work on such issues as fair trade. TIRN supports coalition work on a range of justice issues and belongs to several state, regional, national, and international networks.

for the delegation to consist of women because the maquila workforce in the Matamoros-Reynosa area was overwhelmingly female, and the CFO was interested in connecting with women workers from the United States. It is also women, both in the United States and in Mexico, who are concentrated in the lowest-paid factory jobs and are often most vulnerable when work is contracted out or factories threaten to relocate.

The Tennessee delegation toured factories and community groups in the maquiladoras. They learned why so many corporations move south of the border and so many Mexicans strive to find work in the north. Members of the delegation began to build meaningful solidarity with the workers in Mexico. They also began to ask questions about Latinas and Latinos working in their Tennessee communities. They came home with an understanding that the bad guy was not the Mexican worker in the factory across the border, but the corporations who were driving down wages and worker rights on both sides of the border. Tennessee workers also became aware of the huge gaps between the working conditions and wages paid in Mexico and in Tennessee.

"There I was, just raising hell about 'them damn Mexicans,' " said JoAnn Greene, who worked for thirty years for Magnavox, then for its successor, Philips Electronics. "It was right after the contract my union negotiated with Phillips, a contract that really shafted me royally. They had used the threat of taking our jobs to Mexico to get a rotten, two-tier contract, and I was mad." Then in August of 1994, JoAnn went on a worker exchange to Juarez. "I guess the word would be devastated. Me, growing up in the mountains of east Tennessee, growing up as poor as I was, we didn't have a bathroom, we didn't have running water. I mean, hell, we was dirt poor, let's face it. We carried our drinking water for almost three miles. Then to go down there to see people that are poorer than I was! I really turned away from Mexico with a respect for those people, a respect that I have tried to share with everybody I meet. Those people may not have anything by our standards, but they've got spirit, they've got dignity, they make it day by day by their faith in God. You just can't help but respect people like that."

They understood that the corporations were taking advantage of low wages and relaxed labor and environmental standards in Mexico. They shared their knowledge with friends, unions, community groups, churches, the press, U.S. trade representatives, and members of Congress.

A critical move after this first visit was to form a Fair Trade Committee, which served as a strategic organizing location for TIRN members and staff. From the first exchange we started learning about NAFTA, the North American Free Trade Agreement. The committee developed testimony, slide shows, and materials to describe the dangers of NAFTA. The committee also responded to solidarity requests from workers organizing in Mexico by writing letters to corporations, sending resources to Mexican activists, and hosting workers engaged in specific organizing struggles.

Worker exchanges in one direction or another have followed almost every year since 1991. In 2000, besides hosting a labor leader from Mexico's Frente Autentico del Trabajo (Authentic Worker's Front or FAT), TIRN hosted a delegation from the Cuban Workers Confederation to fight the United States embargo on Cuba.

Supporting the self-organization of immigrants

Not long after TIRN's exchange program began in the early 1990s, Tennesseans saw more and more Latin American workers coming for agricultural work and work in poultry processing plants. People

James Harrell, an organizer for the United Paperworkers International Union in Memphis, Tennessee, also attended the exchange. He said: "I just can't believe that people who are working over forty-eight hours a week in a U.S.-owned factory are living in some of the conditions that I saw in Ciudad Juarez. We have got to get together across what divides us—borders, race, religion, profession—and do something to stop people from getting poorer while companies get richer off of what they tell us is necessary to compete in the global market. What they say is free trade, I see as a free trade ride for a few, with the workers and their children having to pay the price."

Luvernel Clark, a Knoxville resident who has worked in an automotive seat belt factory since 1971, told how she became interested in a worker exchange trip: "I first heard of TIRN from my union. I was in the office one day, and somebody brought a bunch of pictures from the maquila plants down on the Mexico border. He was showing me pictures of the Allied Signal plant—Allied Signal is where I worked—and those pictures got my attention." Barbara Knight, Chairperson of TIRN's Board of Directors and the Vice President of International Union of Electrical Workers Local 796, summed up her experience by saying, "What this is all about is workers here [in Mexico] and in Tennessee fighting the same greedy corporations."

were coming particularly from Mexico as NAFTA, the peso devaluation, and other neoliberal changes devastated certain Mexican communities. These workers are taking the most back-breaking, dirty, and low-paying jobs in the local economy, jobs that most local workers will not fill. But some communities protested the presence of "those Mexicans" in their neighborhood.

In one community, four hundred residents signed a petition and marched to protest a Head Start center being developed in their community for the children of migrant workers. A barn belonging to the owner of the property being leased for the center was burned down. TIRN members who had gone on the worker exchanges were among the strongest to respond and defend immigrants' rights. They talked to preachers in the area, sat in booths at fairs, and talked in their workplaces. At church, the workplace, and home they continue to draw on their own cross-border experiences and speak up against immigrant-bashing.

In 1991, TIRN became actively involved in a fight against the North American Free Trade Agreement. This fight naturally followed for the Tennessee workers who had experienced factory relocations and the exchange in the maquiladoras. TIRN mobilized over five hundred people from union, church, peace, and environmental organizations in six congressional districts in public rallies, forums, and motorcades. We sponsored a speaking tour with a Canadian auto worker and a leader of the FAT. Although Congress did not block the passage of NAFTA, working against the agreement introduced us to many new allies. TIRN thanks NAFTA not for its neoliberal policies, but for giving us the opportunity to build a more international movement for economic justice.

In 1995, TIRN sponsored a statewide "after NAFTA" tour by Mexican and U.S. fair trade activists who described NAFTA's failures in public forums and the media. Similar activities followed in 1999 when NAFTA reached its fifth anniversary.

In 1997 and 1998 TIRN led two statewide campaigns against "Fast Track" trade negotiating authority and organized against treaties affecting Africa and the Caribbean. In 1999 we sent over forty-five demonstrators to the World Trade Organization protests in Seattle and organized our own IMF/World Bank protests in Tennessee in April 2000. These actions helped bring students and environmental activists into our campaign and broadened our base of action. TIRN has also been involved in actions and campaigns involving over thirty plant closings in our state.

Democratic organization

Tennessee workers are the backbone and the brain of TIRN. They have seen the movement of their assembly lines, their jobs, and their plants across national borders. They have acknowledged the growing Latina and Latino communities in their own backyards. They know that these are global issues. Working women and men, with representatives of key organizations that TIRN works with, make up our Board of Directors. This Board guides our activities and keeps us in touch with what is happening in their workplaces and in their organizations across the state. We build our campaigns through local actions and our worker-to-worker exchanges.

Another way that we build our base is through popular education workshops. Popular education involves listening to what people are saying about their lives and their communities. It helps people reflect and build on their own experience, identify problems and solutions, and then move to act on their insights. It values active participation and fosters relationship-building among group members as they share their knowledge and life experiences. TIRN workshops challenge people to talk about class, race, gender, and other power relationships within our regional clusters and the issue work that we do. Popular education allows people to plan their own courses of action instead of being asked to receive the "wisdom" of experts or passively follow a group leader.

Like many other organizations, we have found that people are more likely to carry out actions and remain involved when they work with others to develop action plans. We recognize the importance of theory about globalization but know that in order to be accessible to workers and to serve as an effective guide for analysis and action, theory must be rooted in the everyday lives of people. After learning what energizes people to act, we look for ways to coordinate local actions with national and international ones.

We bring people into our campaigns by reaching out to many different communities: to students, unionized and nonunionized labor, religious communities, environmental groups, and a number of local, regional, national, and international organizations. We keep people involved by sending out regular updates on our economic justice campaigns for living wages and fair trade; through popular education workshops; through actions and lobbying activities around fair trade; through worker exchanges; and through the presentations and discussions that come out of worker exchanges.

Challenges we face

When TIRN started working on fair trade issues, many people misunderstood why free trade is harmful. They had been told that free trade will prevent war and poverty. Some people were reluctant to join us on fair trade issues

TIRN's INF-World Bank protest, April 2000.

even though they had been allies on many other economic justice issues. It was people in the industrial work force who understood these issues right away and led our fair trade movement. The later failures of NAFTA helped bring nonindustrial workers, students, environmentalists, and others into our work on fair trade. Many of our Congressional representatives still don't get it, so we continue to work with them. We were saddened but wiser when six Congressional representatives who made commitments to us to vote against Fast Track turned to vote for it despite their vows.

As people hear more about the failures of free trade, education and action around fair trade becomes easier. The understanding that NAFTA failures brought made it easier to fight Fast Track and will make it easier to fight future trade treaties such as the "Free Trade Area of the Americas" that promises to spread the neoliberal policies of NAFTA.

Organizing a strong local coalition is not an easy thing to do, especially with the lack of materials, funding, and organizers in the Southern United States. Many national campaigns offer what Cheryl Brown, former fair trade organizer for TIRN, calls a "cookie-cutter approach" to organizing that often doesn't fit communities in Appalachia and the South. We need cultural translation to make actions appropriate and effective for specific communities. We have found that many people think that groups in D.C. can do all of the work, but we believe it takes locally rooted action to bring these lessons home and to lay the groundwork for a successful global movement.

The success of the WTO protests in Seattle came out of hundreds of local organizing efforts combined with national and international coordination. Despite the many challenges we face, we continue to work on the local grassroots campaigns that we find essential to building and integrating a successful global movement.

—Kristi Disney is an organizer with the Tennessee Industrial Renewal Network.

Farmers Cross Borders, Cut through Government Fog

Denise O'Brien

Family farmers are an endangered species. We are being forced off our land because the money it takes to grow crops such as corn and soybeans is more than the money we are receiving at the altar of the free market. But the problem for us is not just the low prices. We have also been undermined by propaganda from the government and the National Farm Bureau, who together try to make us believe that the problem is competition from highly subsidized farmers abroad.

Getting through that propaganda was a crucial step in forming the progressive farmers' movement of today—the movement that brought family farmers to Seattle and stood up to the U.S. Secretary of Agriculture and U.S. Trade Representatives in public hearings. What helped us cut through the propaganda? Crossing borders and actually meeting the farmers who were supposed to be our competitors.

My own experience began in the early 1980s when a French Minister of Agriculture visited my husband and me on our farm in Iowa. Arranged by Mark Ritchie, President of the Institute for Agriculture and Trade Policy (IATP), this visit and subsequent meetings held throughout the Midwest began educating small and medium-sized farmers about world trade. We began developing an analysis of how trade was being used to manipulate the farm economy to the benefit of the very few grain traders in the world.

During the farm crisis, women on farms began to understand the dynamics of world trade. Many women on farms were the bookkeepers, so they knew immediately when the debt-to-asset ratio began to shift. We were raising crops for export and yet the prices were so low that we were not able to make enough income to pay expenses. One woman farmer stated, "I know what it is like to sell raw products and not be able to put food on the table." Many women were forced off the farm

to join the workforce in the service sector that paid minimum wage and no benefits. These experiences helped develop a deeper understanding of what it is like to be a farmer in a Third World country.

In Iowa, the rural advocacy organization PrairieFire began farmer-to-farmer exchanges to strengthen their analysis of agriculture's role in world trade. We went to Germany, Belgium, and France and found out that farmers there were experiencing problems similar to ours. Low prices were driving people from the land. Once we talked face to face we began to realize that governments were pitting us against one another as the enemy, when

> *If the American public wants progress, they will have to be guinea pigs.*
>
> —U.S. Food and Drug Administration policymakers, 1998, quoted in Susan Wright, "Molecular Biology—or Molecular Politics?" GeneWatch vol. 13, no. 3 (July 2000): 13.

governmental policies were truly causing the harm.

In 1991, six of us from the National Family Farm Coalition

U.S. farmers at anti-GATT rally, Strasbourg, France, 1992.

went to Strasbourg, France, to participate in the last major rally against GATT, the General Agreement on Tariffs and Trade. Over eighty thousand farmer protesters came from all over Europe. After the rally we six visited different parts of France, staying as guests at farmers' homes and attending local farm meetings. As we heard more and more about the farm debt crisis and the high suicide rate among farmers in France, we began to make the connection to the farm crisis in the United States. "I couldn't believe that I was hearing the same stories in France that I heard in rural Vermont," said Lee Light, a dairy farmer. "Those French farmers that our government told us were highly subsidized were in fact losing their farms."

As a result of this visit, nine French farmers came to the National Family Farm Coalition's annual meeting in 1992. They discussed the GATT and deepened our analysis of agriculture as a pawn in the world of trade negotiations.

The shift in Iowa farmers' attitudes toward farmers around the

Women, food, and agriculture

Women, Food, and Agriculture Network (WFAN) came out of the United Nations 4th World Women's Conference held in Beijing, China, in 1995. I helped Kathy Lawrence, a political activist on issues of food and the environment, organize a workshop at the Beijing Conference called "The Globalization of Agriculture." Women discussed their lack of access to land and capital, the pressure from aid organizations to raise crops for export instead of local consumption, and the effect on the rural economy as men migrated to work in urban areas and women were left in care of family and crop production.

Since Beijing, WFAN has continued with international exchanges to keep educating ourselves about the situation of women farmers in different areas of the world.

In 1996 in Rome, Italy, farmers around the world met for the World Food Summit. WFAN helped sponsor a Rural Women's Workshop before the World Food Summit and we raised money for three U.S. women farmers to attend. At that three-day workshop, thirty-five women from twenty-eight countries put together a "Statement of Action" which they gave to the summit's official delegates. The statement described what women specifically needed in the realm of rural communities and agriculture:

As farming women, peasant women, and indigenous women, we demand witness to . . . our exclusion from the process of food policy deliberation and formulation at the World Food Summit. Though we are producers of at least half the world's food and preservers of most the world's food systems, our rightful democratic representation will be usurped by agribusiness and their cohorts. Twenty years ago, at the first World Food Summit (WFS), world leaders were confident that hunger would be eradicated within ten years through the promotion of high input agriculture and globalization of the marketplace.

The undeniable fact that eight hundred million people, the majority of whom are women and children, face the specter of hunger is proof enough that this plan has failed. Indeed, the policies that were advocated in 1974 have seriously disturbed the equilibrium of life systems on earth and have plunged the human race into a far more critical food crisis than ever before.

This is no surprise to us. We have lost our land to agribusiness, urbanization, and industrialization, through arbitrary and undemocratic processes. We have had our superior traditional and indigenous knowledge systems pirated by giant corporations. We have been forced to renounce our intrinsic right to propagate, improve, and preserve our seeds. We have been coerced into destroying our food systems through monocultures and the use of high, energy-intensive inputs . . . .

We cannot tolerate food insecurity. As women we believe that food *is a fundamental human right which we are obliged to ensure, it must not be trivialized simply as a source of income, a commodity, a weapon, or an object for genetic manipulation. . . .*

An alternative policy to ensure food security must include the following strategies:

The democratization of access to resources especially land, water, seed and intellectual property.

Promotion of sustainable agriculture and community-based resource management.

Establishment of local, people-based trade systems and the infrastructure thereof.

Empowerment of women through equal representation in decision-making bodies at local, regional, national, and global levels.

Access to education for women in general and girl children in particular.

Access to credit and other financial support for women.

Rural appropriate education, health, recreation, child-care, and other infrastructure support systems designed by and for rural communities with considerations to both genders.

Concede the rights of indigenous peoples of the world to their ancestral land.

We place this before you in the certainty that, as women of the land, we represent Mother Earth and therefore have the essential skills to ensure her survival and therefore the survival of all living things. Food security can only be assured when we are empowered and supported to carry out this responsibility.

neoliberalism (nee oh lib' ur ull is um): policies that shift wealth and power from the many to the few. See free trade, structural adjustment, Reaganomics.

world was apparent in September 1999 at a WTO field hearing sponsored by the U.S. Department of Agriculture in Des Moines, Iowa. Several Iowa farmers told Secretary of Agriculture Dan Glickman that they were sick and tired of hearing the U.S. government blaming the French farmers for the problems in world trade.

In the mid-1990s, farmers switched gears and went from working on GATT to working on the North American Free Trade Agreement (NAFTA). The farmer exchange extended to Canadian and Mexican farmers. Relationships with the Canadian Farmers Union and UNORCA of Mexico began to develop and deepen. Working on NAFTA really solidified the international farm movement for us in the United States.

Meanwhile, organizations such as the National Family Farm Coalition, the Rural Coalition, and the National Farmer's Union began to cross sectors in the United States and started developing relationships with labor and environmental organizations. The progressive farm movement

was too small, and within the farm sector itself there was a huge split on the disadvantages and advantages of free trade. The American Farm Bureau Federation, which claims to represent the American farmer, fully embraces the current definition of free trade. AFBF has deep pockets from their insurance industry, giving it a much louder voice in the agriculture sector than those of us who know that free trade hurts most farmers of the world. The progressive farm movement realized that in order to be heard we needed to form alliances with other movements.

During the mid-1990s, while I was president of the National Family Farm Coalition, members of the progressive farm movement joined the efforts of La Via Campesina. In an historic meeting in Tlaxcala, Mexico in April 1996, La Via Campesina laid out strategies to counter neoliberalism. Representatives from sixty-nine organizations in thirty-seven countries gathered for the second conference to respond to the "increasingly hostile environment for peasants and small farmers the world over." Before the meeting, grassroots farmers and peasants from around the world visited projects ranging from farmer cooperatives to women's craft cooperatives. Countering neoliberalism was the common thread that held these local projects together. It was obvious that political activists in the developing countries have much to teach us about globalization. Their analysis is much further along than ours. In the United States where we are living in the belly of the beast, farmers and common people have a diffi-

cult time identifying the problem. We tend to believe, naïvely, that the corporations and government work in our best interest. In the developing countries, they know the beast and call it by name.

Over the years, progressive farm leaders from the United States have been able to attend major world meetings and make statements in support of developing countries' farmers. The progressive movement of small and medium-sized farmers in the United States is hardly acknowledged by other movements within our country, but by

Community Supported Agriculture (CSA) is a strategy becoming more and more popular among smaller, mostly organic farms in the United States. Some farmers regard it as the only way they can make it in a market dominated by corporate food giants.

Usually, community members cover a farm's operating budget by paying for their produce before harvest even begins. Then they go out to the farm during harvest season, usually once or twice a week, to pick up their shares. This process directly links the farmer to the community, thus encouraging land stewardship and developing local economies. Farmers are guaranteed a market and community members are assured about the food they're eating.

To find a CSA farm near you: www.nal.usda.gov/afsic/csa.

joining farmers from all over the world we have made an impact in the fight against globalization.

The farmer internationalism of the 1980s and 1990s bore fruit in Seattle. December 3, 1999, was the food and agriculture day outside the WTO summit meeting. Local organic food was eaten, workshops were held, and a big march took place. We raised the issue of food and farming and brought the impact of globalization to the public during the weeklong gathering. Farmers made a show of solidarity with workers, environmentalists, and students around issues of genetically modified organisms, pollution, and labor rights.

—Denise O'Brien is a leader in the National Family Farm Coalition and the Women, Food, and Agriculture Network.

The Fight Against Boise Cascade

Martin Stephan

The fight against Boise Cascade (BC), an environmentalist's nightmare of a timber company, started in small towns. Destructive, irresponsible logging of old-growth forests in Oregon, Washington, and Idaho motivated local people to launch boycotts of Boise Cascade's paper products, organize rallies at company headquarters in Boise, Idaho, and write leaflets and letters about the issues to local newspapers.

Now our local organizing is becoming national and even global. Since the mid-1990s Boise Cascade has been closing mills in Idaho and moving to places like Mexico and Chile. Their unsustainable logging in Idaho has destroyed the very resources they're dependent upon, motivating them to look for other frontiers from which to profit. Cheaper workforces and lax environmental laws abroad have drawn them to the global South. We have seen the local fight move

South (also global South): the countries at the bottom of the economic heap. Synonyms: Third World, developing nations.

If you're interested in using the Freedom of Information Act get the ACLU's *A Step by Step Guide to Using the Freedom of Information Act* ($2.50 +s/h). Call ACLU Publications (800)775-ACLU or visit www.aclu.org/library.

across the border, adding a whole new element to our campaigns to protect forests.

Environmentalists go global

The American Lands Alliance and Native Forest Network began organizing and educating about Boise Cascade's proposal to build the world's largest chip mill in Chile. We knew we had to join with the Chilean activists to make our voices stronger. We've been in solidarity with them through:

E-mail and phone calls. We send them pictures of clearcut land in Idaho and tell them, "Here is what you can expect from Boise Cascade." With the help of Lighthawk, the environmental air force, we even sent a visiting Chilean up in a flight over Idaho's national forests to see the destruction firsthand. This is a way to cut through corporate rhetoric and let local people learn from local people across borders.

Keeping in touch has been really important for groups here and abroad. To succeed we need to work together and update each other on new developments in the campaign. We use each other as resources. The Chileans know their situation and the actions of BC abroad the best and they share their information. We know Boise Cascade fairly well— their headquarters are in our state—so we can share information about the corporation with the Chileans. We've built a collective watchdog and that is leading to a greater global movement.

Research. Small local groups have been working independently on Boise Cascade for years. Now we are pulling all this information together so we can show a larger pattern of abuses. We collect photos and video footage of logging in the United States and abroad, testimonials by affected people, legal documents, and we use the Freedom of Information Act (FOIA) to get information.

Education. One of the keys to this global economy movement is connecting local issues to the big

focus and not get bogged down with detail when educating people about this.

Market Campaigns. We are working with students who organize their universities to stop using old-growth forest products and switch to better paper suppliers than Boise Cascade. This tells BC that they need to change their business practices and compete for consumers who demand products that are not destroying old-growth forests. Again, the huge, negative impact that this corporation has had on Idaho and the rest of the region is a strong rallying point for these efforts.

Shareholder Activism. In recent years we have been holding outside rallies during BC's shareholder meeting. But we also have begun going inside the meeting to confront the board of directors and its CEO, George Harad. With the help of shareholders who are sympathetic to our cause and proxies that help us get into the meeting, we can actually ask tough questions directly to those in the highest positions of power at BC. This can be a very empowering experience.

picture of the global economy. That's what we're doing here with Boise Cascade. We are educating local environmentalists as well as the hunters, fishermen, outdoors people, and local people who've seen their watersheds destroyed, and we're bringing in a global perspective. We talk about what Boise has done in our backyard, make it real here first, and then say, "Now look where they're going," and tie it into their global offenses. It has required constant education. Globalization is a very complicated issue, so it's important to keep the big picture in

Most people feel quite uneasy inside a corporate setting like a shareholder meeting. The fact is,

Working for change from the inside

While some activists take their protests to the street, others are taking their concerns directly into corporate annual meetings. Held each year, annual meetings provide the opportunity to address your concerns directly with corporate leaders and assembled shareholders who sometimes number in the thousands. Annual meetings usually attract attention from journalists eager for something that reaches beyond the usually highly scripted multimedia company presentations.

Most companies restrict attendance at annual meetings to shareholders. You only need to have a single share to be admitted, but you must buy that share well ahead of time. Companies limit attendance and voting to people who held shares on the annual meeting *record* date, which is usually three months before the actual meeting.

Another way to gain attendance is to find a member or supporter who is a shareholder of the company. Ask that person to write a brief note to the corporate secretary appointing you as their personal representative and proxy at the annual meeting. The name of the corporate secretary and the date of the previous year's annual meeting can be found in the company's annual report, which in many cases is posted on their website or in hard-copy form from the company's investor relations department.

—Scott Klinger is the director of Responsible Wealth, a project of United for a Fair Economy. Its members, people whose income or wealth places them in the top five percent of the United States, speak out and take action for economic justice.

we all must change the way we think about transnational corporations like BC and realize that they were first created to serve our needs (page 173). When these corporations harm the earth we have a right to demand they stop. What better place to make those demands than at a share-holder meeting, face to face with the CEO? In addition we have brought Chileans to the share-holder meetings to speak for themselves and their backyards. These meetings tend to be very official and tightly controlled, but if your group is well prepared with questions you can speak truth to those in power.

> All of the world's forests and people are interconnected and that's how we have to organize.

Rallies and public events. We have rallied outside BC's headquarters for years. These can be great events if the community is involved in the planning. We do sign-making par-ties, phonebanks, and e-mailing. At the last rally we provided street chalk for people to write their mes-sage to BC on the sidewalk around the building. When we went inside BC's headquarters for the share-holder meeting we could see beau-tiful chalk art all the way around the building, which sits on a full square block. I have to imagine that this did something to the people working inside. In addition, it is wonderful when people from Chile come to these events and tell in

their own words how much it means to see people at the rallies supporting this cause. It puts a face on the issue and gives personality and emotion to the campaign. Flesh and blood.

After rallies we often have an open house for community mem-bers to come and meet activists who have traveled here. It's all about building community whether it's right here in Boise or in Chile.

Our international organizing here in Idaho was also strength-ened by our experience in Seattle. One of the agenda items to be dis-cussed in the WTO meetings was the Global Free Logging Agree-ment, which would wreak havoc on environmental protection laws throughout the world. A strong contingent of us drove from Boise to Seattle. The issue of Boise Cas-cade was definitely present in Seattle. In fact, BC has become the poster child of transnational logging companies. The Seattle experience deepened the global analysis of our work against destructive logging practices.

Jobs vs. environment—or common enemy?

We face many challenges including animosity from local

timber workers. During the 1980s and early '90s many logging towns depended on the timber coming off the national forests and private land at unsustainable rates. For years, Boise Cascade company rhetoric suggested that environmentalists were the real problem: "The tree-huggers have closed down the forests, that's why we're moving south." But in the last few years BC's influence on the local media has slackened and allowed the general public to hear another side. As BC divests from Idaho and moves elsewhere, they weaken their base of support in their hometown.

There's still a lot of tension between workers and environmentalists now that production is moving abroad. Some workers recognize that the issue is more complex than jobs versus the environment, but others are still fearful and angry. A big challenge is to get through this rhetoric and ally with laid-off workers to fight this corporation. We're really all in this together.

Martin Stephan lives in Boise, Idaho and has worked with a number of local and national organizations to protect wild places in Idaho and around the world. He is currently working on the Rainforest Action Network's old-growth forest campaign.

Environmental Justice and the Globalization Movement

Heeten Kalan and Ravi Dixit

Massive corporate takeovers are not a new event for people outside the United States. As early as the 1960s, Indian farmers resisted the Green Revolution when major chemical and fertilizer companies disrupted traditional farmers' livelihoods and tried to make India dependent on imported grains. Similar movements and groups sprang up to work on food production, trade, biodiversity, environment, and human health.

The post-Seattle globalization movement in the United States can link up with these groups. The U.S. movement can support their work, strengthen it, and learn from their decades of experience. First, though, we need to redefine international solidarity.

Redefining international solidarity

In the United States, solidarity is a one-way tradition. United States activists in the 1970s and '80s supported South Africans' struggles and helped solve "their" problem, even while recognizing that U.S. corporations were part of it.

In the twenty-first century we have a chance to redefine international solidarity. Two-way linkages are the key. The global North has a wealth of knowledge, research, and technology—how can we get that to the South? Meanwhile, the South has a wealth of knowledge about organizing, protest techniques, and political and economic analysis that people in the North can learn from.

In this two-way relationship, people in the South should have an equal say in determining the agenda. They are the most affected by environmental racism, environmental injustice, and bad trade policies. Imposing a Northern agenda on this increasingly international movement will not work.

Unhappily, we're not there yet. We see conference calls and conferences about globalization where fifty to eighty percent of the participants are still from the global North. Conference organizers bring the big names from Mexico, the Philippines, and southern Africa. That's not enough. We need to bring together rank and file activists from the South and North to really learn from each other. People-to-people linkages, networks, and exchanges are the basis of this way of organizing. The links between people on the ground will sustain us over time, not the links between researchers and academics, though those are important for other purposes.

This is not just a question of movement-building, but of survival. Take Rhone-Poulenc, the giant chemical company. In August 1992, an explosion in Institute, West Virginia, released forty-five thousand pounds of chemicals into the air, killing one Rhone-Poulenc employee and seriously injuring two others. One month later, a practically identical explosion occurred at Rhone-Poulenc's plant in the Midrand, South Africa. Company headquarters knew exactly what happened. Did the two communities know? And if they had been confronting the problem together, how much more power would they have had?

Bringing international work home

International solidarity has meant going to other places and raising money to support their work. The assumption behind this is that the problem is in the South. That kind of analysis builds mistrust in the South and a new kind of colonial attitude in the North, even on the Left. The next step in that attitude is thinking that because we possess scientific knowledge, we know what's best in other countries. Then we try to shape their movements.

In reality, you don't have to travel abroad to work in solidarity. People from other countries often tell Americans, "You have a lot of work to do in your country." When we work on U.S. foreign policy or U.S.-based companies, we build trust abroad.

In the United States there's an unspoken schism between local and international organizers. Local activists see internationalists as not wanting to confront problems down the street. Internationalists say, "You're missing the big picture." We can't afford to deepen this divide because the local and international organizers simply have too much to learn from each other.

North (also global North): industrialized or wealthy countries. Formerly West.

Some suggestions for doing successful international work

- Make sure you have an organizational counterpart in the country where you are working.
- If the campaign suggestion has come from abroad, make sure that you're meeting the needs of the community there rather than the needs of a U.S.-based organization.
- Never let your agenda drive the campaign or project, and do not attempt to set the agenda for communities abroad.
- While many of the financial resources may come from the United States, you must value the knowledge and skills that others bring to the campaign. Respect that and do not let the financial resources set the agenda and tone of the campaign.
- Always bear in mind that communities and organizers in other countries often have a lot more at risk (including their lives). Respect the pace and limits set by them.
- Plan trips, delegations, and exchanges eight to twelve months in advance. Small groups of three to six work better than large delegations where each individual person's skills and expertise are lost.
- Always have a well-thought-out follow-up plan beyond the exchanges, and always plan for counterparts to come to the United States as part of the proposal.

The international organizer can help the local group analyze its issues within a global context. What is the power of knowledge? What is the power of an oppressed community knowing that they are not the only one struggling against an onslaught?

- Plan your media strategy together and always be aware how the media can harm the people you work with. Be careful when exposing names and organizations. U.S. organizations are usually too happy to get the media attention without regard to the after-effects. Make sure that all organizations involved are mentioned in the press releases. Do not hog the spotlight when there is media attention—share it with those who may not be able to tell their story. Remember that they are better conveyors of their story than you are.
- Do not speak for others. Always wait for a mandate to act on behalf of a community when entering negotiations with a corporation or government.
- Ensure that campaigns build and strengthen organizations rather than leave them weak. Always remember that your counterparts are also working on other issues. The campaign you are working on does not always take precedence and should not drain the energies of the organizers.
- Watch your language and always define the buzz words. Be sensitive to other definitions. For example, the word "black" is defined differently in South Africa than it is in the United States, or you will hear about "anti-Irish racism" in northern Ireland. Ask for definitions and do not assume that other countries use words the way you do.

What is the power of a community knowing that another community has challenged the same problem and won?

Similarly, the local organizer offers invaluable insights and skills to the international organizer. The direct on-the-ground organizing strategies, ideas, and victories are important tools for the international counterpart. The local groups usually offer skills in housing development, land tenure, environmental justice, education, community policing, and community banking.

We have to short-circuit the learning curve. There is a rich body of community knowledge and expertise out there. There is an abundance of indigenous knowledge (ignored by most academics and international NGO-types) regarding resource use. We can learn from the West African farmer's response to land degradation, or from the Zimbabwean experience of farming in drought-stricken areas, or from the Native American experiences with medicinal herbs and sustainable living.

The bridging of these gaps, an arduous task, will pool resources to confront the underlying economic conditions and power relations facing societies all over the globe.

Solidarity with the South-in-the-North

In talking about forging these links, let's examine the familiar dichotomy of the North/South divide. That divide is certainly the starting point in our analysis.

However, we need to go further and explore, in addition to South–South links, relationships between the South and what we like to call the South-in-the-North. The South's natural allies are the communities exposed to toxics in Cancer Alley (the corridor between Baton Rouge and New Orleans in Louisiana), and the impoverished, underdeveloped neighborhoods of East and South Central Los Angeles or the housing developments of Chicago. There is a natural connection here and one which each community can relate to. For communities in the global South, there is a strength in identifying with a sister community from the North, and this helps correct perceptions that all is well in the North.

These South–South connections strengthen our analysis as well. The economic and environmental justice movement, which is driven mainly by people of color, offers a profound critique of our present economic system by illuminating the blatant contradictions surrounding development as we know it. The economic and environmental movement in the United States is bringing together all people of color to confront environmental racism and begin to build bridges with communities across borders. Environmental toxins and pollutants know no borders, and they offer us a unique opportunity to mobilize people around a pervasive and destructive issue. The emerging international economic and environmental justice movement is confronting the issues of toxic dumping, transfer of "dirty" industry and, in the words of Samir Amin, "maldevelopment," which points to the structural adjustment programs of the international financial institutions.

This brings us to the mainstream environmental movement in the United States. The more traditional environmental groups need to incorporate a critique of capital in their work. The question is not just "Who will save the rainforest?" but "Who are the companies that are cutting the rainforest down?" The other challenge is to make human connections to the issue. The conservation focus of many U.S. environmental groups looks suspect to people in the South because it is so removed from daily life. We have to make sure we don't pose people as a cost to the environment.

Signs that say "globalization" and "democracy" are very nice, but many people don't feel anything about those words. If you can show the effects on daily lives and communities that are feeling these health crises every day, that bridges the gap between the people who are thinking about these problems and those who are living them.

—Heeten Kalan and Ravi Dixit are the staff of the South African Exchange Program on Environmental Justice.

The Bucket Brigade in South Africa

Heeten Kalan

Since its inception in 1993, the South African Exchange Program on Environmental Justice (SAEPEJ) has organized a number of people-to-people and technical assistance exchanges between the United States and South Africa. The most recent one in May 2000 monitored, sampled, and tested the polluted air that communities have had to contend with for decades. It was called a Bucket Brigade.

Bucket Brigades began in Northern California in 1995, when residents near oil refineries and chemical plants grew tired of toxic releases and the lack of independent information on air pollution. Simple air monitoring devices (called "Buckets") were provided to community members in one refinery neighborhood. Eventually Communities for a Better Environment organized a regional effort to provide Buckets to five industrial communities in the San Francisco Bay area.

In the absence of any strong environmental laws, standards, or an environmental enforcement body, communities must have the

Four large refineries operate in South Africa: the South African Petroleum Refinery (Shell and BP) in Durban, the Engen (Petronas) refinery, also in Durban, the Caltex refinery in Cape Town and the National Petroleum Refiners (Sasol and Total) refinery in Sasolburg, Free State. Current sulfur dioxide (SO_2) emissions from these refineries are well above internationally accepted standards and seriously threaten the health of nearby communities, most of which are low-income communities of color. The South African government has consistently failed to address these concerns.

groundWork, a South African nonprofit organization, has been calling on the South African government to introduce legally binding air emission standards in order to bring emissions down to levels that are no longer a health threat. Currently South Africa has no legally binding air emission standards for refineries, merely non-binding guidelines. The government lacks any kind of regulatory or enforcement body such as an EPA, and instead relies heavily on self-regulation by the industries themselves. groundWork's Bobby Peek says that this self-regulation is like asking a hungry dog not to eat a piece of meat you put in front of it.

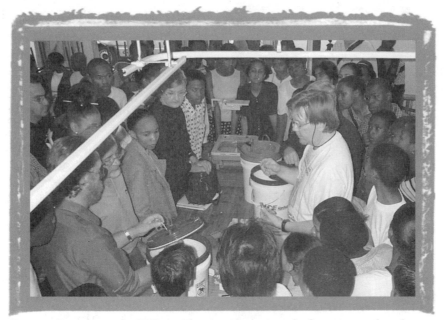

Denny Larson of CBE gathers the crowd for some hands-on experience in assembling the Bucket air sampling devices.

means to monitor their own environments. The Bucket Brigade worked with South African communities adjacent to polluting refineries to develop the skills and knowledge required to monitor their environments and to push for improvements in the laws, standards, and practices of the refinery industry in South Africa. Denny Larson (Communities for a Better Environment), Shipra Bansal (Scientific Advisor), and Heeten Kalan (SAEPEJ) flew to South Africa from the United States and were joined by Bobby Peek from groundWork in South Africa. This trip took close to two

years of intense planning and turned out to be a big success with lots of media attention and continued follow-up.

The Bucket Brigade trained community residents to build a Bucket from scratch and to go out to take an air sample, fill out the documents, and send the sample for analyses. The community was left with the Bucket and manuals for future use. The team visited six cities in two weeks and held three community workshops.

At our first stop, over one hundred residents and youth of South Durban community came by car

Bobby Peek of groundWork and
Michelle Simon, Coordinator of
the South Durban Community Environmental Alliance, take an air
sample of ENGEN's fenceline.

"sniffed" the area and identified the best place to take a sample. The stench was horrible and Bobby and Michelle reminded us that they have to live with this smell.

After signing the chain of custody forms, the air sample was rushed to local couriers so that it would reach the Los Angeles lab within seventy-two hours.

A few days later, the Bucket Brigade landed in Cape Town and learned about local struggles against the Caltex refinery there. The next day we briefed parliamentarians from the Environment and Tourism, Minerals and Energy, Trade and Industry, and Water Affairs Standing Committees on air pollution, oil refineries and incineration. Over twenty parliamentarians came to hear the briefing hosted and chaired by MP Gwen Mahlangu. The meeting was a great success since it focused on alternatives and solutions to filling the information gap prevailing in South Africa.

The Chair, Gwen Mahlangu, was so outraged at the impacts of the oil refineries that she organized a mini-tour of the local refinery for all the parliamentarians and their aides that were present. They came to see firsthand what residents have

and motor taxis to attend the first Bucket air sampling, building, and training outside the United States. The John Dunn House swelled with excitement as people exposed to pollution hungered to discover what they were breathing.

At about 1:00 P.M., the Bucket Brigade was called into action when strange clouds of two-tone smoke and odors erupted from the ENGEN refinery near the training.

Local residents Bobby Peek and Michelle Simon immediately

Flaring at one of the refineries in Sasolburg. Flaring is a usually a sign of off-gassing and leaks from the plant. The company is burning compounds used to manufacture its final product.

been complaining about for many years.

We provided parliamentarians with policy options to strengthen existing legislation to fill some of the data gaps. South Africa does not have the option of making the same mistakes other industrialized countries have made and it needs to adopt creative measures to improve the health and environment of all South Africans.

Media responses and follow-up

Throughout the trip, the media response was exceptional. The two-week trip in South Africa led to nine print media stories and a fifteen-minute piece on Carte Blanche, South Africa's equivalent of *60 Minutes.* Since the trip, we have sent the analysis of three samples to the communities and this has spurred more media coverage. Carte Blanche is doing a follow-up and the print media has reported extensively on the polluted air of South Durban, Sasolburg, and Cape Town.

This trip's success is due in large part to the extensive follow-up we planned before the trip. We also crafted a media strategy that allowed us to feed the sample results back to the media for follow-up stories. The Bucket Brigade continues to provide technical assistance to all the communities we visited. This level of follow-up is often ignored and without it, the original excitement and enthusiasm quickly withers away. As corporations continue to plunder and pollute, communities are being brought closer together by sharing experiences and by challenging corporations with simple and creative tools.

Women Take On Globalization and Militarism

Gwyn Kirk and Margo Okazawa-Rey

Du Rae Bang (My Sister's Place), a bakery near a U.S. base in Korea, provides jobs for women who do not want to be bar hostesses and dancers. At Sae Woom Tuh (Little Sprout), former bar women grow herb plants for sale and make cards and decorative paper from herbs and recycled milk cartons.

Women are creating economic security for themselves in projects like these in Korea, the Philippines, and Okinawa. They—we—are members of the East Asia–U.S. Women's Network Against Militarism.

We are activists, teachers, students, researchers, elected officials, survivors of physical, sexual, and emotional violence; we are daughters, mothers, and wives.

We recognize that the dominant political and economic system has created poverty and misery for many people worldwide, and insecurity for everyone. Militarism with its bloated resources, environmental devastation, vio-

> *Women and girls do two-thirds of the world's work, and two-thirds of their work is unwaged.*

lence against women, and military prostitution is an integral part of this economic system.

We focus on the U.S. military because of U.S. dominance in the world, the vast federal resources devoted to military spending, and because U.S. military bases and

> Militaries reap enormous profits for multinational corporations and stockholders through the development, production, and sale of weapons of destruction. Moreover, militaries maintain control of local populations and repress those who oppose the fundamental principles on which the world economic system is based. The current economic system depends on deep-seated attitudes and relationships characterized by greed, fear, domination, and the objectification of "others" expressed through racism, sexism, imperialism, and the desire to control the physical environment. Vested interests, routine ways of thinking, prejudice, ignorance, and inertia also play their part in maintaining entrenched systems of economic, social, and political inequality.
>
> *—excerpted from the Final Statement of the International Women's Summit held in Okinawa, Japan, June 22-25, 2000 in response to the G-8 meeting on the island.*

operations overseas often threaten host communities and seriously limit their self-determination. The Network is based in the United States because there are resources here to support it, but it is not only a solidarity group to support activists in East Asia. Those of us who live in the United States try to make connections between U.S. domestic and foreign policy. We take issue with the way the military harms people in this country. Social programs that especially benefit women and children like health, welfare, education, and elder care, have been cut while the military budget remains sacrosanct. We connect a variety of issues: military violence against women, environ-

Alma Bulawan (Buklod Center, Philippines) speaks at a rally opposing a new U.S. Marines base on Okinawa, June 2000. *Gwyn Kirk*

mental contamination caused by military operations past and present, and the harmful effects of massive military budgets.

What ties these together is security. The idea of security needs to be demilitarized. Military security is a contradiction in terms. Genuine security includes environmental security, economic security, respect for human dignity, and protection from avoidable harm. We are interested in movements that are democratic, genuinely diverse, and use analytical frameworks including gender, race, class, and nation. We are working together as women because many progressive organizations do not have a strong gender analysis, even though women may be a significant part of the membership.

Teens Go Global

Gail Phares

Early on a June morning in 2000, twenty-three U.S. teenagers stood outside the Free Trade Zone in Managua, Nicaragua. With them were sweatshop workers recently fired from the Mil Colores and Chentex factories, protesting their illegal firing. Thousands of young Nicaraguans streamed through the gates. Many of them were teens just like those of the Witness for Peace youth delegation. Instead of streaming into high schools, they are going to work in sweatshops producing clothing for Target and Kohl's stores here in the United States for three dollars a day.

Each year during the last two weeks of June, Witness for Peace Southeast brings an intercultural group of teenagers to Nicaragua to learn first hand about the impact of debt and of World Bank and International Monetary Fund (IMF) policies on the people of Nicaragua. Our delegation includes African-American teens from inner-city Charlotte as well as Native American, Asian, and Euro-American teens from high schools in North Carolina, South Dakota, Kansas, and Pennsylvania.

Before leaving the States, we have a day and a half of trainings in nonviolence, group building, intercultural communication, and the background and history of Nicaragua. We watch videos such as "Cancel the Debt" from Jubilee 2000 and "Zoned for Slavery" on sweatshops in Central America from the National Labor Committee and "Affluenza" from National Public Radio. The teens read about World Bank and IMF policies on Nicaragua which force cutbacks in funds for education and health care and other social services.

While in Nicaragua, we spend three days living with families on a rural cooperative in Matagalpa, and three days with working class families in Managua. We meet children who work on the streets selling tortillas, shining shoes, and so on, to help their families survive. These are the human faces of World Bank/IMF policies. We visit a sweatshop in the free trade zone and meet with sweatshop workers. In June 2000, two former Chentex workers told us of sexual harassment and denial of health care in Managua's free trade zone. "We've been threatened with attacks and with death by gang members because of our union activities," the two fired workers said. They asked us to return home and put pressure on Target and Kohl's department stores, which buy from Nicaraguan factories. "Ask them to negotiate with the union and to rehire fired workers."

Each evening, we share what we are learning about the impact of Nicaragua's debt and World Bank/IMF policies on the eighty percent of Nicaraguans who live in poverty. The last day, we prepare to return to the States. We have workshops on working with the media, giving talks in our churches and schools, and influencing public policy makers. Together, we write a group report to summarize what we learned while in Nicaragua.

In October, we gather in Washington, D.C., for a reunion to share what we have done since returning home. We meet with our U.S. Senators and Representatives and also with Treasury Department officials responsible for U.S. policy at the World Bank and IMF.

These high school students go on to be organizers with Students Against Sweatshops at Duke, UNC-Chapel Hill, Swarthmore, and other colleges across the United States. Some work with the Farmworkers Labor Organizing Committee (FLOC). Others help organize Students

United for a Responsible Global Environment (SURGE), which is now a national e-mail network of high school and college students working for global justice.

"Our recent trip has given us the experience and the knowledge to take action in our own country and in our own communities, and to educate those around us," said fifteen-year-old Joyce Chapman from Chapel Hill High School. "We must make our voices and the voices of the friends and families that we left behind in Nicaragua be heard."

—Gail Phares is Director of the Carolina Interfaith Task Force on Central America and Regional Coordinator of Witness for Peace Southeast, 1105 Sapling Place Raleigh, NC 27615, (919)856-9468. For information on how to organize a Spring Break or a Teen Delegation to Central America, call Witness for Peace at (202)588-1471.

Used by permission of Jerry Markados.

Building Coalitions

The need for coalitions and alliances is clear. Each individual or group in the globalization movement has its own resources, ideas, creativity, contacts, and power. Linking them strengthens the overall movement.

When these alliances form and our movement is broad, loud, and making the front-page news on a regular basis, our collective voice will be diverse in demands and message. We will run into strong differences of opinion and we'll have to compromise with each other. A blockade on the street involving environmentalists, labor supporters, and global justice activists is a beautiful thing, but this alliance can quickly become strained when it comes time to work out a message, talk to constituencies, and deal with tensions among interests.

Elizabeth Martinez's "Where Was the Color in Seattle?" critiqued the narrow social base of the movement. The sea of white faces in Seattle and Washington, D.C., didn't represent the wide movement affected by corporate globalization. Nor did it give a proper face to the actions being taken against our unjust system. Youth of color standing up to police brutality in their neighborhoods and immigrant farmworkers educating themselves about globalization are taking powerful actions that can transform the system. Alliances between these underrepresented activist groups, as well as work between these groups and the largely middle-class, self-defined global justice movement, are going to be key as we move forward.

Then there is the class divide. Middle-class and working-class activists are separated by more than attitudes and short-term interests. There are different cultures and organizing methods, well defined by Fred Rose in *Coalitions Across the Class Divide.* Middle-class people, says Rose, have an individual relationship to authority. They can get ahead with their own skills and knowledge. They often think changes happen by getting the truth out, convincing those in power to change their views, and using information. But workers, Rose says, have little individual power against the boss. They win through disciplined collective action that forces the powerful to give in.

Middle-class campaigns often start with an idea—a brainstorm, a breakthrough, an "aha" about what's wrong. Working-class campaigns often arise from a local problem so urgent it brings people together to organize. It's surprisingly difficult for these two organizing ideologies to work together.

—Laura Raymond and Mike Prokosch

Globalizing SOA Watch

Bruce Triggs

"I am a survivor of the World Bank," said Carlos Chen Osorio at the Bank's April 2000 meeting in Washington, D.C. He came with a huge banner naming three hundred women and children from his village in Guatemala who were murdered in 1983 for opposing a World Bank dam project.

Along with the names, the banner read, "This dam was constructed with the blood and tears of the community of Rio Negro." Osorio's village is buried underwater today. Survivors know they can't bring back the dead, but they want reparations for their land and for the lives taken to build the World Bank's dam.

The commander who gave the orders to destroy Osorio's village was trained at the U.S. Army's School of the Americas.

The SOA is located at Fort Benning, Georgia. It trains sol-

The IMF, the World Bank, and the other global economic institutions do not keep millions of people in poverty peacefully. Their unpopular economic policies are enforced by military power. Over the last forty years sixty thousand soldiers from some of the most repressive militaries in Latin America have sharpened their skills at the U.S. Army's School of the Americas (SOA).

Years of citizen research and activism have built a movement against the School. Now SOA Watch activists are broadening their focus to include other questionable military training, and at the same time, strengthening their voice by connecting with organized labor and other activist communities. One hundred fifty SOA Watch activists at the IMF's April 2000 meeting linked the SOA's repressive military training with IMF and World Bank economic repression, and showed how united opposition can connect many movements as one. Research is revealing connections between the SOA and the environment, student movements, sweatshops, repression of indigenous communities, and other military training around the world.

diers in counterinsurgency warfare. Until recently, its course materials targeted union activists, religious workers, students, and anyone who questioned government or economic policies. It earned the name "The School of Coups" after Latin American journalists watched SOA graduates overthrow their governments. After the 1989 massacre of six Jesuit priests and two women in El Salvador by soldiers who had just returned from the SOA, Father Roy Bourgeois started "SOA Watch" in a tiny office just outside Fort Benning. Since then, SOA Watch protests have grown to November 2000's twelve-thousand-person civil disobedience vigil.

Building a movement from the inside out

SOA Watch is a true grassroots movement. It grew slowly at first, with very limited media attention. After ten years, though, it may be the largest civil disobedience movement in the country to come mainly from faith communities.

One key event that boosted the SOA from an issue to a movement was a forty-day fast on the U.S. Capitol steps in 1994. Before this, people around the country knew about the School from Father Bourgeois's speaking

---

The SOA and Bolivia's "Water War"

The Bolivian city of Cochabamba knows how the SOA's military muscle backs up the World Bank's corporate agenda. Cochabamba's "Water War" began under a World Bank privatization plan that sold the city's water system to an affiliate of the Bechtel corporation. Water rates immediately doubled and sometimes tripled in many poor neighborhoods. Protests against the rate hike united many different groups in the city.

The Bolivian protests escalated in February of 2000, with a series of massive actions culminating in a citywide and then nationwide general strike. City residents and peasants from rural areas blockaded main roads into town. Finally, public outrage reached its peak when an army officer in civilian clothes was filmed shooting into a crowd of civilians, killing one boy and wounding others. The government backed down and cancelled Bechtel's water contract after these pictures were broadcast on TV.

The political chain of command behind the fatal shooting—the mayor of the city, the governor of the state, and the president of Bolivia, ex-dictator Hugo Banzer—all graduated from the School of the Americas. They showed the truth behind the SOA's claim to be "training for democracy."

For a gripping film about Bolivia's water wars, see This Is Our Water, Damn It! *in the Yellow Pages section. For photos from Cochabamba, see www.americas.org.*

---

tours, but didn't know one another. The long fast was like a convention of the SOA Watch movement-to-be. Different local groups discovered they weren't alone, and they started building a national community.

Lobbyists on Capitol Hill once asked SOA Watch staffers what public relations firm we had hired to get so much popular support. They didn't believe us when we said there was no way to buy what we had built. Grassroots work, old-fashioned speaking tours, and local organizing made this happen.

SOA Watch is driven by the ever-present knowledge of the suffering of people in Latin America. What built its local strength, though, was people performing civil disobedience at the School and receiving long prison terms. SOA "witnesses" were jailed up to a year for carrying a cross or a coffin onto the base. This outraged people back home, and they decided to get involved. Now SOA Watch is organized around these regional "seeds" of prison witnesses, with each person ("missing" in prison) replaced by many others.

Vigils have grown at the SOA in Georgia and in Washington, D.C., for ten years. When they were small, the vigils functioned as informal planning gatherings too, but in the last few years as the actions have grown, we've organized separate meetings for strategizing. These "Suits and Roots" weekends invite activists from many different constituencies to plan legislative and action strategy each year.

Our decade of legislative attempts to close the School keep getting closer. It may only be a matter of time before citizens' acts of conscience finally overwhelm the Army and the State Department and close the SOA (or at least its present incarnation and location) forever. Some of us are starting to look beyond that one training site. Human rights are threatened by other programs, like Green Berets training abusive Colombian and Mexican soldiers. We're analyzing the larger system of poverty that soldiers in Latin America defend using military aid and training. Thinking beyond the SOA brought one hundred fifty SOA Watchers to the World Bank/IMF meeting in Washington, where we met Osorio with his banner. Meeting him, and other witnesses from the global economy, it was clear how

SOA-backed repression supports economic victimization.

Creating alliances

Alliance-building has helped SOA Watch grow. Leading up to the IMF protests, several SOA Watch activists looked for the connections between SOA graduates and IMF/World Bank economic issues. Now we're seeking links between human rights,

> The SOA—that's about killing Indians, isn't it?
> —Native American man in Tacoma, Washington

environmental, and indigenous concerns.

How do we do this? Well, to start with, we check the lists. After fighting to get them under the Freedom of Information Act, we now have public access to lists of tens of thousands of SOA graduates. People can identify specific human rights abusers or entire military units as SOA graduates.

Identifying mutual opponents helps us identify natural allies. The SOA-trained Colombian military's support for oil drilling on the indigenous U'Wa people's land draws together human rights, military accountability, environmental, and indigenous communities. The SOA's lists make it clear that SOA graduates are deeply involved in countries repressing indigenous rights.

SOA Watch is now producing link sheets detailing the needs and possibilities for specific alliances. We've been working ten years to close this one school. We know it'll take much more time, and many more people together, to bring bigger changes. The first of these links was SOA's Ultimate Union Buster sheet. It started with a campaign aimed at one politician, but opened doors for much wider cooperation between human rights and labor activists.

SOA Watch joins with labor

SOA Watch's link with labor

Economic oppression and military repression are flip sides of the same globalization coin. The economic rape of the poor that accompanies globalization could not stand without the repressive military apparatus that brutalizes people who rise up to resist. Those who oppose the globalization of greed and those who work to end U.S. training of repressive foreign armies are joined in one effort.

—Hendrik Voss, SOA Watch

came from brainstorming among activists in Tacoma. We wanted to get our Congressman, Norm Dicks, a pro-military, pro-labor Democrat, to vote against the SOA. We figured if we could get local labor even threatening to back our fight, he might do the right thing. We started digging for research linking SOA graduates with abuses against labor organizers in Latin America. It was worse than we had imagined: The Canadian Federation of Labour reported that one out of four (now one out of three) labor organizers murdered worldwide is Colombian.

We already knew that Colombia's atrocity-prone military had ten thousand SOA graduates—more than any other country—so we started making our case.

At the 1998 Labor Day picnic in Seattle, we brought out our fliers and our secret weapon: bright orange T-shirts calling the SOA "The Ultimate Union Buster." Bigwigs were present, and AFL-CIO President John Sweeney signed one of our shirts in front of video cameras. Ken Little, a union carpenter, took that orange shirt and traveled the country collecting signatures from dozens of union leaders, with hundreds of matching resolutions calling for closing the School.

Organized labor may be learning that antiunion repression knows no borders. "An Injury to One Is An Injury To All" is not just a slogan of goodwill between unions, it's a threat of what happens when we forget to support each other. SOA Watch's labor campaign opened doors for the AFL-CIO to call to close the School, and back home, our own Norm Dicks voted to close it down.

Bruce Triggs has lived at the Tacoma Catholic Worker house for eight years, working with homeless guests. He gets away from the pressures of work on the streets by taking "vacations for justice" to places like the School of the Americas. His favorite alliance in the SOA movement is with the Radical Fairies of Tennessee who in their SOA manifesto demand that RuPaul be appointed SOA dance instructor and Tonya Harding teach ice skating there to Zapatista rebels.

Crossing Borders with Labor

Cross-Border Labor Organizing Coalition

International labor solidarity is an idea whose time has come. After NAFTA many local union leaders and rank and file activists recognize the need for cross-border labor organizing. How can nonlabor activists help?

For its first year and a half, the very small Cross-Border Committee of Portland, Oregon Jobs with Justice, worked on a variety of campaigns, often with the Portland Central America Solidarity Committee (PCASC). We supported Mexico City bus drivers, we helped pressure Starbucks to adopt a code of conduct, and we brought these solidarity struggles into the labor movement at Jobs with Justice's well attended steering committee meetings.

After co-hosting a Mexican labor leader and labor history professor, we consolidated our ideas and organization in two important ways. First, we taught a class based on *Global Village or Global Pillage,* by Jeremy Brecher and Tim Costello, in a local progressive school and we adopted its overall vision of the interconnectedness of world labor and the need to raise the floor worldwide. Second, we asked PCASC to formally join our projects.

One of our long-range goals was to become an organization whose members actively represented a wide variety of labor and community organizations. Our work in Jobs with Justice already brought in a staff member of the hotel workers' union and a representative of the Communications Workers of America who is now the president of the large local. We continued to engage in cross-border campaigns and we started working on issues involving immigrant workers.

From the beginning, our committee's members participated in and organized campaigns for local workers' rights with Jobs with Justice. As key organizers in the successful campaign to raise Oregon's minimum wage, we helped with trainings, petition drives, and demonstrations. We walked on picket lines with farm workers, UPS Teamsters, and hotel maids. We sat in and sometimes got arrested with steelworkers and hospital workers. We see ourselves as part of the local and worldwide labor movements, and we see most of the issues we work on as part of the vision of raising the economic floor worldwide.

Paint-a-thon

In January 1997, the cross-border committee decided to do a "paint-a-thon." We wanted the project to include union people, other workers, and participants in solidarity groups. We also wanted to use the paint-a-thon to begin our support-an-organizer campaign and create awareness of cross-border labor issues, and we wanted to have a political event that was fun and artistically expressive. Most importantly, we wanted a way to get into local union meetings with our message that we need to unite across borders to raise the floor, and give the unions a concrete project they could join.

Our initial idea of creating a mural on work-a-thon day evolved into a project of making banners to sell to unions. The small cross-border committee, which now had six core members, made connections with more than fifteen union locals and other community groups. Many of our initial connections were made through our contacts in Jobs with Justice. We scheduled very short appearances at union meetings to explain the banner project and our cross-border campaigns, always attempting to discuss the effects of globalization on all of us. We then asked if they would like to purchase a banner with the proceeds going to labor organizers in Mexico and El Salvador. Every union we approached wanted to buy a banner for $250 to $500.

We were stunned by how easy it was to talk to union people about the global economy, the need to raise the floor worldwide, and the need to support labor campaigns across the border—especially considering that the core members of the committee were not themselves union members at the time. What we did have going for us was the reality of the destructive force of the global economy, the really cool banner project (unions need banners), and the legitimacy we had as supporters of working people.

At the same time we brought together eleven artists who made drawings based on the logos and other designs the unions and other groups wanted. The artists and their helpers made transparencies at a copy shop and projected the small drawings onto the large blank banners, tracing the designs onto the banners.

Jobs with Justice and PCASC mobilized their phone trees to do outreach. On the day of the paint-a-thon, almost one hundred people

Women workers from the National O-Ring maquiladora demonstrate for women's rights during the May Day parade in Tijuana. Their factory was closed, and the women laid off and blacklisted, after they filed charges of sexual harassment against their employer in courts in Tijuana and Los Angeles. *David Bacon © 1990-1999*

came to donate their creative labor. Participants arrived to find eighteen large tables set up, each with a banner to paint, trays containing little cups of beautiful and very expensive paint, and artists to help them with the finer points of painting in the lettering and choosing colors. Dulcimer music entertained the volunteers during their work and they sang union songs during lunch. Most were so involved in painting that they stayed for almost six hours and hardly took time to eat. Not only were there no mishaps, the quality of the work was outstanding. In addition to nineteen completed banners for unions and other groups, we painted three banners to present to the unions we are working with in Mexico and El Salvador. We raised over $3,000 after expenses, more than meeting our goal. The atmosphere at the paint-a-thon was one of cheerful, unalienated labor. It was the way life should be.

After the paint-a-thon we rolled the dried banner on cardboard carpet cores, prepared care-and-feeding instructions, and made follow-up appointments to present the unions with their beautiful banners. (Unions have very full agendas so you should be able to be in and out in ten minutes). Not only was the event memorable, but the relationships we built with local union leaders and rank and file have been lasting. Whenever we are involved in a campaign we can call on local leaders and union activists to join us in demonstrations or forums. Since the paint-a-thon, labor leaders from Mexico and El Salvador have visited us, and it is easy to bring together local union activists and leaders and our international guests in lively, intimate meetings. In some of these sessions, local activists have learned new approaches from their guests. Ideas of powerful support actions have been born in these meetings. After the paint-a-thon, cross-border labor organizing was on the map as an accepted part of Portland's labor community.

Lessons

- International labor solidarity is an idea whose time has come. After NAFTA many local union leaders and rank and file activists recognize the need for cross-border labor organizing. The trick is finding attractive projects that will allow cross-border activists to get to speak to unions and offer them some concrete action they can take.
- It is critical to interconnect cross-border work and local labor support. This means slowly building relationships in both the labor and solidarity movements, and helping to bring the two together through work on their day-to-day struggles.
- International labor solidarity and power are essential to preventing further erosion of living standards, cultures, and the environment, whether in the United States or El Salvador. It is the workers who hold the switches that make society move, and workers can stop the whole thing. Workers are ultimately the most powerful group in society, and they're on the move.

Tips to get started

In any city, there are labor activists who support other unions' pickets and actions, help with boycotts and corporate campaigns, and lobby for workers' interests. They can be found in Jobs with Justice, Central Labor Councils, or informal groups. Look under "labor" in the yellow pages and examine every listing if you are starting from scratch.

Because labor unions and councils represent so many people of such different political stripes, they need time to think through proposed actions—and to come to trust you. Be patient and allow plenty of time.

Immigrants and the Globalization Movement

Angela Sanbrano

The global economy destroys the economies of developing countries. According to the United Nations, three hundred million more people live in extreme poverty around the world than ten years ago. A billion live on less than a dollar a day. The developed countries are experiencing unprecedented economic growth and dazzling technology, yet half the world's people have never made a phone call.

Governments from developing countries, desperate for foreign capital, welcome multinational corporations that profit from low wages, lack of basic workers' rights and lax environmental regulation. These countries rarely respect workers' rights or protect the environment.

At the same time, under pressure from international lending institutions such as the World Bank and the International Monetary Fund, developing countries are spending far more to repay

March for immigrants killed crossing the U.S.-Mexico border. Crosses say "Unidentified." © *Charles Slay*

loans than to meet the basic needs of the people. The result has been a resurgence in sweatshops, child labor, prison labor, forced labor, growing income inequality, and migration.

In the global economy, goods, information, and capital move freely from one country to another. Labor does not. The globalization of the economy fuels immigration, but international immigration is suppressed through border police actions and with punitive immigration policies. To prevent undocumented workers from crossing the U.S.-Mexico border, the United States has militarized the border. INS agents are allowed to remove undocumented aliens quickly without judicial review. Undocumented workers are taking greater risks in crossing the border and over five hundred died in the first eight months of the year 2000.

Issues affecting immigrants in the United States

Low wages, exploitation, discrimination, and violation of human rights are some of the most pressing issues affecting the immigrant community in the United States. Immigrants are "the South in the North"—the second-class workers who swell the profits of U.S. employers.

Seventy-five percent of the low-wage market is made up of immigrants working in jobs that nonimmigrant workers shun. Many immigrants, especially undocumented workers, take the dirtiest, the lowest-paid, the heaviest jobs and probably the jobs where people get hurt the most. Often workers must work for twelve to fourteen hours a day, six days a week, for only six dollars an hour. One Guatemalan woman I know has been working for seven years in the same sweatshop. Her only time off was to have a baby. She got one month.

When workers complain or seek a decent wage, management often retaliates by turning them in to immigration officials.

Immigrants organize to improve their situation

Day laborers, domestic workers, restaurant workers, and street vendors are not what you visualize when you hear "organized labor." But these informal workers have formed associations under the umbrella of regional immigrant rights coalitions, such as the Coalition for Humane Immi-

Immigrant rights march. Signs say "Amnesty and total unioniza-
tion with a general strike." © *Charles Slay*

grant Rights in Los Angeles. There are about seven regional coalitions in Texas, New York, Chicago, San Francisco, and other parts of the United States. These coalitions were founded as a result of the 1986 Immigration Reform and Control Act.

The AFL-CIO's recent resolution calling for immigrant amnesty has energized the immigrant rights movement. On June 10, 2000, more than twenty thousand immigrant workers attended a forum that the AFL-CIO organized in Los Angeles to support general amnesty; a strong coalition of labor, religious, and immigrant rights organizations was formed. The Coalition for Immigration Reform is presently working for passage of the Latino and Immigrant Fairness Act. Passage of this legislation is an essential first step to building political and legislative support and win full rights for more than six million immigrant workers.

How can global justice activists and immigrants work together?

Global activists and immigrants

should join forces and find solutions to a global economy that destroys developing economies, forces workers to emigrate, forces them into harsh working conditions, hampers their ability to organize, and pulls down wages and working conditions for all wage-earners in the United States.

The right to organize is key. It is the civil rights challenge of the twenty-first century. If global activists support that right, and help win citizenship for all immigrants, they will be helping themselves and other U.S. workers. What is good for immigrants is good for all of us.

What capacity and interest do immigrants have in transforming the global economy? They definitely have an interest. The Central American Refugee Center (CARECEN) and other immigrant organizations participated in the key protests during the 2000 Democratic National Convention in Los Angeles. The theme of the whole four days was globalization and justice in the economy. On the last day, a march against sweatshops and for immigrant workers drew thousands.

Unfortunately, immigrants' capacity is limited. People working fourteen hours a day, six days a week, do not have time to organize global economy actions on their own. But given the opportunity to join events and actions without risking deportation or repression, they will participate. And as immigrant workers build up unions, they will gain the organizational strength to make a difference in the global balance of power. Workers are the bridge between immigration and globalization, and unions are the key to gaining power.

Angela Sanbrano is the director of the Central American Refugee Center in Los Angeles (LA. CARECEN).

Prisons as a Globalization Issue

Laura Raymond

Why does the United States have two million people locked up (the majority for nonviolent offenses) when in 1999 the FBI reported that the '90s had seen the longest, most steady reduction in crime in U.S. history? Why, according to the Department of Justice, are one-third of black males going to serve a prison term at some point in their lives? The number of black men in prison in July 2001 (792,000) equaled the number of black men enslaved in 1820. Why?

Most people probably wouldn't answer "globalization" when thinking through the reasons behind our prison explosion. But with closer scrutiny, economic globalization is a major explanation.

Policing and prisons enable globalization, and the inequality it creates, to occur smoothly. They are a complex form of social control that regulates those left behind by globalization. In many ways, the prison industrial complex is a necessary limb of globalization. For this reason, people concerned about the current global economy need to understand and become active against the prison system.

How is the prison industrial complex a form of social control?

Those who suffer the most under the poverty created by the global economy are disproportionately darker-skinned than those who benefit from the system. This is a major way that white privilege operates in terms of globalization; white people usually don't have to deal with the worst of the ramifications. Within the United States, neoliberal policies widen inequality among Americans along racial and class lines.

Enter policing and prisons. Multilayered discipline and intense scapegoating are required to keep globalization's race and class oppression operating and legitimized. This helps to explain why whole communities have been labeled criminal, lazy, and undeserving. This is also why graffiti, rap, and baggy clothes have been labeled "gang-related." This legitimizes the regulation of the poor. It is the hidden story behind the fact that about seventy percent of prisoners are people of color. (The story is huge; for more information and deeper analysis read *Lockdown America* by Chris Parenti.)

How is social control a part of globalization?

Bruce Triggs of SOA Watch writes that "The School of the Americas' military muscle backs up the World Bank's corporate agenda." The militarization of Latin America and other impoverished countries keeps the people down so that business interests can profit off their exploitation.

The same is true within the United States. The prison-industrial complex enables globalization to create poverty here. This is a necessary part of globalization because, broadly, when people are poor, wages go down and businesses make more of a profit.

SLAM! Protesting the criminal injustice system, Washington, D.C. © Diane Greene Lent

However, a conflict of interest is involved, as Chris Parenti writes:

If the economic restructuring of the eighties and nineties intensified urban poverty, it has also created new, gilded spaces that are increasingly threatened by poverty. This polarization of urban space and social relations has in turn required a new layer of regulation and exclusion, so as to protect the new hyper-aestheticized, playground quarter of the postmodern metropolis from their flipsides of misery.

Parenti's analysis is similar to how Angela Davis talks about imprisonment as the first response and catchall solution to problems created by capitalism in the first place (see Davis' article, "Masked Racism: Reflections on the Prison Industrial Complex," in the Fall 1998 *ColorLines* magazine or on www.corpwatch.org).

The prison industry is instrumental to *how* globalization happens. Just as protesters recognize how the WTO creates laws that further

Jails not Schools? Some numbers from California

- California has the third largest prison system in the world after the United States as a whole and China.
- Between 1993–1995 California decreased investment in primary/secondary public schools by more than 7% and in higher education just under 5%. During the same period of time its investment in the correctional system rose by 43.5%.

- Between 1984 and 1997, California constructed twenty-one prisons and one university.

- Over the last twenty years in California:

Spending on K-12 dropped 33.4% while spending on prisons rose 541.4%.
The number of K-12 teachers fell 8% while the number of prison guards rose 250%.
The number of K-12 schools rose 2.6% while the number of prisons rose 200%.
The number of people in prison rose 400% while the number of kids graduating high school fell 2.7%.

- The majority of students in California's primary and secondary schools are youth of color (58%). Lack of investment in programs for students of color and simultaneous criminalization of youth of color have played a large role in the apartheid-like racial disparities in California prisons (see p. 66).

unequal economic processes, so too must globalization protesters recognize how prisons and victim-blaming create a society where this inequality is tolerated, dissent is repressed, and the poor are locked away and hidden from view.

How can globalization activists join in the struggle against prisons?

First, we must recognize that the struggle has been ongoing for decades. There is much to learn from this history of resistance.

Prison activists have witnessed many concerned white activists engaging in antiprison organizing in recent years. While this is fundamentally needed, it also can be potentially harmful to the prison movement because of "deracialization." This term coming from Critical Resistance East refers to analysis of a racial issue that is devoid of any concrete race analysis. The prison-industrial complex is based upon racial oppression so race analysis is necessary to prison organizing. However, since white people are not directly oppressed by race and are more familiar with the oppression created by capitalism, we often tend to analyze the prison industry in terms of economics.

As the globalization movement develops its analysis of prisons, social control, and globalization, the movement may meet up with the ever-growing resistance to the prison industrial complex. As some of us join with this struggle we need to learn how to lead any organizing and actions with a concrete racial analysis.

There are many links between the prison explosion and issues such as welfare reform and economic restructuring in general, the downgrading of wages and working conditions in certain sectors, and other globalization processes that increase inequality. Let's research these connections and build multi-issue coalitions built on common struggle.

One example to learn from is the broad coalition pioneered by Critical Resistance in California. In the winter of 2001, I attended a conference in Fresno, California, hosted by Critical Resistance. It was called "Joining Forces: Environmental Justice and the Fight Against Prison Expansion." The conference aimed to explore how prisons constituted environmental racism and injustice and how tactics from the environmental justice movement could be used to stop prison expansion.

	LATINO	AFRICAN AMERICAN	EUROPEAN AMERICAN	"OTHER"
Proportion of California's population	30%	7%	47%	16%
Proportion of California's state prisoners	34.3%	31.1%	29.4%	5.2%

Among the speakers and sponsers were organizers from the United Farm Workers, the Center on Race, Poverty, and the Environment, the West County Toxics Coalition, and MEChA. The conference focused on a proposed new prison in Delano, California, the second to be built in this largely Latino farmworker community.

By getting together to discuss the links between their issue areas, organizers in the environmental justice movement and the prison reform movement were able to devise a united message. The main message was that prisons constitute environmental racism (just as a toxic site would) to both the rural communities where prisons are sited and the urban centers from which most prisoners are taken. When Critical Resistance launched a legal battle against the California Department of Corrections, they had a broad base of support among movements in California. The judge in charge of the case ended up barring construction of the new prison until a new environmental impact report is completed.

This is similar to the vision I have for the linkup between globalization and prison reform activists. We need to understand the connections between our issues and organize with a common analysis and shared resources.

Laura Raymond is a writer and activist who lives in California. She can be reached at laurjuliet@excite.com

Youth Fight the American Lockdown

Kevin Pranis

To win serious reform, the prison movement must draw in new constituencies not traditionally associated with criminal justice reform. And it must involve youth, both because young people have a special stake in reform and because their vitality and creativity are desperately needed for this uphill battle. Pioneers in doing this include the Berkeley-based Prison Activist Resource Center; the Critical Resistance conference convened in 1999 by Angela Davis; and the Prison Moratorium Project (PMP).

While college campuses aren't the only place where we operate (PMP has also worked in high schools, Alternatives To Incarceration programs, and on the street), they are an important site of political struggle, and they offer valuable resources. Over the past four years, we have developed new strategies and tactics to build links between prison and campus, and help students and educators become effective advocates for progressive criminal justice reform. The most promising strategies have blossomed into full-fledged programs including:

- Education Not Incarceration (ENI) helps students at underfunded community colleges and state universities make the connection between ballooning corrections budgets and declining support for public higher education. Working closely with Justice Policy Institute, which documented a nationwide dollar-to-dollar shift from higher education to corrections, and the U.S. Student Association, which represents two million students at colleges and universities across the country, we have helped to make criminal justice reform a "student issue." ENI activities have included press conferences (one of which brought together Congressman Charles Rangel, Angela Davis, and former NYPD Commissioner Patrick Murphy) and a weekend organizing training. Guerrilla theater actions in the New York state capitol highlighted the release of a Justice Policy Institute report on the state's higher education and prison spending.

- No More Prisons uses hip hop music to reach both college students and youth from low-income urban communities of color who are often at risk of involvement in the criminal justice system. Produced by progressive

Prison protest in D.C., February 2000. © *Diane Greene Lent*

Hip Hop label Raptivism Records, No More Prisons has generated tremendous support from hip hop artists, producers, and journalists, many of whom donated time and talent to the production of the No More Prisons hip hop Compilation CD. The full-length CD features twenty-three original tracks of prison music, poetry, and performance recorded by the likes of Last Poets, Dead Prez, The Coup, Danny Hoch, and Cornel West. It is available in major record stores and on line. A forty-city and campus tour featured young organizers and artists from the CD.

• Not With Our Money is a coalition campaign that publicizes the role of for-profit private prisons in the expanding prison-industrial complex, and holds the companies and their investors responsible. Two years of research on various aspects of the prison-industrial complex, including prison labor and prison contracting, uncovered an unholy alliance between a multinational caterer (Sodexho Alliance) and an infamous purveyor of prisons-for-profit (Corrections Corporation of America). Sodexho has long held a controlling interest (currently 10.1%) in CCA, but Sodexho's recent acquisition of North America's largest food service provider—now called Sodexho-Marriott Services—made students at more than five hundred campuses unwitting and unwilling accomplices to the biggest corporate crime of the decade. Tired of seeing their dining dollars go to line the pockets of prison profiteers, students responded by kicking off a national boycott of Sodexho in April, 2000 with actions on ten campuses. Thirty more campuses in the United States and Canada joined campaign, while students at four schools "Dumped Sodexho."

Fortunately, young people aren't alone in the grassroots struggle against the prison-industrial complex. The Public Safety and Justice Campaign, for example, was recently founded to join labor unions, criminal justice activists, and community organizations in a Southern-led fight against prison privatization. We are also heartened by the efforts of groups like California Prison Moratorium Project and documentarian Tracy Huling to document the impact of prisons on rural communities, and to develop strategies to block prison sitings. With creative strategies and a little determination, we can start chipping away at the prison industry.

Kevin Pranis is a board member of Prison Moratorium Project and a national organizer for the Public Safety and Justice Campaign.

Not Just Lobbying: The Minnesota Fair Trade Coalition

Larry Weiss

The Minnesota Fair Trade Coalition includes over fifty unions, religious organizations, and solidarity groups across the state. It mobilizes them against harmful new trade treaties, Fast Track, and global institutions like the World Trade Organization and the International Monetary Fund.

But those campaigns wax and wane with the legislative season. What sustains the Coalition is direct solidarity work and an organization that may shrink when crises are over, but doesn't go away.

The Coalition started in March 1991 as a group of community and labor activists: the president of a United Auto Workers local, a staffer with UNITE, and others. We wrote and called every union in the state saying, "We want to come do a presentation to your local and talk about what NAFTA will mean for you." We also said, "This isn't just a coalition about NAFTA. It's a coalition against corporate globalization." From the beginning we tried to bring in direct solidarity with workers in other countries. We got people sending faxes to support labor struggles in Mexico and we worked with the Coalition for Justice in the Maquiladoras.

By the time of the NAFTA vote in 1994 we had one hundred and one Minnesota organizations: unions that had done some education of their members and had contacted congressional offices, several state environmental groups,

> The Coalition brought three hundred people to Seattle, which we think was the largest contingent from east of the Rockies.

churches, and solidarity groups. We participated in a rally on the border called by the Minnesota AFL-CIO and the Manitoba Federation of Labour. We organized a big rally in the iron ore mining

district near Duluth, where the labor movement and environmentalists had a long history of conflict. The head of the state Sierra Club came and spoke about all the issues in NAFTA and why environmentalists and labor had the same interests. After her speech, a big steelworker came up to her in the parking lot and said, "I never thought I'd see the day when I had anything to do with you folks, but I'd like to give you the shirt off my back." And he did—a United Steelworkers of America T-shirt.

We won the NAFTA vote in our state congressional delegation, six to two, but we lost nationally. Then we held a big meeting about what to do next. Forty-seven of our one hundred and one groups came and said, "We don't want to give up the coalition. Globalization isn't going to go away." They committed to paying dues at a level that would support part-time year-round staff.

Since then we've worked on the big national trade fights against Fast Track, the Caribbean Basin Initiative, and Most Favored Nation status for China. But when these legislative campaigns end, most of the Fair Trade

Campaigns I know die off. They come back to life when Congress returns, they rebuild their coalitions and have a few more good months, but that's not enough to sustain a coalition on our scale.

One thing that sustains us year-round is direct solidarity. In 2000 we hosted two Nicaraguan sweatshop workers who were touring the United States with the National Labor Committee. Over one hundred people came to protest at Kohl's local store, which sold clothes made in Nicaraguan sweatshops. We had significant contingents from the steelworkers, UNITE, the Teamsters, the hotel workers, and other unions. During the civil disobedience, the regional UNITE head, a UAW local president, clergy, nuns, and students were arrested.

However, the national anti-sweatshop campaigns don't give us everything we need either. They have the same stop-and-start quality as legislative campaigns. We get alerts about a new sweatshop, mobilize pickets, build up pressure—and then the alerts stop coming. You can't build a local campaign that way. People have to know they're part of something that has a beginning,

middle, and end, and you have to have a good chance of winning. You have to ask: Did this

Having a real functioning organization, even if it's minimal, allows us to be in touch with people, gather information, get it out to them, and mobilize.

campaign add up, did it build something local, did it involve local people in the planning?

What has kept the coalition going? I think it is the combination of a big-picture issue (corporate globalization versus human rights) which is constantly compelling, and an organization that can keep one or more aspects of that big picture in front of folks. Very seldom in these nine years has nothing at all been happening to keep people involved. About every month we send out a memo with updates on four or five issues that winds up in plants and on union bulletin boards.

It also helps to have one very committed group in the Coalition—the Resource Center of the Americas, where I work. Our work here is to build the local component of national campaigns and an international movement, so we've worked to build an institution in the community that people trust. We have our own building where hundreds of people come to take Spanish classes, use the library, visit the coffee shop, take popular education workshops, do labor support, and organize civil disobedience and lobbying. The Center is known and respected, it has a track record, and that anchors the Coalition.

Larry Weiss serves as coordinator of the Minnesota Fair Trade Coalition and coordinates the Labor, Globalization and Human Rights Project at the Resource Center of the Americas.

Coalition-Building: Lessons from the Jobs with Justice Model

Mary Beth Maxwell

Across the land, globalization activists are building new networks and coalitions. Jobs with Justice is one of several new forces helping to build a new sense of solidarity, a broader movement for economic justice with an international perspective, and more power for working people in local communities. Two key contributions of Jobs with Justice are a solid and expanding base in the labor movement and a model of local coalition building that grows broader and deeper over years of collective action.

Here are some lessons that Jobs with Justice has learned in those years.

Coalitions should win tangible victories

It matters that we have tangible wins: workers winning increased wages, winning union representation, keeping jobs in a local community. Winning concrete victories is crucial to building the movement. It's not enough to have an analysis of what's wrong or to articulate a utopian vision. People need their own experience of making demands and winning them to sustain the hope that greater change is possible and so struggle is worthwhile.

Solidarity

Organizations and their members need to support one another's struggles and that needs to be a two-way street.

Jobs with Justice builds this culture of solidarity with a very basic tool—the "I'll Be There" pledge card. Our coalitions build their bases of activists through this simple pledge card that we ask folks to sign. It says, "I'll Be There five times in the next year for someone else's struggle as well as my own." Many of our coalitions have been doing this for years and now have thousands of pledge-card signers that are called out to actions by phonebanks and phone trees. The culture of solidarity puts into practice the old saying, "An injury to one is an injury to all."

Let's take an example. A few years ago, the American Federation of Musicians in Seattle was in contract negotiations with the Fifth Avenue Theatre. Things weren't going so well. The multi-million dollar company was balking at modest wage increases and workplace improvements. The musicians decided to strike just as the theatre was opening its run of *Beauty and the Beast.*

Fifth Avenue, expecting a picket line of eighteen musicians in front of the theatre, brought in scabs for the show and assumed they could get away with it. What they did not expect was a thousand people shutting down the whole street on opening night and several nights thereafter. Jobs with Justice and the King County Labor Council had been building their coalition for several years, building relationships and mobilization capacity. Labor unions, community groups, and students were out in the street saying, "Not in our town, we will not let workers be treated this way in our town."

The workers were bolstered by this dramatic support. Management could not sustain the bad publicity or their losses at the box office. They came back to the bargaining table and the musicians negotiated their best contract in years.

Later that year, Justice for

A CODE OF BEHAVIOR FOR COALITIONS AND NETWORKS

S.M. Miller

Coalitions are marriages of convenience, not overpowering romantic couplings. The partners have to learn how to live with each other. Here are some relatively simple things you can do to build trust and effective working relations within a coalition.

Understanding

Many difficulties between members of a coalition arise because they do not understand what the other members stand for, how they make decisions, and what their problems are—internally and externally.

- Each member of the coalition should be aware of how other members reach decisions, and the internal constraints, pressures, and disagreements that shape their organizations.
- Also clarify what brings the coalitions' members together and what divides them. What are they likely to work together on? What are the likely clashing points or turf battles you should avoid or downplay?

Norms

Norms—what things to do or avoid—are crucial in shaping effective coalitions. How should the members of a coalition behave?

- Accept differences and a division of labor. What one group can do, others cannot. Recognizing this helps avoid the feeling that a group is not carrying its weight. See a coalition as involving a division of labor and ideology. A coalition cannot expect sameness in action or belief, but must respect differences among its members.

- Get information before you holler. When there is disagreement or criticism, don't undermine the coalition—find out the other side of the story.
- Clean up the language of disagreement.
- Separate what is done as a coalition from what is done as an organization. Joining a coalition does not mean giving up the particular qualities of a group. Groups continue to speak in their own names, but they must make clear that they speak for themselves and not the coalition as a whole.
- Avoid using the media to voice disagreements within the coalition.
- Share the credit.

Procedures

Make clear early in the life of the coalition how decisions are going to be made: by consensus, voting, majority rule, or blocking. Keep to the process you adopt.

- Work out in advance a procedure for what to do when strong disagreements emerge or persist.
- Clarify in advance how much room coalition staff and leadership have to make decisions.

Excerpted by permission from "Coalition Etiquette: Ground Rules for Building Unity." For a copy of the entire paper, contact S.M. Miller at fivegood@aol.com.

Janitors organized a strike. Libby Poole, one of the musicians from the *Beauty and the Beast* fight, put her body on the line and got arrested. She said, "I had to do it. It was so amazing that so many people came out for us and our strike. I had to be there for the janitors." That is the power of solidarity. If enough of us are there, we'll all start winning.

Militancy

Along with a culture of solidarity we try to build a culture of militancy to support workers' rights. This means creative direct action and if need be civil disobedience. We believe it takes more than being right to win—it takes more than good arguments. Direct action means saying to the boss, to the corporation, "No more business as usual." We seek in this direct action to strategically pressure targets that can meet our demands so our action can yield victories.

Investing in long-term relationships

In Jobs with Justice we often say that it takes a long time to build relationships and a short time to ruin them. The old way that labor often sought solidarity was to wait for a crisis to reach out for support. That's often too late to engage a broader range of allies or to mobilize seriously. What's worse, it reinforces the notion that labor too often takes community support for granted. And let's face it, many of our organizations—not just unions—only reach out at the last minute when the agenda is already established. Or we never really reach out. We just try to go it alone, whether it's a strike or a housing campaign or a rally.

The Seattle musicians could not have won if we had to rebuild community support and coalition power from scratch each time a crisis presented itself. We believe in building relationships not simply because it is the right thing to do but because it is one of the only ways we are ever going to sustain a movement and build enough power to challenge corporations, governments, and other institutions that affect our lives.

Working across differences takes time and trust. Unions, community organizations, student organizations, and faith-based activists have much in common and very different organizational self-interests, ways of operating, histories, leadership structures, and accountabilities to membership. Common targets or well-articulated issue linkages are not enough to build and sustain coalitions. People need face-to-face time, working together time, experience overcoming conflicts, the kind of trust that only develops over time because I see what you actually *do*, not just what you say in a meeting. And sometimes, when we really get down to it, self-interest is not mutual and we need enough history together to agree to disagree on this one and reunite on the next.

Mary Beth Maxwell is a national organizer with Jobs with Justice.

Challenging White Supremacy

Helen Luu

When Elizabeth (Betita) Martinez first posed the question, "Where was the Color in Seattle?" in her now infamous article (p. 80), she shone the spotlight on an issue that had been up until then largely ignored, brushed aside, overlooked. While chants of "This is What Democracy Looks Like!" were echoing throughout the streets of Seattle, people of color such as youth organizer Jinee Kim were thinking, "Is this really what democracy looks like? Nobody here looks like me." In image after image of the "Battle of Seattle," a disconcerting reality reared its head: the protesters were overwhelmingly white, despite the fact that people of color are often the ones hardest hit by capitalist globalization.

Over one year later, numerous mass demonstrations have taken place as part of the growing globalization movement in the West. Resistance has been demonstrated and continues to be demonstrated in city after city, making it very clear that capitalist globalization is not welcome on our planet. But in city after city in the United States, the overwhelming whiteness of the protesters and organizers has continued with few exceptions. Meanwhile, the long history of struggle and resistance against capitalist globalization of peoples in the South and of people of color and indigenous peoples in the West continues to be ignored while Seattle is credited again and again by the media—and even by activists—as the official beginning of the movement.

It is easy enough to be swept up in the energy and excitement of the globalization movement—and without a doubt it has been an extremely exciting time—but it is far more challenging to point out the problems within it. This challenge is one that we must face, however, if we are to progress any further in our movement. As the articles in this section demonstrate, challenging and dismantling the racial oppression that has been crippling the movement is crucial, and antiracist work must be at the core of our organizing and strategizing for the future.

Both Colin Rajah (p. 85) and Chris Crass (p. 89) offer reasons why we need to make genuine antiracist work a priority in our movement building, and offer suggestions for ways to begin doing this work. Both stress the need to go beyond merely recruiting people of color to join in the demonstrations: that undermines the fact that people of color have already been organizing for decades. Crass brings attention to the role of white supremacy and how it operates not only in larger society but also in activist settings. He outlines a strategy for white activists to do genuine antiracist work. Both Crass and Rajah stress the importance of building alliances with people of color, of recognizing the need to struggle alongside communities of color, of respecting the leadership of people of color. Both also stress the need to make the connection between local issues and global issues.

The "Tools for White Guys . . . " (p. 96) challenge activists to look at the ways that power and privilege manifest themselves in activist settings such as meetings, and offer some practical suggestions that individuals can use to begin chipping away at them.

Challenging and dismantling different forms of oppression within our movement *simultaneously* with resisting capitalist globalization is absolutely crucial if we are serious about fighting for a world that is free and just for all. Already, the impact of Martinez's article and the observations about the whiteness of the movement have triggered positive responses from people who are working towards making the movement truly antiracist. For example, Colours of Resistance (COR) is a grassroots network that was conceived to work on developing multiracial, antiracist politics in the movement against global capitalism, and that advocates for and works towards a movement that is dedicated to ending all forms of oppression. This is the kind of movement we must endeavor to work towards if we are serious about fighting capitalist globalization.

—Helen Luu is an organizer with Colours of Resistance who resides mainly in Toronto, Canada.

Where Was the Color in Seattle?

Looking for reasons why the Great Battle was so white

Elizabeth 'Betita' Martinez

I was at the jail where a lot of protesters were being held and a big crowd of people was chanting 'This Is What Democracy Looks Like!' At first it sounded kind of nice. But then I thought: is this really what democracy looks like? Nobody here looks like me.

—Jinee Kim, Bay Area youth organizer

In the vast acreage of published analysis about the splendid victory over the World Trade Organization in 1999, it is almost impossible to find anyone wondering why the forty to fifty thousand demonstrators were overwhelmingly Anglo. How can that be, when the WTO's main victims around the world are people of color? Understanding the reasons for the low level of color, and what can be learned from it, is absolutely crucial if we are to make Seattle's promise of a new, international movement against imperialist globalization come true.

The overall turnout of color from the United States at the protests remained around five percent of the total. In personal interviews, activists from the Bay Area and the Southwest gave me several reasons for this. Some mentioned concern about the likelihood of brutal police repression. Other obstacles: lack of funds for the trip, inability to be absent from work during the week, and problems in finding child care.

Yet several experienced activists of color in the Bay Area who had even been offered full scholarships chose not to go. A major reason for not participating, and the reason given by many others, was lack of knowledge about the WTO. As one Filipina said, "I didn't see the political significance of it—how the protest would be antiimperialist. We didn't know anything about the WTO except that lots of people were going to the meeting."

One of the few groups that did feel informed, and did participate, was the hip hop group Company of Prophets. According to African-American member Rashidi Omari of Oakland, this happened as a result of their attending teach-ins by predominantly white groups like Art and Revolution. Com-

pany of Prophets, rapping from a big white van, was in the front ranks of the 6 A.M. march that closed down the WTO on November 30. The problem of unfamiliarity with the WTO was aggravated by the fact that black and Latino communities across the United States lack Internet access compared to many white communities. Information about the WTO and all the plans for Seattle did not reach many people of color.

Limited knowledge meant a failure to see how the WTO affected the daily lives of U.S. communities of color. "Activists of color felt they had more immediate issues," said Rashidi. "Also, when we returned people told me of being worried that family and peers would say they were neglecting their own communities, if they went to Seattle. They would be asked, 'Why are you going? You should stay here and help your people.' "

Along with such concerns about linkage came the assumption that the protest would be overwhelmingly white as it was. Coumba Toure, a Bay Area activist originally from Mali, West Africa, said she had originally thought, "the whites will take care of the

WTO, I don't need to go." Others were more openly apprehensive. For example, Carlos ("Los" for short) Windham of Company of Prophets told me, "I think even Bay Area activists of color who understood the linkage didn't want to go to a protest dominated by fifty thousand white hippies."

People of color had reason to expect the protest to be white-dominated. Roberto Maestas, director of Seattle's Centro de la Raza, told me that in the massive local press coverage before the WTO meeting, not a single person of color appeared as a spokesperson for the opposition.

"Day after day, you saw only white faces in the news. The publicity was a real deterrent to people of color. I think some of the unions or church groups should have had representatives of color, to encourage people of color to participate."

Four protesters of color from different Bay Area organizations talked about the culture shock they experienced when they first visited the Convergence, the protest center set up by the Direct Action Network, a coalition of many organizations. Said one, "When we walked in, the room was filled with young whites calling themselves anarchists. There was a pungent smell, many had not showered. We just couldn't relate to the scene so our whole group left right away." Another told me, "They sounded dogmatic and paranoid." "I just freaked and left," said another. "It wasn't just race, it was also culture, although race was key."

In retrospect, observed Van Jones of STORM (Standing Together to Organize a Revolutionary Movement) in the Bay Area, "We should have stayed. We didn't see that we had a lot to learn from them. And they had a lot of materials for making banners, signs, puppets." "Later I went back and talked to people," recalled Rashidi, "and they were discussing tactics, very smart. Those folks were really ready for action. It was limiting for people of color to let that one experience affect their whole picture of white activists." Jinee Kim, a Korean-American with the Third Eye Movement in

Convergence (n). 1. Gathering of activists and affinity groups, esp. to prepare for a direct action. 2. Convergence center or convergence space: "I dropped off the puppets at the Convergence."

the Bay Area, also thought it was a mistake. "We realized we didn't know how to do a blockade. We had no gas masks. They made sure everybody had food and water, they took care of people. We could have learned from them."

Reflecting the more positive evaluation of white protesters in general, Richard Moore, coordinator of the Southwest Network for Environmental and Economic Justice, told me that "the white activists were very disciplined." "We sat down with whites, we didn't take the attitude that 'we can't work with white folks,' " concluded Rashidi. "It was a liberating experience."

Few predominantly white groups in the Bay Area made a serious effort to get people of color to Seattle. Juliette Beck of Global Exchange worked hard with others to help people from developing (Third World) countries to come. But for U.S. people of color, the main organizations that made a serious effort to do so were JustAct (Youth ACTion for Global JUSTice), formerly the Overseas Development Network, and Art and Revolution, which mostly helped artists. Many activists of color have mentioned Alli Chaggi-Starr of Art and Revolution, who not only helped

people come but for the big march in Seattle she obtained a van with a sound system that was used by musicians and rappers.

In JustAct, Coumba Toure and two other members of color—Raj Jayadev and Malachi Larabee—pushed hard for support from the group. As a result, about forty people of color were enabled to go, thanks to special fundraising and whites staying at people's homes in Seattle so their hotel money could be used instead on plane tickets for people of color. Reflecting on the whole issue of working with whites, Coumba talked not only about pushing JustAct but also pushing people of color to apply for the help that became available.

One of the problems Coumba said she encountered in doing this was "a legacy of distrust of middle-class white activists that has emerged from experiences of 'being used.' Or not having our issues taken seriously. Involving people of color must be done in a way that gives them real space. Whites must understand a whole new approach is needed that includes respect (if you go to people of color thinking you know more, it creates a barrier). Also, you cannot approach people simply in terms of numbers, like 'let's give two scholarships.'

People of color must be central to the project."

Jia Ching Chen recalled that once during the week of protest, in a jail holding cell, he was one of only two people of color among many Anglos. He tried to discuss with some of them the need to involve more activists of color and the importance of white support in this. "Some would say, 'We want to diversify,' but didn't understand the dynamics of this." In other words, they didn't understand the kinds of problems described by Coumba Toure. "Other personal conversations were more productive," he said, "and some white people started to recognize why people of color could view the process of developing working relations with whites as oppressive."

Unfortunately the heritage of distrust was intensified by some of the AFL-CIO leadership of labor on the November 30 march. They chose to take a different route through downtown rather than marching with others to the Convention Center and helping to block the WTO. Also, on the march to downtown they reportedly had a conflict with the Third World People's Assembly contingent when they rudely told the people of color to move aside so they could be in the lead.

Yet if only a small number of people of color went to Seattle, all those with whom I spoke found the experience extraordinary. They spoke of being changed forever. "I saw the future." "I saw the possibility of people working together." They called the giant mobilization "a shot in the arm" if you had been feeling stagnant. "Being there was an incredible awakening." Naomi, a Filipina dancer and musician, recalled how "at first a lot of my group were tired, grumpy, wanting to go home. That really changed. One of the artists with us, who never considered herself a political activist, now wants to get involved back in Oakland. Seattle created a lot of strong bonds in my small community of coworkers and friends."

They seem to feel they had seen why, as the chant popularized by the Chicano/a students of MEChA goes, "Ain't no power like the power of the people, 'cause the power of the people don't stop!"

There must be effective follow-up and increased communication between people of color across the nation: grassroots organizers, activists, cultural workers, and educators. We need to build on the contacts made (or that need to be made) from Seattle. Even within the Bay Area, activists who could form working alliances still do not know of each other's existence.

The opportunity to build on the WTO victory shines brightly. More than ever, we need to work on our ignorance about global issues with study groups, youth workshops, conferences. We need to draw specific links between WTO and our close-to-home struggles in communities of color, as has been emphasized by Raj Jayadev and Lisa Juachon in *The Silicon Valley Reader: Localizing the Effects of the Global Economy* (1999), which they edited. As Jinee

Kim said at a San Francisco report-back by youth of color, "We have to work with people who may not know the word 'globalization' but they live globalization."

Elizabeth 'Betita' Martinez is a longtime Chicana activist, author and educator based in San Francisco. She has published six books and many articles on popular struggles in the Americas, taught Women's Studies in the California state university system, and worked with youth on antiracist issues. Currently she heads the Institute for MultiRacial Justice, a resource center to help build alliances among peoples of color and combat divisions. This article is excerpted from a longer version printed in ColorLines Magazine, Spring 2000, vol. 3 no. 1.

Race in the Globalization Movement

Colin Rajah

When I first came to the United States to go to college back in 1989, I had already spent more than six years intensely involved in political activism in Malaysia and other parts of Southeast Asia. A veteran activist, one might say. Large conferences and training camps, strategizing meetings, street demonstrations, police arrests and the resulting brutality,

were all significant parts of my life by then. I expected the following years here to be no different. The quest for liberation and justice would continue to inform and drive me, I assumed.

Strangely, the process of assimilation into U.S. college culture, specifically the activist one, proved problematic. I realized that I had to relearn a lot of the language, tactics, approaches, and structures in academia as well as within campus activism. My frustration with my U.S. peer activists and vice versa often pushed the limits of my dedication. It soon became apparent that stratified social constructions and structures that exist in the larger U.S. context, were often manifested in social subsets, including that of the political left.

What was most difficult in this realization, however, was that I needed to alter my behavior, attitudes, and way of thinking to the dominant patterns of U.S. leftist organizing if I was to fully integrate myself into this form of activism. This included changing how I prioritized social issues of importance, how I approached these issues strategically/tactically, how I communicated it to my fellow organizers and the general public.

What this inevitably meant was that my previous years of activism were pretty much meaningless. The resulting loss of self-confidence made me constantly question why I was doing this and what greater purpose this process would contribute to.

Ten years later, and now we find ourselves in a moment of significant historical importance. You can't take a trip to the restroom without running into an article about the protest movement and the growing resistance to corporate-led globalization. Seattle, D.C., Philadelphia, L.A., and undoubtedly other cities to follow have all catapulted the issues of global capitalist political economy to the forefront of national and international attention.

Yet we cannot escape from the harsh reality that confronts us at every strategizing meeting, at every sit-in, and at every protest and rally that has accompanied this movement, and to a larger extent the globalization struggle. It is predominantly white, and perhaps even more troubling, it is predominantly middle class.

At the risk of stating the obvious, none of us should be comfortable about this for many reasons. For one thing, it strategically limits the movement's public appeal. Not everyone will be able to relate to young white middle-class people. In fact statistically, among college-aged young people in this country, only about one quarter are enrolled in a four-year college or university. Others are in community colleges, vocational schools, working, or incarcerated by the police state. It can be substantially argued that this is a larger reflection of social stratification in this country. Most people's attraction to the liberating potential of this movement will be miniscule because, quite frankly, the people on the covers of the newspaper articles about the protests look, talk, and act different from most.

Such a movement will also have trouble forging powerful alliances with other people and sectors of society. Yes, this movement has publicly exposed capitalist deficiencies in the World Bank and WTO. However, if the movement remains sectarian and esoteric, and unable to link with community struggles of people of color, immigrants, indigenous peoples, and others, the ruling class will only find it easier to ignore or even terminate the movement.

But arguably most important, a mostly homogenous force will undoubtedly have significant holes in its ideology. Its relevance to oppression everywhere will be limited by its lack of inclusivity of those other realities not experienced by the inherent privileges that comes from being a white middle-class person. This is

serious because if we claim to speak a truth at a global level, we will already have failed in the very formulation stage of that truth.

The attention being paid to this issue has in one sense been comforting. It is good to know that organizations and individuals alike are acknowledging the stark stratification of this movement. On the other hand, the approaches they are taking is oftentimes alarming and difficult to manage. The common reaction of "we need to diversify our outreach" is not only short-sighted and myopic, it singlehandedly ignores decades of community organizing by working class people and people of color, and approaches our communities as if we need to once again be incorporated or assimilated into this movement. There should first and foremost be a recognition of the level of political mobilization that has been happening at the community level for years.

The seemingly Berlin Wall divide between globalization and community organizing, centers on impact. Most communities of color direct our efforts toward bread and butter issues such as housing, jobs, the police state, access to education, and health that have a direct impact on our working class communities. It's a matter of survival. The middle-class, college-educated-led globalization movement can afford and has the access to broaden their efforts towards other injustices that don't necessarily oppress them directly—sweatshops, Third World debt, or international trade.

Since we more and more recognize the root or structural similarities of these struggles, this movement needs to be able to struggle *alongside* our communities on these other community issues as well. At the same time, the movement needs to be conscious of not *taking over* these struggles (since communities and individuals of color have led them for ages) but play strategic and important ally roles. There is a space for that, and undoubtedly communities of color will be appreciative and very welcoming of such efforts to engage.

Another key aspect that needs addressing is leadership. While many claim a leaderless movement as an ideal, the reality is that certain individuals play significant roles in leading and directing struggles. To ignore such leadership is not only strategically weak, it also shows a high amount of disrespect for individuals who have dedicated their lives at great expense and who hold the trust of their mobilizations. Direct engagement amongst these leaders is a critical step to forging real and lasting alliances.

However, perhaps the most challenging aspect of building such cross-race, cross-class alliances is the ability to acknowledge that we all carry certain cultural, language, and behavioral traits. While these should be celebrated and embraced, alliance-building and mobilization require an ability to be respectful and not overwhelm any space with a dominant culture that might be alienating to others who do not share it. While in principle this appears obviously agreeable, it might sometimes mean sacrificing certain traits that individuals or groups hold dear.

If the U.S. movement against corporate-led globalization seeks to maintain its momentum and have a lasting impact on sociopolitical change, two things are for certain. First, it should never seek to diversify itself. It should embrace itself for what it is, while sharing leadership and working together with community activists and movements in forging new alliances and reinventing how it approaches its activism.

The other certainty in this mix of variables is that the effort to build cross-race, cross-class alliances and share strategies and struggles is by no means an easy task. We will have to counter and overcome centuries of social stratification and segregation at multiple levels. But our collective moral obligation is to do just that and not to remain divided in our struggles for justice and liberation.

Colin Rajah is the Director of Programs for JustAct—Youth ACTion for Global JUSTice, a national nonprofit organization dedicated to promoting youth education and activism for global justice. A youth activist for more than seventeen years, Colin currently directs all of JustAct's programmatic aspects of education, organizing, and action for thousands of youth activists nationally, and coordinates working alliances with youth movements internationally.

Beyond the Whiteness—Global Capitalism and White Supremacy

Thoughts on movement building and antiracist organizing

Chris Crass

One of the most exciting developments that has come out of the globalization movement's mass actions is the movement-wide discussion about racism, white supremacy, and organizing strategies to build a multiracial radical movement for global justice.

Elizabeth 'Betita' Martinez's widely distributed essay, "Where Was the Color in Seattle," put forward the question: Why, if global capitalism has the greatest negative impact on people of color around the world and in the United States, was the direct action against the WTO so overwhelmingly white? Her essay helped launch a dialogue in alternative media and in activists groups throughout the United States and beyond.

Among activists of color, the question has generally been, "How can we bring an analysis of global capitalism and global justice to our local organizing efforts?" White activists have responded to Betita's essay by asking themselves, "How can we get people of color to join our groups and movement?" But this isn't the most useful question that we should be asking. The question to struggle with is, "How can we be antiracist activists dedicated to bringing down white supremacy?" White activists need to work on developing our understanding of white supremacy, how white privilege operates in the activist movement, and how we can bring a solid antiracist politics to the work that we do.

It's more than diversity

The idea that we just need to get more people of color to join our groups is an example of how white activists have internalized white supremacy. It carries the idea that we have all the answers and now they just need to be delivered to people of color. The alternative would be something like this: people of color have been organizing for a long time (500+ years), and we (white

activists) have a lot to learn, so maybe we should find ways to form alliances, relationships, and coalitions to work with people of color and be prepared to learn as well as share.

The other major problem with "how can we get more people of color to join our group" is the idea that antiracist consciousness develops through osmosis—that if white people sit in the same room as people of color, we will begin to understand how white supremacy operates and therefore we won't really need to talk about it. We need to be clear that multiracial doesn't automatically mean antiracist. The U.S. military is multiracial in composition, but clearly serves the interests of imperialism and white supremacy. Similarly, an antiracist group of whites can work to end white supremacy. What we are envisioning is a consciously antiracist and multiracial movement against global capitalism.

White people do learn about racism through interactions and relationships with people of color. But our goal cannot be to bring in people of color and expect that they will teach us. Organizers of color have enough work already. In our pursuit to get educated, we need to go to more events and actions organized by people of color and show support, listen, and learn.

We need to read the amazing writers that are out there. We can pay attention to how the system works (when we are in jail, in court, in classrooms, at work, and on the street). We can build relationships and learn from each other. But, just as men cannot expect women to educate them about sexism, and heteros cannot expect queers to give them the Homophobia 101 class whenever it is deemed appropriate, white people have a responsibility to work on racism together and not just wait until a person of color brings it up.

Here's an example of this kind of dynamic. Men in Food Not Bombs, the group I've worked with, would often talk about sexism in terms of how can we get more women taking on more responsibility and create equal power. The conversations would sometimes turn to such questions as, "How can we check our behavior that is preventing women from taking on responsibility?" And, "What kind of internal culture do we have and how does it privilege men and

keep women down?" These conversations about what men should do were very useful—men should worry less about what women are and aren't doing, and think more about what they as men are and aren't doing. The women in the group are just as capable, just as responsible, just as intelligent, once men stop occupying all of the space and learn to share power. Men worrying less about appeasing women and more about ending sexism is what must happen.

This is how we need to think about racism. Too often I hear white activists talk about why more people of color aren't in the group—not whether we really understand how deeply racism affects the issues we're working on, and how we can form working relationships with organizations and activists of color already working on these issues.

White supremacy is a system of power

The definition of white supremacy that I use comes from Sharon Martinas and the Challenging White Supremacy Workshop. White supremacy is a historically based, institutionally perpetuated system of exploitation and oppression of continents, nations, and people of color by white people and nations of the European continent. Its purpose is to maintain and defend a system of wealth, power, and privilege. White supremacy operates through racial oppression against people of color: slavery, genocide, antiimmigration, driving while black—and white privilege to white people: not being thought of as a criminal every time you walk into a store, for example. All the while, white supremacy maintains real power for the ruling class who control the major institutions of society.

The effect white supremacy has on white folks is rarely looked at, especially in relationship to activism and organizing. White privilege means that white people don't have to think about racism. White privilege means that white people can think of themselves as normal and generalize universally that what they experience is the standard. White privilege is a major barrier to activism and has historically undermined radical, multiracial, and antiracist movement building. An example is

Republican Convention protest, Philadelphia, August 2000.
© Diane Greene Lent

white radicals organizing actions that involve possible arrest without thinking about how people of color have a very different relationship to the police. Police brutality is a daily reality in communities of color and police generally treat people of color more harshly than whites.

White privilege often leads to white activists thinking that their way of organizing is the only way to organize and that their tactics are the most radical tactics. In the political punk zine *HeartAttack*, activist Helen Luu wrote about the whiteness of the protests in Seattle as well as the left/anarchist movement generally. Luu looked at how middle-class white activists often have the privilege to choose issues and tactics, and stated that they generally have less to lose by engaging in activism. People of color, on the other hand, generally have to focus their activism on survival issues—like police brutality, housing, welfare rights, environmental toxins next door—that affect their lives and communities in concrete ways. Luu argued that we need to rethink the way we define activism and I would argue that white radicals need to examine how we talk about

"radical" issues and "militant" tactics in relationship to the way white supremacy operates.

White privilege undermines solidarity when white activists are "blinded by the white." By this, I mean that white activists often fail to comprehend the implications of communities of color organizing and building the strength to get toxins out of their neighborhood, get improved public transportation, get accountable public schools, end police violence, or end INS deportation.

Jason Wade and Steve Stewart took up the discussion about organizing and anti-racism in their article, "The Battle for our Lives" from the anarchist journal *The Arsenal.* They argue that activists/organizers must develop analysis that connects sweatshop labor in Indonesia to sweatshop labor in the United States and demonstrate that global capitalism creates misery in the Third World and misery in the United States as well. They write, "We need to take the momentum from the antiglobal capitalism struggles and connect them with struggles against police brutality, for health care, against welfare cutbacks, for better access to education, struggles that grow from our neighborhoods, and build a serious revolutionary critique, vision, and movement to redistribute power back to our everyday lives." They argue, "We have to struggle around these 'everyday life' issues if we hope to build a more multiracial movement."

Allies in solidarity

With this in mind, white activists need to think about antiracist organizing in at least a couple of ways. One, white privilege is the flipside of racial oppression and each must be challenged if we are to move towards equality. Two, when people of color oppose racism they are also reaffirming their humanity in a social order that denies it. That is why struggles around racism have been such catalysts for revolutionary social change: they challenge the foundation of this society—white supremacy. White radicals need to think about ways of talking about and organizing against white privilege—in the predominately white sectors of the movement and in general white society. White radicals should remember that organizing against racism is also about freeing our own humanity from the grip of the slave society.

White radicals also need to think about how we go about forming working relationships with people of color. Gloria Anzaldúa, queer Chicana author/activist, writes about how white activists often talk about helping other people— helping the people at Big Mountain, the farm workers, indigenous communities working to keep toxins out of their neighborhoods, political prisoners, etc. Anzaldúa writes that as they (white folks) learn our histories and understand our struggles, "They will come to see that they are not helping us but following our lead." This is a major distinction—no white savior coming to make it all better, but rather white allies working in solidarity with people of color in a way that respects leadership and builds trust and respect.

White activists must find ways to show solidarity and act as allies with people of color. It's not about helping other people with their issues or acting from a sense of guilt, but rather taking responsibility for racial injustice and recognizing how those issues affect us. As black feminist author/activist Barbara Smith says, "In political struggles there wouldn't be any 'your' and 'my' issues, if we saw each form of oppression as integrally linked to the others."

Criminal injustice protest, D.C., February 2000.
© *Diane Greene Lent*

This is an exciting time with great possibilities. We need to be ready to make mistakes, make hard decisions, and experiment with antiracist organizing that really challenges white supremacy while confronting global capitalism.

In doing our work, it is important to have vision and hold on to it. When I think about and imagine the kind of movement of which I want to be a part, it is: multiracial and antiracist— absolutely dedicated to self-determination for all oppressed people and ending white supremacy; feminist with a commitment to develop new social relationships based on equality and bring down the social structures based on domination; queer liberationist with a commitment to challenging heterosexism and creating freedom to safely define our own sexualities and genders; multigenerational and full of energy, wisdom, and a desire to make healthy communities for all of us to care for and learn from each other; anticapitalist with a deep analysis of how the system deforms and dehumanizes us joined with a vision of a new order based on social cooperation and ecological sustainability; and democratic with a passion for col-

lective liberation and empowerment, along with an eye for organizing strategies that have direct
action, collective action and soli-
darity-building at their core.

Together we can, forever we
must.

*Chris Crass is a writer/organizer
working to bridge race, class, and
gender analysis of power with
anarchist theory and practice. He*

*is an antiracist trainer/organizer
in San Francisco; he works with the
Direct Action Network and Colours
of Resistance. He would like to
thank his mentors Sharon Martinas,
Elizabeth 'Betita' Martinez, and
Roxanne Dunbar-Ortiz.*

Tools for White Guys Who Are Working for Social Change

and other people socialized in a society based on domination

Chris Crass

1.   Practice noticing who's in the room at meetings—how many men, how many women, how many white people, how many people of color. Are the majority heterosexual, are there out queers, what are people's class backgrounds? Don't assume to know people, but also work at being more aware.

2a. Count how many times you speak and keep track of how long you speak.

2b. Count how many times other people speak and keep track of how long they speak.

3.   Be conscious of how often you are actively listening to what other people are saying as opposed to just waiting your turn and/or thinking about what you'll say next.

4.   Practice going to meetings focused on listening and learning; go to some meetings and do not speak at all.

5a. Count how many times you put ideas out to the group.

5b. Count how many times you support other people's ideas for the group.

6.   Practice supporting people by asking them to expand on ideas and dig more deeply before you decide to support the idea or not.

7a. Think about whose work and contribution to the group gets recognized.

7b. Practice recognizing more people for the work they do and try to do it more often.

8. Practice asking more people what they think about meetings, ideas, actions, strategy, and vision. White guys tend to talk amongst themselves and develop strong bonds that manifest in organizing. This creates an internal organizing culture that is alienating for most people. Developing respect and solidarity across race, class, gender, and sexuality is complex and difficult, but absolutely critical—and liberating.

9. Be aware of how often you ask people to do something as opposed to asking other people "what needs to be done."

10. Think about and struggle with the saying, "You will be needed in the movement when you realize that you are not needed in the movement."

11. Struggle with and work with the model of group leadership that says that the responsibility of leaders is to help develop more leaders, and think about what this means to you.

12. Remember that social change is a process, and that our individual transformation and individual liberation is intimately interconnected with social transformation and social liberation. Life is profoundly complex and there are many contradictions. Remember that the path we travel is guided by love, dignity, and respect—even when it is bumpy and difficult to navigate.

13. This list is not limited to white guys, nor is it intended to reduce all white guys into one category. This list is intended to disrupt patterns of domination that hurt our movement and hurt each other. White guys have a lot of work to do, but it is the kind of work that makes life worth living.

14. Day-to-day patterns of domination are the glue that holds together systems of domination. The struggle against capitalism, white supremacy, patriarchy, heterosexism, and the state, is also the struggle towards collective liberation.

15. No one is free until all of us are free.

Antiracism Workshop This three-hour workshop for white people was

used for the August, 2000, Democratic Convention protests in Los Angeles.

```
              Goals for Workshop

1. Build an awareness around power and privilege
as it is tied to white racial identity.
2. Look at what it means to be white people par-
ticipating in the Convergence space daily actions,
and in the growing movement.
3. Gain some basic tools for communication on
issues of racism.
4. Challenge ourselves and each other to keep
active and conscious about issues of racism.
```

Introductions of facilitators, Ground rules, Tools for communication on issues of racism

Philosophy of workshop

We are going to be working together and taking action together in the streets. We need to understand that we come from different places and experiences. We need to look at how these differences affect our interactions with one another and affect people's participation in our movements. Today we are going to focus on racism because this is one of the core things that still divides our movements.

We take it as given that racism exists in this society. Racism = Race Prejudice + Power. Power is passed on by controlling the institutions and systems of governing. Racism includes institutional/systemic racism, individual acts of racism, and racist ideas. Racism gives a series of advantages, rewards, or benefits to those in the dominant group (whites, males, Christians, heterosexuals, etc). Privileges are bestowed unintentionally, unconsciously, and automatically. Often, these privileges are invisible to the receiver.

Internalized racial superiority is a multigenerational process of receiving, acting on, internalizing, making invisible, and legitimizing a system of privilege. If we are going to practice antiracist behavior we have to do work to unlearn racism. We need spaces where we feel safe enough to take risks, grow, and unlearn.

Introductions and Sentence Completion
"When I think about my racial identity I feel _____"

Identity Exercise
Break into pairs and select partner A and partner B. Partner A will go first and answer the questions and B will listen silently. Then they will switch and do the same thing. We will then switch partners.

Questions for exercise
When was the first time that you realized you were white?

What did you learn from your family about being white?

What did you learn from society about being white?

What is one thing that is negative about being white?

What is one thing that is positive about being white?

What do you think it means for you to be white and a part of the globalization movement?

Debrief exercise
What was it like to talk about your racial identity?

What was hard to discuss about your racial identity?

Testimony
Ask for one or two people to share a short story that illuminates a specific experience of racism in Seattle, D.C., or other action in which their privilege as a white person played out.

Breakouts on power and privilege
Break into small groups of three to four people. Discuss your privilege in relationship to institutions that we will be interacting with during the course of the actions. Answer this question: A privilege that I have in (choose one below) as a white person would be _____.

| Criminal Justice System | Media | Education |

Debrief small group discussion in large group

Ask people to share what they discussed in their small groups.
Ask them what they learned about their white privilege and how they benefit from it.

Interrupting racism role play

Ask for volunteers to role play and have them act out the situation. During the situation freeze the action and ask for a volunteer to step in and try other ways to interrupt the racism. Do this a couple of times discussing the effectiveness of each strategy.

Role play 1: Rock affinity group has just finished meeting and two white members of this racially mixed affinity group are talking after the meeting. One person is complaining that the people of color in the group were not committed enough because they had concerns about getting arrested. The other person challenges the first about their racist attitudes. The role play begins with the first person complaining about the people of color in the group.

Role play 2: This takes place at the convergence center. A group of people of color walks into the space and immediately leaves. Two white people are talking about what just happened. One person is complaining that the community is so unappreciative of the work that is being done and they do not understand why these people just left. The other white person needs to engage this person about their racist attitudes.

Debrief the Exercise

Why is it important to interrupt racism?
What can get in the way of you interrupting racism?
What are some strategies we can brainstorm to help us interrupt racism?

What all this means for the movement

What do we want the globalization movement to look like?
What does it mean to have antiracism as a main focus?
How can we as white people be allies to people of color and other white people?

Close

Building Today's Global Movement

Walda Katz-Fishman and Jerome Scott

Three essential building blocks for our economic and social justice movement are critical consciousness, vision, and strategy. Critical consciousness is our understanding of how the world works and our place in it, including our sense of history. Vision is the big and bold picture we create of the world we want for our families, our communities, and our planet. Strategy is the plan we collectively make to change the world in which we live into the world we envision.

To build today's global movement for economic and social justice we must be clear about the answers to the following three questions:

What is today's globalization and what does it mean?
Why do we need a global movement and why can we win?
Where is our movement today and how can it lead to victory?

What is today's globalization and what does it mean?

Today's globalization is globalization in the electronic age. It brings together high technology, global capital, the dominant power of global corporations, and neoliberal policies. Together these forces create maximum profit for global corporations through their unrestricted access to all markets—for finance, goods and services, and labor— around the world.

High technology—for example, electronics, computers, information technology, automation—has revolutionized the tools and technologies of production, transportation, communication, and domination. Goods and services are produced and distributed with less and less human labor more and more quickly, and knowledge itself is an increasingly valuable commodity. The technologies of domination are more and more powerful and deadly.

Global capital, employing these new technologies, has restructured production, distribution, and power relations. The historic driving force of capital—maximizing profit—now takes place in increasingly global markets for labor and goods and services, for finance and communication. Capital flows electronically and instantaneously around the globe twenty-four hours a day. Goods and services are sold in markets around the globe twenty-four hours a day. And people communicate in cyberspace around the globe twenty-four hours a day.

The dominant power of global corporations now rules the world through international institutions such as the International Monetary Fund (IMF), World Bank (WB), and World Trade Organization (WTO). Global corporations' need to maximize profit in the new global economy is the driving force for today's neoliberal policies in developing as well as developed countries around the world. The race to the bottom is on, the social contract is gone, oppression is on the rise, and the rich are richer than they have ever been.

The primary justifications for WTO have been arguments about the inevitability of globalization . . . [free trade theorists argued] that we could not stop or reverse globalization because it was like a bicycle—if it stopped, we would fall. [They] clearly had not ridden a bicycle, because every bicycle rider knows that all you have to do to stop a bicycle is put your foot down. That is what the citizens and Third World governments did in Seattle. They put their foot down and the machinery came grinding to a halt. All mythology of "natural phenomena" and "inevitability" evaporated in thin air.

—Vandana Shiva, "Spinning a new mythology: W.T.O. as the protector of the poor," December 14, 1999.

Why do we need a global movement and why can we win?

Armed with this understanding of today's globalization, we can say with confidence that we need a global movement. The economic and political forces we are fighting are global—the global corporations, international institutions, and neoliberal policies. The nation state and, of course, local and state governments, are losing power to global corporations and international institutions. And, from our bottom-up perspective, we have to have a global vision and global strategy, which can only emerge from a global movement.

Global corporations, with all of their wealth, are totally immoral. Scarcity is alive and growing in a world that is technologically capable of killing it off. Today's high technology has created a world of abundance. There is no objective reason for hunger, homelessness, lack of health care and education, environmental destruction, and so on, except for the greed and power of global corporations and their drive for maximum profit.

We can win because we have the technology and abundance to provide a wonderful life for all the world's 6+ billion people—not just the rich and super rich. The future hangs in the leadership and strategic direction of our movement.

Where is our movement today and how can it lead to victory?

Today the global movement for economic and social justice is at the beginning stage of coalescing. We all know about the thousands who demonstated in Seattle 1999 and Washington, D.C., 2000 against globalization and neoliberalism. But fewer know about the thousands who demonstrated in Columbia, S.C., against the Confederate flag flying over the state capital and in Tallahassee, Florida, against Jeb Bush's policy to end affirmative action.

Clearly, the movement is gathering momentum. It is drawing in more and more people, and getting closer to a leap in activity and intensity. This leap will mean a new quality in the movement—a critical mass of people who are conscious of the global and systemic root causes of our problems and who are engaged in the struggles to fundamentally transform our world.

We are in the leadership development phase in the movement-building process. How we prepare for the upsurge when millions enter the fight will, in large measure, determine which direction it will go—ours or theirs.

What this means for conscious movement-building folk is that we must focus on developing a bottom-up leadership that is broad and deep. It must include leaders from all sections of society, but concentrate on those most adversely affected. This phase of leadership development requires a process of education, with popular education being an important tool, to create a shared vision and winning strategy. This is essential if we are to be ready for the leap in our movement—to ensure that it does not compromise, and to secure and hold onto victory. Our movement depends on people who are ready—who come to the truth of the moment and are prepared to engage.

Make it happen!

Walda Katz-Fishman and Jerome Scott work at Project South: Institute for the Elimination of Poverty and Genocide.

Popular Education

Steve Schnapp

Popular education, developed in the 1960s and 1970s by the Brazilian educator Paulo Freire, is a nontraditional method of education that tries to empower adults through democratically structured cooperative study and action.

Popular education is carried out within a political vision that sees women and men at the community and grassroots level as the primary agents for social change. It is a deeply democratic process, equipping communities to name and create their own vision of the alternatives for which they struggle.

The popular education process begins by critically reflecting on, sharing, and articulating with a group or community what is known from lived experience. The participants define their own struggles. They critically examine and learn from the lessons of past struggles and from concrete everyday situations in the present.

The process continues with analysis and critical reflection upon reality aimed at enabling people to discover solutions to their own problems and set in motion concrete actions for the transformation of that reality. In Freire's model, the teacher becomes a facilitator, the traditional class becomes a cultural circle, the emphasis shifts from lecture to problem-posing strategies, and the content, previously removed from the learners' experience, becomes relevant to the group.

Popular education has always had an intimate connection to organizing for social change. In the early 1960s, Freire began by using the principles of dialogue and critical consciousness-raising—fundamental to popular education—to teach literacy to peasants struggling for land reform in Brazil. Freire argued that action was the source of knowledge, not the reverse, and that education, to be transformative, involved a process of dialogue based on action and reflection on action.

In the United States, the Highlander Center in Tennessee—committed to the civil rights movement, labor organizing, and, more recently, environmental struggles—is an example of how education is critical for effective organizing.

Organizing guided by the following principles at the core of popular education helps to address two key interrelated challenges many organizations face: how to make our organizations more democratic, and how to get people involved who will work to make the organization represent their interests and achieve its goals.

- Encourage participation.
- Develop democratic practices.
- Promote participants' control of the process and actions.
- Focus action around the issues in people's daily lives.
- Involve the entire person, including the heart, mind, body, and spirit.
- Respect the histories and cultures of those involved.
- Take power relationships into account.
- Integrate a gender and race perspective.
- Challenge all privileges (e.g. race, gender, class, sexuality, ability, age).
- Affirm identity.
- Emphasize movement and/or organizational base-building.
- Have long-term goals and visions.

If we want to build the base of our organizations with active and involved constituents who believe everyone can make a difference, we need to understand and practice organizing in this way and empower people to be the subjects of their own learning and development.

Steve Schnapp is the lead trainer and curriculum development specialist at United for a Fair Economy. With more than thirty years' experience as a community organizer and trainer, he has studied popular education theory and practice, and has trained organizers, community educators, and social justice activists.

Books on popular education

Arnold, Rick, Carl James, D'Arcy Martin, and Barb Thomas. *Educating for a Change.* Toronto, Canada: Doris Marshall Institute for Education and Action, 1991. Popular education methodology applied to community organizing. In this book the issue of power is central. Education must empower all people to act for change, and education must be based on a democratic practice, creating the conditions for full and equal participation in discussion, debate, and decision-making.

Freire, Paulo. *Pedagogy of the Oppressed.* New York: Continuum Publishing Company, 1970. This book lays out Freire's theory of popular education—every human being, no matter how "ignorant" or submerged in "the culture of silence," is capable of looking critically at the world in a dialogical encounter with others. As a new awareness of one's self and a new sense of dignity emerge, individuals are no longer willing to be mere objects but more likely to engage in a struggle, with others, to change the structures of society that are oppressive.

Freire, Paulo, and Myles Horton. *We Make the Road by Walking—Conversations on Education and Social Change.* Edited by Brenda Bell, John Gaventa, and John Peters. Philadelphia, PA: Temple University Press, 1990. Edited transcript of conversations between Horton (the director of the Highlander Center in Tennessee) and Freire in 1987.

Nadeau, D. *Counting Our Victories: Popular Education and Organizing.* New Westminster, BC: Repeal the Deal Productions, 1996.

Pretty, J.N., and I. Guijt, J. Thompson, and I. Scoones. *A Trainers Guide for Participatory Learning and Action.* London: International Institute for Environment and Development, 1995.

Vella, Jane. *Taking Learning to Task: Creative Strategies for Teaching Adults.* San Francisco, CA: Jossey-Bass Inc, Publishers, 2000.

Workshops

Child Labor Is Not Cheap (3 sessions) for grades 8–12 and adult study groups. Forty-one pages, including maps, charts, worksheets, handouts, and clear instructions for workshop leaders. $14.95 from the Resource Center of the Americas, www.americas.org, 3019 Minnehaha Avenue, So., Minneapolis, MN 55406, (612) 276-0788.

Demystifying Global Economics for Women and *The East Asian Financial Crisis,* two workshops from Center for Popular Economics, P.O. Box 785, Amherst, MA 01004.

Unpacking Globalization: A Popular Education Tool Kit. Economic Literacy Action Network, c/o Highlander Research and Education Center, 1959 Highlander Way, New Market, TN 37820, 865-933-3443, $24. Includes workshops on women and the global assembly line, the Asian financial crisis, privatization, sweatshops, welfare, women's labor, and globalization.

Women's Education in the Global Economy (WEdGE), an interactive workbook that connects the global economy to local organizing and develops strategies to "bring global sisterhood home." $25 from Women of Color Resource Center, www.coloredgirls.org, (510) 848-9272.

Organizations
See Yellow Pages.

Organizing Farmworkers through Popular Education

El Comité de Apoyo a Los Trabajadores Agrícolas (CATA)

Since 1979, CATA has helped farmworkers in the eastern United States organize to improve their living and working conditions. CATA believes that only through organizing and collective action will farmworkers be able to achieve justice.

CATA's method is popular education. The organizer's role is to facilitate, to raise consciousness, and to empower farmworkers, rather than to convince or to serve them. Solutions come from the affected community and not from the outside. Likewise,

In an increasingly globalized world where the capitalist interests of a rich few dominate, agriculture has veered away from its original purpose of feeding people and has become a competitive profit race based upon exploitation. Our current food system exploits the land by raping its future potential for present profits, deceives consumers by disregarding the health effects of pesticides used to increase production, exploits farmers by forcing them into debt to compete with subsidized corporate agriculture, and exploits farmworkers by lowering their working and living conditions to substandard levels far worse than endured by almost every other sector of society. The large majority of farmworkers migrate to the United States because the same economic and political forces that have transformed agriculture into a profit race have transformed their home countries to be fraught with debt, high inflation, high unemployment, and little opportunity to provide for their children. Faced with no alternatives, farmworkers are forced to deal with poor living and working conditions they find in the United States in the hopes that their suffering will allow their children a better future.

leadership development is an essential element in a campaign based upon popular education, as well as a result.

This methodology consists of continual visits and discussions with workers, requiring a long-term commitment of time and resources. The effort results in long-lasting community involvement with a strong potential for growth. CATA uses this methodology because it enables workers to make informed decisions based on comprehensive information. Through this process, farmworkers become aware of alternative solutions and their consequences. They become ready to work collectively and in coalition, changing public policies in their own interest.

CATA's program objectives are threefold: farmworker leadership

One hundred fifty mushroom workers and community supporters march at Philadelphia City Hall during Pennsylvannia Supreme Court hearings on mushroom workers' right to organize, October 2000. © *Tamer El-Shakhs*

development and empowerment, coalition building, and affecting public policy.

Leadership development

CATA engages workers in farm labor camps or apartment complexes, visiting them repeatedly to discuss their living and working conditions, health and safety dangers, discriminatory labor practices, and environmental justice issues. To raise workers' awareness, CATA discusses the outside factors that create oppressive conditions in the agricultural industry. Workers interested in organizing collectively form local committees and determine what steps will improve their working and living conditions. CATA is committed to have programs and actions come from the community most affected by the injustice.

Farmworkers develop their leadership capacity by participating actively in CATA. As leaders emerge they join Concilios (Farmworker Councils), which review the regional situation of farmworkers, then determine and coordinate efforts to improve conditions. CATA's Board of Directors comes from this leadership and gives direction to the entire organization. The General Assembly of farmworker members along with the Board of Directors evaluates the past year's work and sets the agenda for future activities. In addition, CATA's organizing staff is recruited from the farmworker community, which speaks to CATA's commitment of empowering farmworkers and involving them at all stages of the organization.

Coalition building

Active participation in coalitions strengthens the farmworkers' struggle for justice by increasing awareness within the larger community, creating allies, and influencing public policy. Farmworkers have reached out to allies at the local, state, national, and international levels in order to bring about social change for all. Over the years, CATA has developed relationships with labor unions, religious groups, progressive organizations, consumer, environmental, and agricultural groups in order to support each others' struggles for a fair and just society.

Affecting public policy

CATA testifies at public hearings and government commissions so that farmworkers' concerns are documented as decisions and policies are being formed. CATA participates in policy-making committees to improve public policies for farmworkers and all oppressed workers. H2A guest-worker legislation, Migrant and Seasonal Farmworker Protections Act, Right-to-Know laws, Worker Protection Standards, organic farming standards, and international labor laws are some of the laws CATA has tried to change.

Despite the many obstacles facing agricultural workers, including a legal and economic framework intentionally designed to prevent them from organizing, CATA's efforts have borne fruit. This success is most evident among the mushroom harvesters in eastern Pennsylvania. Since 1993, CATA has helped organize workers at three of the largest mushroom farms in Chester and Berks Counties. Workers voted to unionize in historic elections supervised by the Pennsylvania Labor Relations Board with two

(from left) Luis Tlaseca, President of Kaolin Mushroom Workers Union and Co-chair of UTAH, and Antonio Gutierres, UTAH Co-chair and President of CATA's Board of Directors, address October 2000 rally. © *Tamer El-Shakhs*

of the elections won by a two-to-one margin. In February 2000, two of the independent unions joined to form La Unión de Trabajadores Agrícolas y del Hongo (United Agricultural and Mushroom Workers Union). UTAH's members are farmworkers who provide the leadership for CATA. As the nonprofit arm for the union, CATA provides the education and training needed to bring other farmworkers into the fight for justice.

In the farmworkers' struggle for social justice, CATA operates under the concept that all people are entitled to the same rights and should be treated with dignity and respect regardless of whether they are working in this country or abroad. We believe that a worker, no matter what their circumstances, has the right to: work, support his/her family, receive a living wage, work collectively, live in adequate housing, and be treated with human dignity. It is these ideals that permeate CATA's work, and this philosophy that helps farm-workers become their own agents of social change, to get to the root of the problem.

CATA is a migrant farmworkers' organization with a membership base from Mexico and the Caribbean. They work in the north-eastern United States, mostly in New Jersey and Pennsylvania. CATA's role is to empower farm-workers to take control of their lives in terms of their communi-ties and workplace. Being a farm-workers' organization, they work with issues affecting low wage workers, safety and health, immi-gration, and workplace abuse. Through the use of popular educa-tion methodology, CATA aims to enable workers to be the main pro-ponents in their decision making process.

Ain't I a Mother?! Ain't I a Worker?! Ain't I a Woman?! Sparking a New Grassroots Women's Movement in the U.S.

National Mobilization Against Sweatshops

In 1998, a group of Chinese gar-ment workers from Brooklyn, New York, won almost $300,000 in back wages from a clothing manufacturer named StreetBeat Sportswear. Although Streetbeat had twice signed compliance agreements with the Department of Labor to abide by labor laws and to contract only with sweat-shop-free factories, workers testi-fied that they had worked up to 137 hours a week for wages as low as $2 an hour.

A woman named Mrs. Lai heard about how the StreetBeat workers—nonEnglish-speaking, immigrant women like herself—were fighting back despite black-listing and intimidation. She was sewing expensive dresses for Donna Karan, the famous designer of the DKNY clothing line, in a unionized factory in mid-town Manhattan. Supposedly the conditions in Midtown were supe-rior to those in Chinatown and other places. In reality, workers were forced to work with their heads lowered at all times. The bathrooms were padlocked. Sur-veillance cameras monitored their every move. They worked more than eighty hours a week with no overtime pay. Latina workers were even subjected to frequent body searches.

Mrs. Lai's first attempts to take

> ## Why target retailers like Donna Karan?
>
> Today big retailers such as DKNY are allowed to walk away with billions of dollars by stripping women of their rights and crushing the life out of them. They sit on the top of a subcontracting pyramid and claim zero responsibility. Who's responsible for inhuman and illegal working conditions in the sweatshops? Retailers hang back looking innocent and let the blame fall on the manufacturers. Manufacturers subcontract the work out to factory owners, then duck and run from the blame. Factory owners squeeze profits out of their workers while portraying themselves as victims.
>
> Retailers, as the sellers of the clothing made in garment factories, hold the most power in this subcontracting system. They decide what goods they will sell and what price they will pay for them. Manufacturers, who design the clothes, must offer them a good deal. Competition among manufacturers to sell their garments to retailers, on top of manufacturers' thirst for profits, drives down the prices for production.

action could easily have broken her spirit to fight back. The union told her to stop being a troublemaker or she would lose her job and her actions would push Donna Karan to take her work abroad. The Department of Labor said it could not change conditions in the factory. Emboldened by the courage of the Street-Beat workers, Mrs. Lai decided to take on her own factory conditions and fight to hold Donna Karan accountable.

Joined by the National Mobilization Against Sweatshops (NMASS) and community members from around the city, Mrs. Lai began to speak out. Donna Karan's sole response was to shut down the factory, leaving seventy women without a job. But instead of giving up, seven Latina women coworkers joined Mrs. Lai to expose not only basic wage and hour violations and terrible conditions, but severe racist tactics used to divide the women. The Latina women were continually told they were too stupid and clumsy to use the machines.

Instead, they were forced to do strenuous handwork because "they had bigger eyes than the Chinese," and they were paid less than the Chinese to do so.

The DKNY campaign

The DKNY workers are fighting for the wages owed them and for reinstatement to their jobs. NMASS is also demanding that Donna Karan commit to pro-

> Women's groups in some Third World countries, shocked to learn about the working and living conditions here, are supporting the fight of the DKNY women workers.

ducing one hundred percent of her clothing in law-abiding factories. To prevent the company from moving work away in retaliation for our organizing, we are demanding that the company produce at least three-quarters of its goods locally.

As a result of our organizing efforts in the heart of the Manhattan garment district, over twenty workers from DKNY-contracted factory shops have come forward to expose similar injustices, including twelve-hour workdays and seven-day work-

weeks. Some of these Chinese and Latina workers say conditions are even worse than what they experienced back home. They are now leading a ground-breaking class action lawsuit that holds Donna Karan directly accountable for the abuses they and hundreds of other workers have endured for years.

Beyond legal action, the workers themselves are inspiring other garment workers, restaurant workers, injured workers, college students, and youth to come forward. While we are launching a national "Girl"cott of Donna Karan, we are not limiting participation to those who can purchase DKNY clothing. Instead, we are using the "Girl"cott to expose sweatshop conditions right here in the United States.

Why fight sweatshops here in this country?

If you want a close-up of the global sweatshop, you can see it right here at home, in the United States. Unemployment in minority communities, the super-exploitation of immigrant workers, the proliferation of downsizing, and temporary jobs are different parts of a common system that attacks and

smartly divides working people in general. Immigrants, people of color, and women are the hardest hit, but sweatshop conditions no longer stop there. More and more white-collar office workers, for example, are experiencing long hours and health risks despite the so-called booming economy.

We cannot forget the long history of Third World exploitation. However, to participate effectively in a global movement for fundamental change, we must start where we can make the most difference: right here, in the belly of the global beast. We need a worker-led, fighting movement in this country that will change its institutions, the relations of power governing them, and as importantly, its culture. To do so, we must start not only in our communities but with ourselves.

With this new perspective, NMASS was formed. We wanted to create a membership-driven workers center, bringing together working people and youth from all different communities, professions, native-born and immigrant backgrounds. Four years after starting, we have grown into a multiracial, multiethnic, multi-trade organization. Through our educational and organizing work, we are demanding the right to work forty hours a week at a living wage whether we are overworked, underemployed, or working at home caring for our children.

We emphasize women's leadership in the charge against sweatshops because women see most clearly how sweatshop conditions affect them and their families. Lilia Gutierrez, one of the original seven Latina DKNY workers, sums up her experience as she recalls working "ten, eleven hours a day, six days a week. I woke up at 5:30 in the morning to get my kids ready for school. Sometimes I sent them without breakfast. I left at 7 and came back at 8 or 9 at night. I would pick up my kids, make dinner and prepare for the next day. All I did was work."

Sparking a new grassroots women's movement

According to the Bureau of Labor Statistics, members of U.S. households now work more hours than those of any other industrialized country, and the average couple works six weeks per year more in 1996 than in 1989. More and more, mandatory overtime is becoming a fact of life, and the forty-hour work-week is now perceived as part-time. Meanwhile, more than 6,575,000 people reported work-related injuries and illnesses in 1999 in the United States.

For most women in this country, working and living conditions are especially deteriorating. Women are disproportionately concentrated in clerical, service-sector, and manufacturing jobs that, while important, are devalued and lower-paid. Many immigrant women, like the DKNY workers, find they have no option but to work as garment workers, domestic workers, hotel and restaurant workers, toiling long hours under unhealthy and unsafe conditions while their wages decline. Long hours are also stealing the life away from office workers, including professionals such as lawyers and graphic artists, particularly as companies downsize and lay staff members off.

On the other hand, many women cannot find a full-time job; they settle for working several part-time or temp jobs without benefits. Mothers on welfare are often told to get a real job as if being a single parent raising a family did not qualify as work. Women workers injured on the job and no longer able to work say that the long hours and hazardous working conditions are not worth the sacrifices that came along with it, being robbed not only of their time raising their children but of their health.

On top of these "official" jobs, women are usually the primary

> If we don't change this system, we cannot live and fully enjoy life as human beings.

caretakers of children and elderly relatives, and they still take on a disproportionate responsibility for housework. This "women's work" is never recognized or valued as work. It is estimated that the average woman worker in the United States works seventy to ninety hours a week when employment, childcare, and housework are accounted for. Meanwhile, an estimated one-third of our country's children are taking care of themselves and are spending more and more time without parents. Deepening economic instability forces young ones to begin assuming adult responsibilities early on: attending doctors' visits, translating at appointments, interpreting their parents' documents, and taking

on part-time jobs to make up for the family's lost income.

Most women workers feel that to survive, they must give up control over their time and their lives. However, many women are fed up. Even professional women have started changing careers for the sake of their health, family, or sanity. Others are searching for a way out.

Unfortunately women, while experiencing similar trends, are very much separated from one another. We are divided by race, trade, community, and education. Much women's activism has reinforced these divisions, focusing on strategies that enable only a few women to rise out of poverty, and even fewer women to gain high positions in government, academia, and business. Little effort has been made to address the issues that unite working women, the systemic problems that keep the majority of women in this country down.

In April 2000, NMASS brought together women from all walks of life: South Asian domestic workers, Latina factory workers, Chinese garment workers, Polish home attendants, office workers, mothers, artists, and high school and college students at our

National Ain't I a Woman?! Conference, named after a speech by former slave Sojourner Truth. We came together to talk about our lives as women and how to fight the sweatshop system that exploits us all, especially immigrants, women of color, and youth. We came together because we value our time, our health and our families. Because this sweatshop system does not value raising children and taking care of the home, mothers have no choice but to work full-time outside of the house to survive. Because this sweatshop system does not value youth, young people have to pay thousands of dollars for school, and work for money on top of studying. Because this sweatshop system does not value life, most of us work more than forty hours a week at our jobs, are forced to put in overtime, and are called in whenever the company is short-staffed. Because this sweatshop system wants to control us, it teaches us that our lives are secondary to money. Because we need to build a new grassroots women's movement, we are beginning by making an example of Donna Karan and showing that women workers are no longer going to tolerate abuse to themselves or their families.

We need to build a grassroots women's movement led by low-income immigrants and no-income immigrants, women of color, and youth because our issues are ignored by the mainstream movements in this country. By organizing to hold DKNY accountable to workers, the DKNY garment workers inspired a much broader campaign, the Ain't I a Woman?! Campaign, to examine our own lives and recognize the ways in which we are not being valued. A hundred years ago, Sojourner Truth broke out of slavery and demanded recognition as a woman and a human being. We hope you join NMASS in ending this modern-day slave system and organize to build this new women's movement that will free us all.

Three Organizing Models

Mike Prokosch

Many global activists started their social change careers in the anti-sweatshop movement. Others cut their teeth on direct action or local organizing. None of these is an adequate social change strategy. The U.S. movement is using three competing organizing models, and none alone can transform the global economy.

Direct action is a sometimes revolutionary strategy for stopping business as usual and opening up the space for direct democracy. It is utopian and punk: it's acting to bring the future into being—now. But it's hard to translate that experience into systemic change, and many direct activists are asking, "Where's the strategy?"

If the direct action movement is young, *institutional campaigns* feel older, aimed at reform and education. The Citigroup campaign may change a global bank's lending policies; it will certainly teach us that the financial sector pulls the strings in the global economy (p. 171). The World Bank Bond Boycott has opened up space inside the Bank for liberal Bank staffers to push

reforms; outside, it is teaching new audiences about the Bank's many fiascos (p. 232).

Campaigns like these can awaken new activists and train them as organizers. However, they don't always build local organization. "Many national campaigns offer a cookie-cutter approach to organizing," says Kristi Disney, an organizer with the Tennessee Industrial Renewal Network. "We believe it takes locally rooted action to bring these lessons home and to lay the groundwork for a successful global movement."

The third organizing model is *local and coalitional.* Environmental groups, labor unions, and community-based organizations pledge to support each others' actions. This strategy builds solidarity across sector and race lines. In the fall of 2000, Jobs with Justice and its partners called for local solidarity actions that turned the globalization movement homeward and started building sustainable ties with labor and communities of color.

Coalitions take the postmodern place of parties that used to unite many interests behind a single program. They project solidarity, but how far can that go? Can it overcome the conservatizing influence of many community-based organizations, with the strings that attach them to foundation funding and politically diverse memberships?

All these strategies arose to challenge power at times when progressive influence was ebbing. Thus, instead of building a larger movement, each strategy was expected to *be* the movement—to defend, extend, recruit, train, and project a national progressive presence all by itself.

Now we are in a time of movement expansion. Perhaps we can put these three strategies together in a model that overcomes the weaknesses of each. In this integrated organizing model, direct action could be used more strategically. National campaigns could support local organizing but not substitute for it. Local coalitions would gain a larger political agenda and apply effective national pressure. And the globalization movement would put its energies where most people live, work, and organize.

Organizing for the Long Haul:

The View from Western Massachusetts

Frank Borgers

The eruption of the U.S. globalization movement in Seattle was met with jubilation by the U.S. left, with most rushing in to celebrate the birth of a new broad coalition. Many activists were inspired to form new action groups and networks. One was MassAction. This western Massachusetts group mobilized an astonishing six hundred people for the IMF–World Bank protests in April 2000, and went on to organize a dizzying series of teach-ins, protests, conferences, local solidarity actions, and for-credit classes. At the same time, MassAction's struggles over race, class, leadership, and process may help other new groups reflect on their own internal challenges.

MassAction's home, the Pioneer Valley, is anchored at its southern end by the medium-sized industrial cities of Springfield and Holyoke. Their working-class and increasingly poor African-American and Latino populations were devastated by the erosion of the industrial economic base, especially in the 1980s and 1990s. In contrast, the Valley's universities concentrate over forty thousand students in an idyllic cluster of small college towns. The countercultural soup of ashrams and communes, and the concentration of left and progressive groups have earned the Pioneer Valley its nickname "Granola Valley" or "the Tofu Curtain."

MassAction emerged from the left-progressive off-campus community after Seattle. However, it really took off when it started to organize for the IMF–World Bank protests in Washington, D.C., in April of 2000. During this transition the group moved rapidly from the community onto the campuses of the five colleges. Extraordinary student interest and excitement led to huge planning and informational meetings of seventy participants at a time. While many wanted to recreate Seattle after having missed the show, others hoped that invigorated student activism would spill over into long-term local organizing.

In just two months MassAction educated, mobilized, transported, and supported some six hundred local activists at the IMF–World Bank rallies and direct actions. The group subsequently coordinated intensive jail solidarity work for those arrested. Following the D.C. mobilization, MassAction engaged in an exhausting range of actions from Windsor, Ontario, to Philadelphia and Boston, and from local solidarity actions to a monthly, valley-wide progressive newspaper.

MassAction's history mirrors the extraordinary eruption of the globalization movement after Seattle. At the same time, the group has faced many of the organizational challenges confronting the larger movement.

The challenge of race and class

Since Seattle, the movement has taken up the challenge of becoming more inclusive in both its membership and in its alliances. MassAction is largely white, and overwhelmingly comprised of students, albeit from a wide variety of class backgrounds. Much debate has focused on the nature of the group's culture and how it might alienate potential working-class and minority activists.

While MassAction engaged in some outreach to on-campus groups representing students and activists of color, these efforts elicited little interest. One possible reason is the way the group organized for the IMF–World Bank protest. MassAction ended up operating as a stand-alone, five-campus organizing committee instead of trying to coordinate and mobilize the efforts of preexistent student groups, including those of color. If it had adopted the latter approach, it may have had more success in its outreach efforts.

MassAction was more successful in building coalitions with off-campus organizations that represent working class and people of color in the valley. Western Mass Jobs With Justice and the Pioneer Valley Labor Council were key partners in a demonstration against Wal-Mart's global sweatshop apparel sourcing and domestic union-busting. MassAction worked with ARISE for Social Justice (a Kensington Welfare Rights Union affiliate representing mostly poor black and Latin populations in nearby Springfield) to get its members down to Philadelphia for the Republican National Convention protests. MassAction has also supported a number of local strikes and organizing drives.

Moving MassAction in this direction was not easy. The coalition-building was led by a few core organizers within MassAction. Their preexisting organizing experience and ties to off-campus groups allowed them to transcend the cultural and organizational distance between the on- and off-campus communities. Focusing on this "bridging" strategy created tensions in MassAction. After the D.C. protests, the group faced a dizzying choice of actions that interested different members. The dispute over direction was settled less by establishing consensus than by the ability of the informal leadership to establish its agenda against a fragmented and more weakly defined opposition.

Leadership

One of the movement's biggest challenges is to work within direct action parameters of consensus decision-making and nonhierarchical organizational structure. MassAction tried to adhere to these principles but still saw at least three levels of participation emerge.

Informal leadership took on heavy logistical loads and was very influential in framing the broad direction, as well as setting the broad goals and tasks of the group. While critics acknowledge the intense workload, they charge that leaders took on the more high-profile "sexy" tasks. Overlaying this critique is the observation that this group was exclusively male.

Informal mid-level organizers and activists also took on heavy logistical loads. Again, according to critics (who belonged to this second group), these tasks were often more mundane, invisible, and framed within goals set by the informal leadership. Activists at this level felt that they had diminishing influence in shaping the group's broader direction, goals, and tasks.

A floating base of members participated sporadically in group meetings or went to D.C. as relatively autonomous and disengaged group participants.

MassAction created multiple committees to handle the various organizing tasks for the D.C. mobilization. However, many of these committees either stopped functioning or functioned only sporadically. Committee missions were often unclear or even conflicting, meetings were numerous, and key individuals would drop out and reappear randomly. While meetings were very good at generating task proposals, they were far less effective at assigning volunteers

While the D.C. mobilization was numerically very impressive, it is unclear how well it developed a broad base of long-term local activists. The goal of helping huge numbers of participants get to D.C. may, in retrospect (and with 20/20 vision), not have been the best way to build the organization's base. In fact, the very success of MassAction's logistical effort allowed many local participants simply to attend the permitted rally and march without developing a deeper engagement in the movement. As such, the goal of massive mobilization in this manner facilitated the type of casual summit-hopping that our critics have accused us of. Meanwhile, the organizers who took on this logistical work were swamped by the sheer enormity of the task and suffered severe exhaustion and burnout on return.

and accountability. Key committee tasks were often not carried out due to a lack of follow through or a lack of clear assignment of responsibilities.

Consequently, individuals at the mid-organizer level were often left holding the bag and were sometimes castigated by the leadership when they failed to deliver. On the other hand, informal leaders, frustrated that crucial tasks were not being accomplished in a timely manner, often ended up assuming the work and making decisions themselves. At times these two groups communicated poorly with one another.

The net result was escalating tension, with individuals in both groups ending up with huge workloads and responsibilities. While difficult for all involved, it may have been hardest for those in the organizer group who were engaged in relatively thankless work while receiving little or no organizational recognition. Meanwhile, despite MassAction's anti-hierarchical rhetoric, this dynamic created informal leaders who were, given the lack of formal structures, fairly unaccountable to the rest of the group.

These tendencies proved quite destructive, heightening tension and conflict among the most active leaders and organizers, while generating lots of criticism but little support from the rest of the group. Many key activists became increasingly bitter and burnt out. While MassAction's informal leaders have managed to sustain themselves, a number of organizers and affinity groups have exited. This dynamic has likely damaged the group's ability to build a long-term activist base and to repeat large direct action mobilizations in the future.

Process

While MassAction has attempted to follow rough rules of consensus, the challenges and tensions around the group's decision-making process are quite complex.

At times, consensus decision-making gave participants, especially those in the mid-level organizer group, a great sense of empowerment and ownership of the movement. This sense was particularly strong during the IMF–World Bank protest in Washington where consensus decision-making was used in the local spokescouncils and during the direct actions.

On the other hand, consensus decision-making within MassAction itself often fell apart. This

A useful historical comparison is provided by Barbara Epstein's 1988 "The Politics of Prefigurative Community: the Non-Violent Direct Action Movement" (published in *Reshaping the U.S. Left*, vol. 3, Verso, 1988). Epstein's analysis is based on her participation in the 1980s antinuclear movement, which also framed its protests and organizing work within direct action principles.

All of the groups that Epstein describes experienced rapid growth accompanied by an escalation of internal tensions that led quite quickly to groups splitting and even collapsing. The splits were caused mainly by disagreements over the tactics of nonviolence, consensus decision-making, and leadership-group dynamics.

While Epstein is supportive of direct action principles, she concludes that they proved to have significant organizational limitations. According to Epstein, the most problematic failure of the direct action model lies in its attempt to build a strictly nonhierarchical, leaderless organizational structure. Informal, de facto leadership emerged in every antinuclear group, and Epstein implies that this was probably unavoidable. The contradiction between this tendency and direct action's antihierarchical principles created intensely destructive organizational outcomes. These outcomes are identical to those ascribed to MassAction.

Epstein concludes that, while the direct action model has very attractive qualities, its organizational limits must be recognized and dealt with. Her final statement is worth noting: "The Direct Action movement is organizationally fragile and often lacking in political direction, and it cannot substitute for other sections of the movement: short of a moment of broadly perceived crisis, it is likely to remain predominantly white, middle-class, and made up of people with flexible schedules who are willing to assume a degree of political marginality, at least politically" (p. 90) was partly due to the inexperience of many of the group's facilitators and the challenge of facilitating consensus decision making within groups of over fifty participants. Leadership dynamics within MassAction also harmed the decision-making process. Informal leaders tended to override or dominate group decision-making. Sometimes this happened during meetings through sheer force of personality (and some would charge, through patriarchal dynamics). Informal leaders also subverted group consensus by making some important decisions independently. Usually they justified those decisions on the basis of a lack of follow through from committees, or the urgency of getting critical tasks accomplished.

Time and operational pressures were central to MassAction's destructive dynamics. The mobilization for D.C. and every subsequent event was marked by an intense sense of crisis and urgency. This may be partially attributable to the rhetorical militancy of the informal leadership. More significant may be the group's mostly implicit assumption that every major summit must be protested, and that the group's mobilizations should equal the impact of Seattle.

These goals are almost unachievable and set the group up for failure. The institutions of corporate neoliberalism are too numerous and their meetings are too frequent. Furthermore, the rapid escalation of state sophistication and preparedness, the centrality of surprise and chance during the WTO protests, and an increasingly jaded media make it highly improbable that future direct actions will match Seattle's impact.

Conclusions

First, the leaders and activists of MassAction are an incredibly dedicated, smart, and talented group of individuals. Further, while the group has, at times, operated quite dysfunctionally, its participants have been deeply well intentioned. However, the group processes discussed should not be dismissed, for they have proven to be deeply destructive. The analysis reveals (at least) three crucial challenges.

There is a real need for *training on organizing and leadership development.* Some of the group dysfunction could be reduced by fairly basic educational interventions, including training on running larger meetings under consensus decision rules. Beyond this, it would probably be helpful to set up activist retreats (perhaps organized regionally) during organizing lulls, that create a space for learning, reflection and mending, away from the heat of battle.

The applicability of *direct action principles* to long-term group building is a complex issue. While consensus decision-making has produced mixed results, this may have as much to do with a poor application of principles and inhospitable context as it does with inherent failures in the model. In contrast, the antihierarchy rhetoric that accompanies the direct action model has been quite destructive. There is a real need for groups like MassAction to address this rhetoric, and to create and maintain more formal governance structures and group accountability. While MassAction could try to create a permanent spokescouncil-affinity group structure, it does not currently operate as a network of groups, and some alternate structure, such as a steering committee with elected representatives, may be more appropriate.

MassAction's *crisis-driven organizing* has greatly amplified its more destructive group dynamics.

The most immediate danger is continued burnout among leaders and activists. Further, it is extremely difficult to create democratic and participatory spaces under crisis conditions. The group's ability to delegate, trust, and allow for learning through failure is severely compromised by the scale and frequency of its mobilizations. Ultimately, crisis-driven organizing will lead Mass-Action to fail in what should be one of the movement's central goals—the birth and nourishment of an expanding network of activists.

The author teaches in the Labor Studies program at UMass-Amherst and has been active in the globalization movement in western Massachusetts. This paper is based on his personal experiences and observations and a critical examination of e-mails distributed across various local listservs. It also draws extensively on interviews with and responses by key organizers and activists within MassAction to an earlier draft of the article. He would like to acknowledge their achievements, tenacity, and remarkable sense of sharing and solidarity that have made MassAction a reality and contributed immensely to the writing of this article.

Direct Action

What is the public face of the globalization movement? For some, it is the youth-led swarm that emerged in Seattle and went on to confront meeting after meeting around the world. The direct actions in these massive protests engaged the media and public, and added crucial energy to the movement. Several articles in this section trace direct action's history and dissect its workings. Andrew Boyd adds a study of a widely successful creative action, reminding us that direct action isn't necessarily civil disobedience (p. 152).

As the protest wing of the movement travelled from city to city, proving its staying power, hard questions emerged. Some activists wondered if "summit-hopping" would build a lasting movement. Activists of color and antiracist activists critiqued the privilege and exclusive culture of this direct action-oriented protest movement. Still others called for serious dialogue about long-term strategy. They argued that some activists and organizations had elevated the tactic of direct action to the movement's main strategy without a real vision behind it.

With each new city and each new shutdown, activists tried to incorporate these critiques into actual protest organizing. During August 2000's protests in Los Angeles, for example, the actions were based on a long-term strategy for sustainable movement building. Los Angeles community-based organizers said the young movement's insistence on civil disobedience tactics and mass arrests wouldn't work for the city's communities of color or advance the vision of organizers there (p. 140).

That same summer, mostly white direct action-oriented activists from New York Direct Action Network and radical youth of color in New York City worked to build a multiracial front against the criminal injustice system in Philadelphia during protests against the Republican National Convention. They combined the tactical skills of the direct action group and the analysis, networks, and strategy of SLAM!, a group rooted in communities of color (p. 160). This action set an example for future multiracial coalitions.

—Laura Raymond

From the Salt Marches to Seattle: Direct Action's History

Denis Moynihan and David Solnit

> The exploitation of the poor can be extinguished not by effecting the destruction of a few millionaires but by removing the ignorance of the poor and teaching them to noncooperate with the exploiters.
>
> —Mohandas K. Gandhi, Haryan, July 28, 1940.

Direct action has a colorful and potent history. Early exemplars include the taking and tilling of public land by the Diggers in 1650 to protest the conditions that followed the English civil war. The Boston Tea Party is an early and patriotic example in the United States. Abolitionists established the Underground Railroad, and Henry David Thoreau refused to pay his taxes as a protest against slavery.

Early in the twentieth century, Gandhi in South Africa and the Industrial Workers of the World (IWW) in the United States began organizing direct actions. The IWW used the phrase "direct action" and sought immediate redress for workers' grievances at the point of production: the mines, mills, factories and fields. They used work slowdowns and strikes, mass nonviolent parades, civil disobedience, art, and song. Under the Alien and Sedition Act of 1919, many leaders of the IWW were imprisoned for up to twenty years for their effective organizing.

Gandhi's development of nonviolent noncooperation, which he named satyagraha, inspired mass civil disobedience in India in opposition to British rule. Gandhi's Salt March of 1930 led to over one hundred thousand arrests and reverberated around the world.

But it was in Spain that direct action's characteristic affinity group structure arose. The Iberian Anarchist Federation used *grupos de afinidad* as their local, regional, and national form of coordination. These small groups of friends and activists were so resilient that outlawing them had little impact. Instead, their model of direct democracy led to the CNT, a national rank and file-controlled trade union federation with two million members. When the fascists staged a coup against Spain's social democratic government in 1934, six million people created a social revolution, taking over their land and factories, workplaces and towns, and running them directly and democratically based on people's needs. They showed that large urban and rural areas could manage their own lives and communities without bosses or the state.

Civil rights and Seabrook

The U.S. civil rights movement was pivotal in popularizing direct action. Bayard Rustin was arrested in 1942 for refusing to move to the back of a segregated bus. The successful Montgomery bus boycotts in 1955–56 were consciously modeled on Gandhi's strategies, and they propelled direct action to the center of public attention. Groups such as the Southern Christian Leadership Conference, the Congress of Racial Equality (CORE), and the Student Nonviolent Coordinating Committee organized lunch counter sit-ins, the Freedom Rides, and the quarter million-person march on Washington, D.C., in 1963.

Antiwar activists also used direct action, with protests at the U.S. Army's School of the Americas original location in Panama starting as early as 1959. Demonstrations against the war in Vietnam began in 1964. A rally in 1965 numbered twenty thousand people; one in the spring of 1967 drew four hundred thousand in New York City. Mass creative actions included a light-hearted attempt to levitate the Pentagon. A mass action in Washington, D.C., on May Day, 1971, attempted to stop all traffic from entering the city and resulted in thirteen thousand arrests. Since 1980, members of the Plowshares movement have damaged military hardware with hammers and poured blood thereon.

The use of direct action to take over the Seabrook, N.H., nuclear power station in 1977 set the modern standard for affinity group-based mass action organizing. Its decentralized, nonhierarchical model insulated the action from infiltration by the authorities and demonstrated the power of consensus-based decision making. Its success, emulated at over a dozen other nuclear plants under construction, put the antinuclear movement firmly in the public's mind. As a result of this movement, hundreds of planned nuclear plants never made it off the drawing table, and not one new one has been built in the United States since. The mass occupations and blockades at Seabrook were inspired in part by similar actions in Germany and the affinity group was borrowed from the Spanish anarchist movement.

In the 1980s, antiapartheid activism led to mass arrests on campuses and in front of the South African Embassy. Campus activists constructed mock shantytowns and lived in them, and the divestment campaign pulled four billion dollars out of the South African economy. Critical to its success were grassroots consumer boycotts within South Africa.

The Central America solidarity movement also used civil disobedience, with the Pledge of Resistance in the 1980s leading to over five thousand arrests. The Sanctuary movement clandestinely moved political refugees north from Central America in the spirit of the Underground Railroad. An annual protest at the School of the Americas at Fort Benning, Georgia, has grown from few people in 1989 to over twelve thousand in 1999, with more than five thousand risking arrest.

Theater in the streets

The AIDS Coalition to Unleash Power (ACT UP) brought a new and lasting theatricality to the direct action movement. ACT UP uses small "zap" actions, such as disruptions of politicians' campaign events, composite banners made of hundreds of placards displayed at stadiums during professional sports events, and body blockades in front of buildings. Mass actions have included a large civil disobedience on the steps of the U.S. Supreme Court in 1987.

Environmental activists have also married spectacle with direct action. Greenpeace's intervention in whale hunting and ocean-based nuclear bomb testing with inflatable boats and their banner hangings from skyscrapers have proven to be very mediagenic.

However, it took more cross-border crossfertilization to bring direct action to its present level of theatricality and decentralization.

Children of the Zapatistas

On January 1, 1994—the day the North American Free Trade Agreement went into effect—masked armed rebels from poverty-stricken indigenous communities in southern Mexico rose up, taking over towns across the state of Chiapas. They used laptop computers and the Internet to bypass mainstream media censorship. Their statements were poetic and humorous, capturing people's imagination. They were not a traditional guerrilla movement attempting to seize power. Instead they acted as a catalyst calling on people to "do it yourself." The sense of possibility this gave to millions of people across the globe was extraordinary. Zapatistas offered the greatest threat to the Mexican dictatorship in over thirty years and they were a slap in the face of the myth that corporate globalization was inevitable, or as British Prime Minister Margaret Thatcher had said, "There is no alternative."

Our global resistance is like an ecosystem—a shifting web of relationships, ideas, events, and local struggles that cross-fertilize movements and people. Seattle was a big audacious blossom that grew from this cross-fertilization. Its bright and powerful roots are in direct democracy movements like Mexico's Zapatistas, Reclaim the Streets in Britain, and Art and Revolution in the United States. Before them, though, came a century of creative direct action and innovative cultural resistance.

—David Solnit

In 1996, the Zapatistas, with trepidation as they thought no one might come, sent out an e-mail calling for a gathering in the Chiapas jungle. Six thousand people showed up for the first *Encuentro* and spent days talking and sharing their stories of struggle against the common enemy: capitalism.

A second *Encuentro* took place a year later in Spain, where the idea for a more action-focused network to be named People's Global Action (PGA) was hatched by activists from ten of the largest and most innovative social movements. They included the Zapatistas, the Brazilian Landless Peasants Movement, India's Karnataka State Farmers Union, and Reclaim the Streets in Britain. The emerging network outlined its goals and principles:

- a rejection of appeals to those in power for reforms to the present world order;
- support for nonviolent direct action as a means of communities taking back power; and
- an organizational philosophy of decentralization and autonomy.

PGA's first gathering was held in February 1998 in Geneva, home of the World Trade Organization. More than three hundred delegates from seventy-one countries came together, gave birth to PGA, and confronted the WTO meeting held the following day. The world's grassroots movements were beginning to talk and share experiences without the mediation of the media or nongovernmental organizations (NGOs).

In the global South, PGA drew on a flood of direct action against global capital and environmental destruction. The practice of satyagraha was still strong in India. Women in the foothills of the Himalayas, whose collection of firewood for fuel became extremely onerous with increased deforestation, started a movement known as chipko, which means *embrace.* They protected the trees with their bodies and won significant protections for the forests on which they depend. Adivisis and indigenous people of India's Narmada Valley annually practice satyagraha in an ongoing campaign against such mega-projects as the Sardar Sarovar dam. In *Operation Cremation Monsanto,* the Karnataka State Farmers Association uproots genetically engineered crops and burns them. Networks of indigenous groups in Ecuador have organized several recent mass mobilizations, one of which nonviolently deposed the president. Their tactics shut down traffic into and out of cities.

In Europe and North America, PGA brought together rave culture, political puppeteering, and the direct action traditions from Seabrook through ACT UP. Today's globalization movement is the latest in a very long lineage.

Denis Moynihan and David Solnit volunteer with the Direct Action Network and many other groups.

How We Really Shut Down the WTO

Starhawk

Some 50,000 people—armed only with their convictions—made the whole building rock and this happened within the boundaries of the mightiest military and economic power on Earth. The apparently impossible seems to be—after this—becoming possible.
—World Rainforest Movement Bulletin #29, editorial,
"The Battle of Seattle."

The police, in defending their brutal and stupid mishandling of the direct action in Seattle, said they were "not prepared for the violence." In reality, they were unprepared for the nonviolence and the numbers and commitment of the nonviolent activists— even though the blockade was organized in open, public meetings and there was nothing secret about our strategy. My suspicion is that our model of organization and decision making was so foreign to their picture of what constitutes leadership that they literally could not see what was going on in front of them. When authoritarians think about leadership, the picture in their minds is of one person—usually a guy—or a small group standing up and telling other people what to do. Power is centralized and requires obedience.

In contrast, our model of

power was decentralized, and leadership was invested in the group as a whole. People were empowered to make their own decisions, and the centralized structures were for coordination, not control. As a result, we had great flexibility and resilience and many people were inspired to acts of courage they could never have been ordered to do.

Here are some of the key aspects of our model of organizing.

Training and preparation

In the weeks and days before the blockade, thousands of people were given nonviolence training— a three-hour course that combined the history and philosophy of nonviolence with real-life practice through role plays in staying calm in tense situations, using nonviolent tactics, responding to brutality, and making decisions together. Thousands also went through a second-level training in jail preparation, solidarity strategies and tactics, and legal aspects. As well, there were first aid trainings, trainings in blockade tactics, street theater, meeting facilitation, and other skills. While many more thousands of people took part in the blockade who had not attended any of these trainings, a nucleus of groups existed who were prepared to face police brutality and who could provide a core of resistance and strength. And in jail, I saw many situations that played out just like the role plays. Activists were able to protect members of their group from being singled out or removed by using tactics introduced in the trainings. The solidarity tactics we had prepared became a real block to the functioning of the system.

Each participant in the action was asked to agree to the nonviolence guidelines: To refrain from violence, physical or verbal; not to carry weapons, not to bring or use illegal drugs or alcohol, and not to destroy property. We were asked to agree only for the purpose of the November 30 action—not to sign on to any of these as a life philosophy, and the group acknowledged that there is much diversity of opinion around some of these guidelines.

Affinity groups, clusters, and spokescouncils

The participants in the action were organized into small groups called affinity groups. Each group was empowered to make its own decisions around how it would participate in the blockade. There were groups doing street theater, others preparing to lock themselves to structures, groups with banners and giant puppets, others simply prepared to link arms and nonviolently block delegates. Within each group, there were generally some people prepared to risk arrest and others who would be their support people in jail as well as a first aid person.

Affinity groups were organized into clusters. The area around the Convention Center was broken down into thirteen sections, with affinity groups and clusters committed to hold particular sections. As well, some groups were "flying groups"—free to move to wherever they were most needed. All of this was coordinated at spokescouncil meetings, where affinity groups each sent a representative who was empowered to speak for the group.

In practice, this form of organization meant that groups could move and react with great flexibility during the blockade. If a call went out for more people at a certain location, an affinity group could assess the numbers holding the line where they were and choose whether or not to move. When faced with tear gas, pepper spray, rubber bullets and horses, groups and individuals could

© Jim Harney

assess their own ability to withstand the brutality. As a result, blockade lines held in the face of incredible police violence. When one group was finally swept away by gas and clubs, another would move in to take its place. Yet there was also room for those of us in the middle-aged, bad lungs/bad backs affinity group to hold lines in areas that were relatively peaceful, to interact with the delegates we turned back, and to support the labor march that brought tens of thousands through the area at midday. No centralized leader could have coordinated the scene in the midst of the chaos, and none was needed—the organic, autonomous organization we had proved far more powerful and effective. No authoritarian figure could have compelled people to hold a blockade line while being tear gassed—but empowered people free to make their own decisions did choose to do that.

Consensus decision making

The affinity groups, clusters, spokescouncils, and working groups involved with the Direct Action Network (DAN) made decisions by consensus—a process that allows every voice to be heard and that stresses respect for minority opinions. Consensus was part of the nonviolence and jail trainings and we made a small attempt to also offer some special training in meeting facilitation. We did not interpret consensus to mean unanimity. The only mandatory agreement was to act within the nonviolent guidelines. Beyond that, the DAN organizers set a tone that valued autonomy and freedom over conformity, and stressed co-ordination rather than pressure to conform. So, for example, our jail solidarity strategy involved staying in jail where we could use the pressure of our numbers to protect individuals from being singled out for heavier charges or more brutal treatment. But no one was pressured to stay in jail or made to feel guilty for bailing out before the others. We recognized that each person has their own needs and life situation, and that what was important was to have taken action at whatever level we each could. Had we pressured people to stay in jail, many would have resisted and felt resentful and misused. Because we didn't, because people felt empowered, not manipulated, the vast majority decided for themselves to remain in, and many people pushed

A call to action

Our resistance is diverse in content and expression, and we fiercely affirm that it will remain so.

We are rooted in a belief that a desirable, just world is one directly controlled by the people. We reject capitalism, centralized government, hierarchy, and all forms of discrimination. We will not be controlled by corporations and militaries, nor by their insidious propaganda that passes for truth.

We commit to creating a broad based peoples' movement. We believe in our collective power to overcome the corporate imitation of culture. We don't need to be told how to live. We already know. We desire a certain greatness, in which freedom is a fact and economic, social, and ecological persecution are mere fossils in our history.

When we look around we see immense talent, compassion, and potential. We can use these tools to structure our lives to the benefit of the planet and its peoples. We know this because we have already begun. In the past few years we've seen our actions gain momentum as a swelling movement against global capitalism, corporate domination, and falsely democratic political structures. We are rising up, and we are getting things done.

—Direct Action Network, early 2000.

themselves far beyond the boundaries of what they had expected to do.

I'm writing this for two reasons. First, I want to give credit to the Direct Action Network organizers who did a brilliant and difficult job, who learned and applied the lessons of the last twenty years of nonviolent direct

There are no cookie cutters, recipes, or blueprints for making fundamental social change. The direct action that shut down the WTO in Seattle created its own model, and while we can learn and borrow from that model we can not repeat it.

—David Solnit

Washington D.C., April 2000. © Diane Greene Lent

action, and who created a powerful, successful and life-changing action in the face of enormous odds, an action that has changed the global political landscape and radicalized a new generation. And secondly, because the true story of how this action was organized provides a powerful model that activists can learn from. Seattle was only a beginning. We have before us the task of building a global movement to overthrow corporate control and create a new economy based on fairness and justice, on a sound ecology and a healthy environment, one that protects human rights and serves freedom. We have many campaigns ahead of us, and we deserve to learn the true lessons of our successes.

This article was excerpted from "How We Really Shut Down the WTO," which can be found at www.spectacle.org. Starhawk is a direct action trainer and movement inspirer who can be reached through her website, www.starhawk.org.

Harnessing Direct Action for Community Organizing

Cameron Levin

My name is Cameron Levin and I have been a community organizer in Los Angeles for the past ten years. In January 2000 I and other organizers and artists founded Rise Up/DAN LA (Direct Action Network) in response to the inspirational actions in Seattle. We wanted to cultivate that energy in Los Angeles. When we found out that the Democratic Party was going to be holding its convention in L.A., we knew this was our opportunity to contribute to the globalization movement.

We began with a critique of what we saw happening in Seattle and Washington, D.C. We felt those two protests were unable to link global struggles with community struggles here in the United States. The communities hardest hit here by globalization were not participating; instead, most of the protesters were white middle-class youth. We also felt that the movement had not placed an antiracist, antioppression analysis and practice at the top of its agenda.

With this critique, we set out to do something different in Los Angeles. Our vision was not focused on a single event like the Democratic Convention, but on how we could contribute to the movement for social justice in Los Angeles. This meant organizing for twenty, thirty, or fifty years from now. We understood that no single event was going to bring about the revolution. It is through small victories in local communities that people become inspired to struggle and stand up. It is when people have a sense of their own power, that transformation becomes possible.

Making the actions safe

The direct action organizing model used in Seattle and Washington mobilized activists who were able to get arrested in acts of mass civil disobedience. In contrast, our organizing model tried to build ties with people in L.A.'s various communities and address issues that affected them directly. We partnered with community-based organizations (CBOs) that worked on immigration, welfare, women's issues, youth and education, gay lesbian and transgender issues, police brutality, and the prison-industrial complex. The individual organizers and artists in Rise Up/DAN LA already worked on many of these issues, which made it easier for us to collaborate with CBOs. We approached them offering to help build their work and provide their members training and artistic expression like puppet-making.

However, there were limits to our collaboration. CBOs have to worry about their funders and their membership when they get involved with a movement like the globalization movement. They also have to consider the long-term cost of working with ad hoc groups whose nonhierarchical nature can make them less accountable than community-based organizations.

One challenge we faced was to develop actions where the CBOs' members would be able to participate without getting arrested. We knew civil disobedience wouldn't work for them. Some people already had too much contact with the criminal injustice system. Many lacked legal immigrant status. Others were not ready to use civil disobedience, and the amount of work it

would take to get them ready was far beyond our capacity. Historically, in many communities of color, civil disobedience has been a tactic of last resort when other forms of struggle have failed to achieve the desired outcome.

To create actions that were accessible to the largest group of people in L.A., we got permits for our marches and communicated with the police during some of the actions. This resulted in protests with both a legal side and a civil disobedience piece. For example, at the Ramparts police station action over thirty people were arrested while others stood in solidarity with them. However, other actions were made more powerful because they did not involve civil disobedience. A kiss-in/march/and die-in drew over one thousand people to demonstrate for gay/lesbian/transgender rights. L.A.'s queer community has not seen an action of this size since AIDS Coalition To Unleash Power (ACT UP) was organizing here in the early 1990s. This year's march inspired the formation of Queer and Allies groups here and in San Francisco. Had it been only a civil disobedience action, the opportunity to

Activists march on the Ramparts police station to protect police brutality. © *Geoff Oliver-Bugbee*

involve the queer community broadly would have been lost.

In the globalization movement, civil disobedience has been elevated to a principle that is often used to measure commitment, as in, "Are you willing to get arrested?" We faced many challenges from protesters arriving in town and expecting mass civil disobedience every day. We were accused of not being down with getting arrested and of forcing our concerns about L.A.'s communities onto the movement as a whole. We believe that the globalization movement needs to evaluate the role of civil disobedience in our movement. Connecting with grassroots community struggles is important, and we should discuss whether civil disobedience makes that harder. We should look specifically at how race and class privilege affect people's ability to travel across the country and get arrested.

Working against oppression

Another area in which we put great effort was making sure antiracist, antioppression practice was present in everything we did. Rise Up/DAN LA made a sincere effort to be a racially diverse group. While we succeeded in some ways we failed in others. From the beginning of our organizing, the group struggled to address issues of racism and antioppression. The process began with looking at how we could develop an antioppression practice. While we had established a core group that was relatively diverse, with every new influx of members there came more and more white people. This created a real challenge for us. We began by trying to define an antioppression practice and our commitment to this practice. Initially we started by having discussion in each of our workgroups that asked people to define what they think antioppression practice looks like and how could we do this in our group. We also tracked the makeup of the workgroups in terms of racial and gender balance.

Eventually problems with racism and other forms of oppression started creeping in. A process work group was created in part to troubleshoot and develop strategies to resolve them. During discussions within the organizing collective we identified issues of racism within the larger globalization movement, within Direct Action Network Continental, and within our group. We then discussed examples where people of color had experienced racism within the group and in some cases individuals including myself were called on behavior that was oppressive.

We then analyzed the causes of the problems we had identified. We created a chart that named a specific problem and then listed short-term solutions, long-term solutions, and no solution. We used this chart to identify solutions, create a plan, and implement it.

For example, we identified racism and racial privilege as a dynamic within the group that came from a white-dominated society. We defined a short-term solution: white people need to address issues of racism and continually struggle with issues of privilege and power. For the long term, we need to build social justice movements that have an antiracist analysis, message, and approach at their cores. In the no-solution category we acknowledged that racism is deeply woven into this society and it was not going to be ending any time soon. This means we have to be even more determined to take on issues of racism and other forms of oppression within our organizations, our movements, our world, and ourselves.

We realized that racism was going to happen within the group, and we could not stop that. What we could do was have the commitment and the courage to address racism and other 'isms' when they emerged. We included antioppression work in all our trainings. We posted our antioppression guidelines in the convergence space, in our action handbook, and in our meeting rules. We made our convergence space accessible to diverse groups of people, with all types of artistic expression from puppet-making to graffiti and everything in Spanish and English. We incorporated antioppression themes in our messaging. Whenever we spoke in the media we raised the issue of racism and its use, locally and globally, as a tool for corporate domination.

From the beginning of our organizing we knew that we would have to do antiracism workshops for white people. This turned out to be controversial. But with only white people in the room, they could talk amongst themselves about how they were racist and how they could help one another challenge their racism. By creating a safe space, people could take responsibility for their racist behaviors and attitudes, and learn to unpack the racism within. Meanwhile, a people of color caucus was also taking place to create a safe space for discussing issues of racism.

Ideally there are spaces where people of color and white people come together and have dialogues. Also, facilitating these workshops requires a great deal of skill, and anyone who leads them should have specific training in leading antioppression workshops. Our workshop outline is on page (98).

The workshops got participants to acknowledge their white privilege and the benefits that it brings. They learned some tools for combating racism within themselves and in their organizing. They also gained a positive way to handle their white guilt by taking responsibility for combating racism instead of being immobilized by it. The end result was that people wanted to have more time and more discussion about the role of racism within the movement, and how to become allies to people of color and other white people.

Our work during the Democratic Convention in L.A. was effective in some ways but not in others. We did not get the Democrats to acknowledge our issues and concerns. We did mobilize thousands of people in L.A. for five straight days. We helped the globalization movement grow and raised some very significant issues within it. This movement is still young. We hope it will soon set aside time for critical reflection and strategic planning. If we can continue to learn each time we organize mass mobilizations, we can build a truly powerful movement capable not only of challenging power but also of generating real power.

Cameron Levin works for a community organization that helped get a living wage passed in Los Angeles and that works on economic justice and workers' rights issues. If you would like to engage further or see Rise Up/DAN LA's tools, trainings, or materials, e-mail him at struggle@earthlink.net.

Black Comeback

Kai Lumumba Barrow (excerpts from an interview with LA Kauffman)

What if there was a revolution and nobody noticed?

OK, "revolution" is too grand a term, but the event in question is undeniably historic: the creation, in the United States, of a direct-action-based alliance across racial lines, between the predominantly white movement against corporate globalization and the predominantly people of color movement against criminal injustice.

You won't read about it in the mainstream media, but then, they didn't see Seattle coming either. More troubling is how little discussion there seems to be in radical and progressive circles about this nascent alliance: its necessity, potential, and pitfalls.

Kai Lumumba Barrow has been a major figure behind the recent resurgence of direct action within movements of color. She works full time as an organizer for SLAM!, the Student Liberation Action Movement, based in the City University of New York, especially Manhattan's Hunter College (City College SLAM! (www.geocities.com/Capitol-

SLAM! and NYC-DAN protest the criminal injustice system at the
Republican National Convention in Philadelphia, Summer 2000.
© *Diane Greene Lent*

Hill/Lobby/6353/). Since the mid-nineties, SLAM! has been a pioneering activist force on the East Coast, mobilizing working-class students of color in a series of savvy and daring campaigns for educational
access and economic justice.

SLAM! brought the largely white New York City Direct Action Network (NYC-DAN) and other groups together to plan a joint action
against the Republican Party Convention in Philadelphia, focused on
questions of criminal injustice. The process was a bumpy one—in particular, there was resistance within NYC-DAN to what some felt was a
turn away from the group's focus on corporate globalization, resistance
that many activists of color viewed as racist—but the coalition held.

–LA Kauffman

(Editor's note: A year after this interview was completed, LA
Kauffman said that SLAM! and NYC-DAN weren't actively collaborating, but the multiracial alliance fostered relationships between their
members, and the possibility of future work together is real.)

Kai Lumumba Barrow: I went to college thinking, this is where the revolution is going to happen. I went to a historically black university in Atlanta, and I was really taken aback: It was the Carter years, and Reagan was beginning to show his ugly head, and there was no movement.

COINTELPRO had done a serious job on the Panther Party and then also the Black Liberation Army. There was underground stuff happening but it was way, way submerged. There wasn't any real movement specifically in black communities any more. And I was on this campus with the bourgeoisie, the black bourgeoisie, and I was really freaked out. Like, what is going on? (laughter)

But then I got active around antiapartheid work, building student organizations on campus, and doing a lot of work around Assata Shakur and Joanne Little and other political prisoners.

I also became a member of the Republic of New Africa, whose full name was the Provisional Government of the Republic of New Africa. It focused on establishing a nation for black people in five states in the South. Doing a lot of institution-building, in that sense. We started a school—a Saturday school—did a lot of political prisoner work and a lot of political education. I ended up here in New York in the early nineties, still staying with the same issues, police brutality and prison work.

LA Kauffman: In the U.S., the tactics and techniques of direct action were really pioneered by the black freedom movement of the fifties and sixties, but by the early seventies, those tactics are rarely seen in movements of color, especially in black movements. How did that come to be?

KLB: There was a major shift in the political expression of the black liberation movement in the mid-sixties. I have recollections of looking at the civil rights movement, Dr. King, and the dogs and that sort of thing, and I have recollections of my family saying, Why are they allowing themselves to be beaten and attacked by these pigs, by these racist pigs? Why are they not fighting back?

So there were two predominant tendencies regarding which way forward for our people. It's reductionist to say it, but it was primarily Malcolm X versus Dr. King, and you choose your camp. And I tended to be in the Malcolm X camp—still do, frankly.

The Black Panther Party, as the heirs of Malcolm X, said we're not going to just stand by idly, we're going to utilize self-defense in order to get our movement forward. And at that time the Party did engage in a lot of direct action, such as from taking over the state capitol in California—that was a direct action

Now, though, the black liberation movement is at a really crucial stage in its development. We've seen a lot of our leadership and a lot of our comrades killed and imprisoned and driven crazy, exiled, because we stood up against oppression. And at this point there seems to be a reassessing of which way we should we go. We've engaged in a critique around the standard leadership model, the hierarchical leadership model; we've done a critique around the party model; we've done a critique around every possible model that we know exists, and at this point we're in the process of rebuilding.

So as a people, within different movements, we've been stunned to some degree for a really long time. Since the early to mid-seventies. I think the experiment with armed struggle models, underground models, hit us really hard. The Party as a large movement kind of stopped at that point. There have been smatterings of different things that have occurred since then, but I don't think we've really been able to capture the imagination of our communities in any broad way since that period.

So we've been kind of in this stalemate, and I think what's happening is that we're starting to look back to, well, the fifties. (laughter) This dawned on me maybe about a year or so ago, and I was really pissed. I was like, damn it, we're going backwards. (laughter)

So we're starting to reassess the utilization of direct action and civil disobedience, but we're coming at it, I think, more militantly than in the fifties. We've seen it as a way to engage more of our community. Primarily what we've been doing since the seventies is rallies and permitted protests and those sort of things, that have been more or less nonconfrontational. I think we're starting to say, wait a minute. We've been using a multitude of

Kai Lumumba Barrow (center) at an emergency rally in New York City to protest the killing of Shaka Sankofa in Texas, July 2000. © Diane Greene Lent

nonconfrontational tactics, and I think at this point some of us are starting to escalate some of the tactics that we're utilizing, understanding that we're also the most victimized by the state for participating in those tactics.

We took the position in the past that nonviolent civil disobedience placed us in a very passive position, so we started engaging in armed struggle or at least self-defense. We didn't have enough experience with that perhaps, or we didn't have enough support for that, and we were beat. We were beat pretty badly.

We're trying to come back from that, get it together and figure out how we're going to move forward. Taking the best of both self-defense and militancy while still being accountable to our communities.

LAK: What were your feelings about Seattle when it happened?

KLB: Why the hell am I in New York at a SLAM! meeting? I had planned to go. I was so mad! For all the obvious reasons, I thought it was great. I was really disappointed by the coverage, I don't know if there were more people of color in Seattle than the none I saw in the media.

The morning after, my partner and I were on the train, reading the paper. And we were smiling and high fiving each other. I lived at the time in Bed Stuy, so the train was filled with black folks—and everybody was smiling. I had some good conversations with a couple of folks on the train, about how this is necessary, and it's about time, and this reminds me of the old days. People were overwhelmingly supportive. Nobody said, "Oh, they shouldn't have thrown the rock at the Starbucks." (laughter)

But, in terms of their weaknesses, Seattle, D.C.—even Philly and L.A.—these mass convergences require a week's worth of time in order to participate, dollars in order to travel, support. If a whole group of people go somewhere for a week, there's a whole lot of work that's not getting done, and who's going to do it? Whether that's taking care of the children, or working nine to five. It's very difficult for people of color, even young people of color, young working-class people of color, to participate in mass convergences.

I thought Seattle was a great experiment, and it was great that labor came out. But there was clearly a class distinction between the people who organized and participated in Seattle versus where I come from. Access to cell phones? Please, we're just getting walkie-talkies. The utilization of technology, organizing on the Internet. What's that phrase, the digital divide? It's there. Make no mistake about it, it's there.

So the organizing and the building for that action clearly indicated that an intelligentsia, a bourgeois class, had organized it. They had the equipment, they had the contacts. That's not necessarily a bad thing, but it's really important to acknowledge that.

So to some degree, I thought it was great to see it, and I felt really heartened that people were in the streets. I also felt disconnected, and I felt envious—player hate. (laughter) I felt like, you know, why don't we have the resources to do this kind of work.

If we look at the Vietnam War protests, we see how those protests—because of a capacity to utilize the system, and money, and resources—tended to overtake and co-opt the black liberation movement, the American Indian Movement, the Chicano movement, and the Puerto Rican movement. I'm worried that this network of people doing direct action around corporate globalism is going to do the same thing to emerging movements around criminal injustice. These are issues where people of color are saying no, this is genocide, and we're building a movement. I worry about globalization issues knocking that out of the box.

That's why I think the predominantly white antiglobalization movement has got to engage in a domestic analysis of corporate globalization and what effect it has on disenfranchised communities of color. The movement against corporate globalization has to engage in an ongoing analysis about race and imperialism, and how they play out in the United States, or else it will completely undermine our work and continue to propel a racist and classist system.

That's why I wanted to really look at how we could unite with the Direct Action Network, or build a parallel alliance or network of people of color that were focused on issues that affect people of color, and unite the two major issues—corporate globalization and criminal injustice—as a place that we can spring from.

This interview first appeared as Issue #11 of FREE RADICAL: Chronicle of the New Unrest. The interviewer, LA Kauffman, is a journalist, editor of FREE RADICAL, and organizer active in a number of New York City direct action campaigns. She is the first person she is aware of to be arrested for allegedly committing a crime by fax machine. For the full interview see www.free-radical.org.

Billionaires Crash the Extreme Costume Ball

Andrew Boyd

During the "Shutdown in Seattle" in November 1999, I watched a hundred sea turtles face down riot cops, a gang of Santas stumble through a cloud of tear gas, and a burly Teamster march shoulder to shoulder with a pair of Lesbian Avengers naked to the waist except for a strip of black electrical tape across each nipple. Several months later in Boston, a mutant freakshow with a cast of thousands—including hunchbacked rats, three-headed corn cobs, and strawberry fish—

took the streets against an international gathering of biotech industrialists. Protest has become an extreme costume ball.

To some it's just kids cutting up in the street. To others this brand of theatrical Do-It-Yourself (DIY) street politics represents a new kind of anticorporate movement distinguished by creativity, self-organization, coalition building, and the will to take on global capitalism.

"The costume ball is the one formal convention in which the

Andrew Boyd with the Loan Sharks in Washington © *Diane Greene Lent*

THE GLOBAL ACTIVIST'S MANUAL

There was one sublime moment in Seattle when I realized that the wild yet focused energies in the streets could never be resolved into a folk song—we were now part of Hip Hop Nation. The rhythms of the chants were rougher, more percussive. The energy was fierce and playful. The street resonated with an in-your-face confidence. The costumes—half Native American totems, half whimsical culture-jamming commentaries—made a joyous, friendly cacophony. The activists were comfortable with irony, but not bogged down by it. We were no longer mimicking the '60s nor distancing ourselves from its failures.

Something deep had shifted. This was not a new naïveté. Somehow the movement had taken a Hegelian lurch forward—from thesis to anti-thesis to synthesis. In the '60s was the thesis: "We can change the world." In the '80s came the anti-thesis: "What good did it all do anyway." We knew everything was corrupt. We were bitter and defensive. We distrusted ourselves. We were too cool to care—or we played the self-righteous voice in the wilderness calling out, "Everyone else betrayed the ideals but me."

Maybe it takes the span of a generation to metabolize these kind of historical phases. Maybe the new generation of youthful activists are free to believe in themselves again because they are not invested in either the '60s or the retreat from it.

Whatever the reason, on the streets of Seattle, there was synthesis. Irony was no longer an expression of our lack of confidence; it was a playful tool we could wield and still be intensely passionate about our politics. We had somehow transcended and incorporated thesis and anti-thesis. Before Seattle, irony had the better of us; now we had the better of it. We were neither nostalgic nor snide. We had achieved a new attitude—sly and mischievous, yet full of hope for the future.

desire for individuality and extreme originality does not endanger collective performance but is actually a condition for it," the architect Rem Koolhaas once said, describing the urban chaos of New York City. He could just as easily have been describing the new sensibility of protest. "It works because we're all expressing a similar message in a different way," says Emily Schuch, 22, who was in D.C. for the April 2000 anti-World Bank protest. The phalanx of corporate loan sharks, the Rube Goldbergian contraption that ate pieces of earth and shat out coins, the contingents of indigenous peoples in striking native garb, combined artistically and politically to say: "More World! Less Bank!"

For Schuch, a recent graduate of the School of Visual Arts, the creative invitation offered by a carnival-like protest meshes well with her peers' do-whatever-you-feel-like attitude toward drugs, sex, and music, summed up in her mind by a recent bumper sticker—"My body is not a temple, it's an amusement park." This movement's costumed protest provides an exciting venue for self-discovery and artistic experimentation, where every giant puppet is a barricade and every outrageous act a challenge to the corporate-manufactured consumer sameness that passes for culture.

Its sources are many. In the '80s and '90s groups, like ACT UP, Women's Action Coalition, and the Lesbian Avengers inspired a new style of high-concept shock politics that was both identity-affirming and visually arresting. In 1994 the Zapatistas burst from the Chiapas jungles and into the political imaginations of activists around the world. The "first postmodern revolutionary movement" set aside the dry manifesto and the sectarian vanguard for fable, poetry, theater, and a democratic movement of movements against global capitalism. The U.S. labor movement, hit hard by globalization, began to innovate and seek out new allies. Among them was Earth First, which was experimenting with new technologies of radical direct action in the forests of Northern California. The Critical Mass bicycle rides, dubbed "organized coincidences," provided a home-grown, working model of a celebratory, self-organizing protest. Even the Burning Man festival, while not explicitly political, helped spread an implicit politics of radical self-expression and radical self-organization. The Burning Man slogans "No spectators!" and "You are the entertainment!" were just as evident on the streets of Seattle as in the Nevada desert.

New ideas also migrated across the Atlantic. Reclaim the Streets began in London in the early '90s, a loose collection of ravers, artists, and anticar activists. RTS brought the underground rave dance scene out of the warehouses and clubs and into charged political spaces. An RTS action is part protest, part street party, part a gesture that reclaims the streets from the private exclusive use of the car and returns them to a collective use as a commons. Quickly, a tall three-pronged tripod structure is set up, blocking the street. Someone scampers to the top. A truck with a sound system arrives, and before the police can respond, hundreds are dancing in the streets. It is both a negative act of resistance and a positive act of celebration, community-building, and self-expression. It is a mass civil disobedience in which ravers, performance artists, and fire jugglers set the tone. Exciting and easy to reproduce, these "festivals of resistance" quickly went global.

"We feel that art shouldn't be just an ornament, but rather an integral part of the movement," says David Solnit. "Everything is theatrical. Traditional protest—the march, the rally, the chants—is just bad theater." In the mid-1990s, Solnit helped launch the Art and Revolution collective, which was inspired by RTS and the diverse Do-It-Yourself (DIY) alternative youth cultures of the hip hop, punk, and rave music scenes. Pioneering a powerful fusion of direct action and Bread and Puppet-style street theater, Art and Revolution organized "Convergences" throughout the western United States to train activists and artists in nonviolent tactics, prop and puppet-making, and decentralized decision-making. "We put art and art-making at the center, not only of our actions, but of our organizing," says Solnit. Chapters formed. The model spread.

By the WTO meeting in Seattle, RTS-style protest had taken hold of the activist imagination. The Direct Action Network (DAN), had adapted the Convergence model to handle the democratic planning of a mass blockade. Activists divided a map of downtown Seattle into pie slices. Clusters of independent yet coordinated affinity groups took responsibility for each slice. With this decision-making structure, thousands of people could organize themselves like so many rings in a many-ringed circus. We threw a costume ball that also successfully blockaded the WTO. On the street, each sideshow was part of the whole, every creative gesture was also an interruption of power.

"We were in Seattle for the world and for justice," says one Boston activist. "But we were also there for ourselves, to create a new culture." By bringing people together in a carnival-like format to challenge the major institutions of global capitalism, the movement found a shape that pushes beyond identity politics, yet creates a space for it. Traditional goal-oriented politics links up with the politics of being. People join the movement not only to take action but to feel alive and find out who they are.

At the end of that long week in Seattle, as the last protest was winding down, I met a woman with whom I had the following conversation. I am not making this up. She was white, in her mid-twenties, wearing J.C. Penney slacks and blouse, and she was clearly moved. "This is my first protest," she said. "Well, I hope it won't be your last," I said. "We'll see what happens," she replied, "But I'm feeling very free."

The face that launched a thousand clicks

But not everyone felt the way she did. Those watching on TV might have thought it was just a chaotic party. If you aren't a participant or a direct observer, the true feeling may not come across—and the specific political message may also get lost. The carnival protest, probably by nature, lacks a unified message. One of its great strengths—its plural character—is also one of its weaknesses.

With these concerns in mind, "Billionaires for Bush (or Gore)" was conceived by United for a Fair Economy, an economic justice organization based in Boston. We hoped to tap into the DIY energy, creativity, and daring of the new movement but maintain the tight message discipline and sustained focus of a campaign. As a consultant for UFE, and a member of RTS and DAN, I was at the center of the project.

The Billionaires were also part of a broader movement effort to link up, both conceptually and organizationally, with issues closer to home. For many in DAN, inspired by the influential *ColorLines* article written by Elizabeth "Betita" Martinez, "Where was the Color in Seattle?" this meant linking up with efforts to combat the prison-industrial complex, the death penalty, police brutality, and the threatened execution of Mumia Abu-Jamal, the celebrated radical journalist on death row in Pennsylvania. For others in DAN, and for United for a Fair Economy, this meant linking up with efforts to reform the campaign finance system and combat domestic economic inequality. We wanted to stay with a big broad theme that had worked in Seattle: democracy vs. corporate power.

In early May, I pulled together a team of talented volunteer designers, media producers, and veteran street theater activists—many of them associated with RTS in New York. With support from UFE, we began to put the pieces of the campaign in place. We created a stylish logo by splicing together a donkey and elephant and a "candidate" by digitally morphing photos of Bush and Gore into a single eerie image. Riffing off of slogans like "Free the Forbes 400," "Corporations are people too," "We're paying for America's free elections so you don't have to," and "We don't care who you vote for, we've already bought them," we created bumper stickers, buttons, a series of posters, and a kick-ass website that eventually won more than a few awards (www.billionairesfor-bushorgore.com). We also created more content-rich materials including a political platform, a full campaign speech, and a candidate product comparison chart. We even made mock radio ads, pressed them onto CD, and sent a hundred out to stations across the country. The satire was com-

BILLIONAIRES FOR BUSH (OR GORE)
Because Inequality Is Not Growing Fast Enough.
www.billionairesforbushorgore.com • • • UFE • 37 Temple Pl. • Boston, MA 02111 • 617/423-2148

pact, funny, and politically on target. The look was slick and the message was unified across a whole range of media. It was quite a package. And we launched it all with a "Million Billionaire March" at the Republican and Democratic national conventions.

We designed the campaign to be participatory: a simple concept that was easy to execute yet allowed for rich elaboration. Through the website activists could download all the materials they needed to do actions in their own communities. By June, wildcat chapters were springing up. In Denver a Billionaires squad barged into the Green Party convention and tried to buy off Ralph Nader, much to the delight of delegates and the media.

By the time we arrived in Philadelphia for the Republican convention in late July, we were already a minor sensation. Advance articles and Internet buzz had put us on the map. Our website was getting one hundred thousand hits a day (twenty thousand unique page views). Everybody was asking for our buttons and stickers and posters. Nearly a hundred Billionaires in full dress joined us in the streets, chanting, singing, burning money, smoking cigars. We also staged a "Vigil for Corporate Welfare" and auctioned off merchandising rights to the Liberty Bell (would it become the Taco Bell Liberty Bell or the Ma Bell Liberty Bell . . . ?) The media were all over us. An informal poll of photojournalists voted us "favorite protest." We were certainly one of the more focused and cohesive. The Democratic convention in Los Angeles was more of the same. My Billionaire character, Phil T. Rich, became a hit on the radio interview circuit and web site traffic shot up to two hundred thousand hits per day. An editor at *The Nation* called us "the sea turtles of the convention protests."

As the campaign picked up, a hub-node structure arose. UFE became the organizational hub of an ad hoc network of Do-It-Yourself movement grouplets. In addition to the campaign framework, UFE was providing funding, infrastructure, research capacity, media contacts, and mainstream legitimacy. The grassroots injected energy, street smarts, and creative elaboration of the core ideas. In the weeks after the conventions, we'd get e-mail every day from people across the country, raving about

The Billionaires take Philadelphia. © *Diane Greene Lent*

the project and eager to start local Billionaires chapters or informing us of actions they had already undertaken. Many had checked out the "Be a Billionaire" section of our website, chosen satirical names for themselves, and downloaded the slogans, posters, and sample press releases. New subcampaigns sprung up at the local level, including Billionaires for More Media Mergers, which was adopted by the San Francisco chapter to protest the National Association of Broadcasters meeting there in September 2000. There were some tensions between nodes and hub, but for the most part, a strong synergy emerged.

"The task of an organizer," says one movement veteran, "is to set up structures so people can participate." The Billionaires effort was not totally decentralized; the hub played an essential role shaping and steering the campaign. The hub designed the core ideas and launched the call to action. But what mechanisms helped us steer the campaign once things got rolling? One was the website. Another was the Million Billionaire March, which modeled the kinds of actions people could do in their home cities. Finally, it was the shtick and the materials themselves. Jokes were funny, content was thoroughly researched, graphic production values were high. People liked the package and wanted to use it. Quality matters.

Building the movement one ironic gesture at a time

The Billionaires campaign is an instructive model. It shows how hub and node can work together to invite open-ended DIY participation into creative actions and yet maintain artistic cohesion and a focused message. It demonstrates the potential of the web for disseminating not just information, but ready-made organizing and message-making tools. It also shows how ingenious meme warfare can inject a message into corporate media in spite of editorial frames designed to filter it out.

The campaign was designed to spread like a virus. Our central meme was our name, "Billionaires for Bush (or Gore)." Those five words not only made people chuckle but carried our two core messages: Big Money owns both

meme (meem, n.): information virus.

candidates and both candidates are roughly the same. All we had to do was say our name, which we did relentlessly and in every manner we could muster. Even the most fragmented and decontextualized mention of us in the media tended to carry our name, and thus our message. If they also got our tag line, "Because Inequality is Not Growing Fast Enough," then the message deepened. If they picked up modular parts of our shtick, then it deepened further. None of this could have happened without tight message discipline up and down these layers and across all the materials. In this way, even when the wildcat DIY actions started to get scrappy, the core idea came through and it was all of a piece.

Seattle showed that street protest can be a place where diverse subcultures can mix it up, where steelworkers and treehuggers can learn how to party together, where young people can experiment with new ways of being and then pronounce, as much to themselves as the world, "*This* is what Democracy looks like!" But the cacophony and free-for-all whimsy of the extreme costume ball can also undercut the seriousness of its political intentions, alienating or confusing people we want to reach. Perhaps the message discipline and media savvy of campaigns such as the Billionaires can help to balance this out, without repressing creativity. "It's one thing to use creative expression to celebrate our own marginal subculture," says David Solnit. "It's another thing to use it as a bridge to other cultures. It's the best alliance-building tool I know."

Andrew Boyd (a.k.a. Phil T. Rich) founded the arts and action program at United for a Fair Economy. He also writes weird books including Life's Little Deconstruction Book: Self-Help for the Post Hip *(W.W. Norton, 1998). A modified version of this article appeared in the Village Voice in July 2000 under the title "Extreme Costume Ball."*

Using Direct Action Effectively

Denis Moynihan

Direct action is more than shutting down a meeting. It can also mean boycotting a store, singing

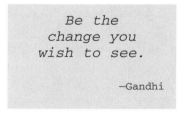

> Be the
> change you
> wish to see.
>
> —Gandhi

in the street, or sitting in at a segregated lunch counter to demand racial integration. It can be used to halt an event that threatens imminent harm, to dramatize an injustice, to gain popular support or media attention, to boost morale amongst campaigners, or to escalate a campaign.

This discussion of direct action is limited to its nonviolent uses. We hope these ideas and resources will encourage you to take direct action in pursuit of your goals, in a manner that is safe, strategic, and effective.

Because direct action pushes

people outside of "normal" behavior, whether it be serious confrontation or intense celebration, it can have a powerful transformative effect. Both participants and spectators can emerge empowered, united, or more skeptical about established channels of change. Direct action can, and some argue, must, serve as a critical component of a campaign. It cannot substitute for a campaign, however. Direct action for its own sake may be an understandable expression of one's passion, but will likely have little impact.

Direct action offers people the opportunity to organize nontraditionally. Alternate models for decision-making can be used, and time can be spent addressing the many deeply-seated oppressive behaviors that affect our interactions. How a direct action is organized is at least as important as the action itself, if not more so. Consensus and affinity

---

7 ways to make our protests more powerful

1. Create more "dilemma demonstrations."
2. Decide specifically whom we're trying to influence, not just "the public."
3. Use campaigns more often, to become proactive rather than reactive.
4. Shift our understanding of the role of mass media.
5. Heighten the contrast between protesters and police behavior.
6. Take a powerful attitude toward the prospect of state repression and collectively take away one of their greatest weapons: fear.
7. Fully commit to strategic nonviolent direct action explicitly.

—from "Mass Action Since Seattle: 7 Ways to Make Our Protests More Powerful" by George Lakey, available from Training for Change, 2719 Springfield Avenue, Philadelphia, PA 19143-3514, (215) 729-7458.

---

groups form the core of the following model. Thorough training and preparation also are crucial.

Direct action is not synonymous with civil disobedience. Civil disobedience explicitly calls for participants to risk arrest (not to want or to try to get arrested). Direct action can and often does include civil disobedience, but can also employ the creative assertion of legally protected behavior. A consumer boycott is an example of this.

Process

The range of tactics, the varying sizes of actions, the differing levels of comfort with direct action that different groups feel, and other variables provide a complex milieu wherein a campaigner may hope to place a direct action. What is the target audience of an action, and what is the goal? How will the action be presented in the media, and how will the public react? What costs will the campaign incur, relative to potential benefits? There are many questions like these to be answered before undertaking a direct action. The answers depend on the strength of one's campaign, one's locality, and the place for direct action in an overall strategy.

If direct action is chosen as a component of a campaign, the task is to do it well. Training is thus a prerequisite. One important goal of these process suggestions is to create alternative systems while struggling against the systems we oppose. Much of what follows comes from the hard-won experience of failed group processes, and from years of dealing with sexism, racism, and other oppressive behaviors that have hampered people's work.

Create more "dilemma demonstrations"
This form of direct action puts the power holders in a dilemma: if they allow us to go ahead and do what we intend to so, we accomplish something worthwhile related to our issue. If they repress us, they put themselves in a bad light, and the public is educated about our message.

—George Lakey

Nonviolence training

Nonviolence training combines theory with role playing to help people carry themselves nonviolently and to prepare people for potentially violent situations. During direct action, conflicts often arise with people who feel their livelihoods are being threatened or their day's progress disturbed. They can become violent verbally and physically. Nonviolence training can prepare activists to interact with such people, using nonthreatening body language and effective listening and responding. Activists learn what to expect when arrested and how to continue deriving power from one's nonviolence while within the justice system, which is designed to disempower. Trainings also provide an opportunity to meet people, form affinity groups, practice consensus decision making, and discuss oppressive behaviors that exist within organizations and groups.

Consensus decision-making

Using consensus, a group can pursue agreement on a proposal, and in the process improve it by incorporating everyone's opinions. This can be better than other systems of decision making, notably voting on an array of options, which could pass a proposal with almost half the group opposed. Even less participatory are bodies that empower a single person or a small group to make decisions for many. Consensus is typically a slower process than these others, and thus is considered less efficient. But when people are going to put their bodies on the line, the extra time is worth it to make sure nobody is overridden by a majority on decisions affecting them so personally.

The first task is to define the group that will make the decision. Is it open to anyone, or to members of an organization or affinity group only? Those who are included in consensus process are considered empowered to speak. Limiting a discussion can save valuable time. The basis of exclusion should be clear, such as, "only those risking arrest are empowered for this discussion," and not arbitrary, but it should also be clear that consensus does not imply "open to anyone who walks in off the street."

Consensus can work in many

settings. The suggestions below are for a more controlled, ideal setting. The process can be adapted to work in the streets, in jail, or elsewhere.

The group should choose a facilitator or two for the discussion. This person will guide the discussion, keep it focused and flowing, and help keep an eye on disruptive or disrespectful behavior, like interrupting. A facilitator should generally exclude her or himself from the discussion and focus on the task of facilitation. If the facilitator feels a need to participate in a part of the discussion or does not feel sufficiently objective, an alternate facilitator should be found. An additional facilitator, sometimes called a vibes watcher, can monitor group dynamics and let people know if their behavior is inappropriate, or if a break is needed. A person to keep stack, that is, to maintain a list of people who want to speak and in what order, is useful, as are a dedicated notetaker and a timekeeper.

Consensus, briefly, works this way: a proposal is made, clarifying questions are answered, concerns are voiced, amendments or counterproposals are made to address the concerns, and the amended proposal or counterproposal is agreed upon. A synthesis of present opinion is pursued in this manner, rather than pursuit of votes to gain passage of one proposal among a field of competing proposals. Unanimity is difficult to achieve in any situation. There are means within this process to express dissent. These include voicing non-support, reservations, standing aside, or blocking.

Blocking is perhaps the most problematic aspect of the consensus process for those unfamiliar with it. An individual may block the group from reaching a decision. This is an important component of the U.S. trial-by-jury system, where one juror can cause a hung jury. As some issues may not demand a formal discussion and pursuit of consensus, the group can agree to use alternate forms, such as voting, or to use a vote to overcome an impasse. Also, the block option often has constraints placed upon it. For example, the blocker may have to justify the block with respect to the group's guiding tenets, or there may be a requirement for two or more to block a decision, to protect against antagonistic solo blockers whose intent is to disrupt the process.

Antioppression training

Identifying behaviors that are oppressive is a vital part of good group process. Racism, sexism, hierarchies within a group, and class and cultural biases all exist and they hurt people. Whether creating a direct action or engaging in other organizing, intentionally addressing these concerns and learning how to identify and hopefully overcome them must be a part of the work.

(See the antioppression workshop on page 98.) In the United States, many communities, such as people of color and gay/lesbian/bi/transgender people, are treated more harshly when in conflict with authorities, and may not agree to direct action tactics.

Affinity groups

Affinity groups are small groups of people, perhaps from five to twenty, who have something in common. The members know each other and trust one another. The affinity group

Some white activists hesitate to take a stand [for] nonviolence because they mistakenly believe that "it's a white thing." That would be a big surprise to the hundreds of thousands of people of color in the United States who have used nonviolent direct action in campaigns for over a century. Not to mention the role of nonviolence in the anticolonial struggles in Africa and Asia. When we think of nonviolence, why do the names of Gandhi, King, and Cesar Chavez so easily leap to mind? They are only the tip of the iceberg. Actually, a far, far higher proportion of people of color have engaged in nonviolent action in the United States than have white people, and continue to do so year in and year out. (I won't even start with the myth that nonviolent action is inherently middle class—that's even more off base than the myth that it's white.)

—George Lakey

forms a unit when engaged in an action.

Many benefits accrue from affinity group organizing. Members can undertake specific, critical roles, and other group members can trust that those roles will be fulfilled. For example, if several members of an affinity group are risking arrest, it is best if they know and trust the person providing jail support. It is not essential that they know the person, but the overall efficacy of the action— and the confidence of the participants—will be boosted. Affinity groups are harder than anonymous groups to infiltrate, which helps people organize direct actions where secrecy or surprise are necessary and helps to exclude people intent on disrupting organizing efforts. Over

Campaigns put us on the offensive

Sometimes a strong reaction to a move of the power holders can be very powerful, as it was in Seattle. The negative side of globalization was put on the public agenda for the first time. The very unleashing of rebel energy itself was positive.

Occasionally reacting is one thing; staying in a posture of reaction is something else. A good word for continuous reaction is *disempowerment*. Mohandas K. Gandhi's first principle of strategy was to stay on the offensive. Having our action agenda dictated by where and when the power holders want to have their meetings is not staying on the offensive.

Campaigns put us on the offensive.

Running a campaign is like taking a magnifying glass and holding it between the sun and a piece of paper. By focusing the energy of the sun, the glass ignites the paper. Successful campaigns focus on their target over time—nine months, two years—with a specific demand that seems achievable.

—George Lakey

time, affinity groups gain experience and expertise, and thus work with increased effectiveness, whether in an autonomous action or a mass action. Consensus process is quickened when people use it together over time.

Roles within the affinity group, in addition to "putting one's body on the line," include media liaison, police liaison, jail support, food and water provider, medic, and videographer/documenter. The specifics of the action will dictate if these or other roles are necessary.

Affinity groups offer an experiment in direct democracy, where all individuals have a role in decision-making. In a mass action, the creation of a spokescouncil allows all affinity groups a place in making decisions about how the action takes shape. Each affinity group empowers a spoke, and that spoke speaks for the group in the spokescouncil. The affinity group is welcome to sit by if logistics allow. The spoke receives instructions throughout any discussion from the affinity group. With a well planned spokescouncil meeting, participating affinity groups will have advance notice of proposals, and their spoke will arrive with the group's position clarified, minimizing the need to return to the group for its consensus. Although this affinity group-based representative democracy is a step removed from allowing every individual to participate in discussions, it has been used to reach decisions quickly with over one thousand people in consensus.

A cluster is a formation of several affinity groups. Clusters are useful when larger numbers of people are needed for actions, and when they need to coordinate closely. Clusters can form and gain momentum over time, and such continuity might well be sought by people interested in affinity group-based organizing.

Training for specific direct action tactics

As the media and the public become more familiar with direct action tactics, these tactics are both more likely to be ignored and more easily dealt with by those whose activities the tactics aim to disrupt. Use of new tactics is accompanied by increased risk of both injury and failure, so proper training is critical. If one hopes to hang a banner, block an intersection, disrupt a campaign stop, or present street theater, learning how to do so safely should be an early step. Seek training in your community or region, or consult the Resources section below.

In all aspects of direct action organizing, an important task is to encourage and train those with less experience. This means giving people opportunities to facilitate meetings, speak with the media, deal with police and public, and take a fair share of responsibility.

Denis Moynihan organized his first march in the fifth grade, and sparked his first small-scale (cafeteria) riot by seventh grade. He credits Bread & Puppet, Augusto Boal, and Spontaneous Celebrations with help in channeling deep contempt for illegitimate authority into direct action against it.

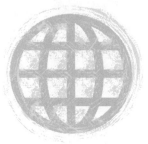

Taking on Corporations

Going after a company like Nike or Citigroup (p. 171) is a powerful educational strategy. Anticorporate campaigns have taught millions of Americans how the global economy works. But can those campaigns actually transform that economy? Even if you force one company to stop using sweatshops—which could take years—its competitors will keep sweating workers and maybe even force the reforming corporation out of business.

Some activists have responded by challenging the legal basis for corporations' very existence. Paul Cienfuegos (p. 175) describes campaigns to revoke corporations' charters and undo their legal "personhood" or campaign financing. Others, like Randy Kehler (p. 181), want to sever the money pipeline that gives corporations power over politicians. The Indymedia movement (p. 187) is attacking another dimension of corporate control—the power to mold our minds.

—Mike Prokosch and Laura Raymond

Beyond the Bottom Line: A Campaign for a Sane Economy

Rainforest Action Network

Citigroup is making a big mess with your money. The largest financial institution in North America needs to stop financing destruction and start supporting a sane and sustainable economy. By focusing the confrontation with corporate globalization on Citigroup, a leader on Wall Street, we will bring the struggle for global justice back home to our communities.

The megabanks behind environmental destruction

The past decade has seen a seven hundred percent increase in funding from corporate financial institutions for development projects around the globe. Many of these projects are causing extensive and irreversible ecological damage and social disintegration. Up to now, the megabanks' role has been nearly invisible.

In response, Rainforest Action Network has launched a campaign targeting Citigroup, the largest financial institution in North America. Citigroup is the top financier of the world's most destructive projects, from mineral exploitation in the Amazon basin to oil pipelines in African rainforests to coal-burning power plants in Southeast Asia. These projects pollute and destroy extensive tracts of land and forest, decimate critical wildlife habitat, and displace indigenous populations. The international Citigroup campaign targets the roots of the corporate globalization that is devastating our environment, working conditions, and communities.

Irresponsible and amoral corporations are fueled by a global

The financial realm constitutes the commanding citadel of the global system—the benefactor that provides essential capital, the enforcer that disciplines multinational corporations as well as nations. Its imperious attitudes and amoral operating assumptions are embedded in every aspect of globalization and implicated in every complaint, from inhumane working conditions to environmental wreckage, from the erosion of national sovereignty to the gross and growing inequalities.

—William Greider, The Nation, *April 24, 2000.*

> *For much of Asia, the ugly face of globalization has been disastrous volatility. As they see it, free investment flows have meant that the little guy got screwed while the wealthy were able to sock away most of their money in Geneva. And, pretty much, they're right.*
>
> *—Robert Hormats, vice chairman of Goldman Sachs International,* Washington Post, *October 9, 2000.*

a deeper understanding of our common adversaries.

RAN's Campaign for a Sane Economy aims to help transform the corporate financial sector. It is challenging a definition of profit that fails to recognize the value of protecting the environment, preserving democracy, and building a just and equitable global society. Now is the time to call for the redirection of global investments toward community and ecological sustainability.

The central role

In our increasingly globalized society, each and every new project and activity requires large amounts of capital. Citigroup has the ability to provide that money, thus effectively deciding which initiatives proceed. However, for the global economy to continue to function, individual buy-in is necessary. If you bank with Citi, have a student loan through Citibank, have a mutual fund or pension fund portfolio with Salomon Smith Barney, or even carry a Citibank credit card, your money contributes to the capital financing activities that result in environmental destruction and destabilized communities around the world.

financial system that refuses to take basic social and environmental standards into account. Citizens concerned with the corporate-led, environmentally and socially destructive model of globalization currently being promoted by Western governments and international institutions are increasingly turning their attention to the corporate players. Citigroup, as a primary architect and beneficiary of globalization, has led environmental and social movements to

Citigroup is the largest corporate finance institution in North America and one of the top in the world. Its operations affect almost every aspect of the global economy. Citigroup offers its services and its capital to back such morally bankrupt projects as Maxxam's clearcutting the last ancient California redwoods, Monsanto's genetic engineering which is threatening global food safety, and Wackenhut's construction of private prisons. In our inner cities, Citi has been exposed for redlining communities of color and for predatory lending practices that drive poor people deeper into poverty. Citigroup reaps daily profits from the massive debt burdens that cripple so many third world countries and from currency speculation like that which led to the Asian financial collapse. Its extensive financial contributions to our elected officials have guaranteed it an unfettered pursuit of profit, often with support from such governmental institutions as the Overseas Private Investment Corporation (OPIC), of whose funds Citi has been a primary recipient.

Historically, the diversity of social and environmental issues needing attention has divided our efforts. The Citigroup campaign offers us an unprecedented opportunity to focus some of our momentum and energy. Only by working together as one movement can we handle the magnitude of the problems that face us. While we are committed to fighting for our own issues, we add strength to each others' work.

There are countless ways to tell Citigroup that financial investments must support communities and the environment, not harm them. As students, concerned citizens, and Citibank customers we have the power to withhold our business and expose Citi's brand name by telling the truth about how they make their money. From colorful street theater and nonviolent civil disobedience at Citibank branches or Salomon Smith Barney offices, to leafleting potential customers at credit card recruitment tables on college campuses, to canceling Citi accounts with a letter explaining why you're unwilling to do business with them, this campaign will help create opportunities to bring pressure on Citigroup.

Rainforest Action Network has street theater ideas, sample editorials, background information, and other organizing materials to help you take on Citigroup. Check www.ran.org. "Ten Things You Can Do" is an especially valuable checklist for on-campus activism.

The time is now

We live in a unique time in the history of the planet. As the sixth great mass extinction unfolds, we are losing up to one hundred species a day. From the oceans to the wetlands to forests, every ecosystem on the planet is in decline. The global climate is being disrupted. We no longer have the time to treat only the symptoms of the problems; we have to attack them at their roots. It's up to all of us to answer the question: will we have a global society based on life-affirming principles or corporate profits?

It is this very step that we must take in order to address the underpinnings of a misguided globalization. Our task now is to bring into the light the intimate relationship between the projects that destroy our forests, burn our atmosphere, evict people from their homes and those who daily fund these projects. Behind bad projects are bad financial decisions.

We stand at the point of an evolutionary leap in the movement toward a sustainable Earth and culture. In the last year, disparate forces have come together to recognize that our visions of a healthy future are one and the same. Recent mass mobilizations in Seattle and Washington, D.C., have shown our power to define a globalization that works for people and the environment, not just the corporate bottom line.

Paradigm Shift: Challenging Corporate Authority

Paul Cienfuegos

In the twentieth century, American citizens got used to challenging corporate harms and corporate abuses of authority one harm at a time—one clearcut Timber Harvest Plan at a time, one toxic spill at a time, one plant closure at a time. It wasn't always like this. "Earlier generations of Americans were quite clear that a corporation was an artificial, subordinate entity with no inherent rights of its own," says Richard Grossman, "and that incorporation was a *privilege* bestowed by the sovereign people. For example, in 1834 the Pennsylvania Legislature declared: 'A corporation in law is just what the incorporation act makes it. It is the creature of the law and may be molded to any shape or for any purpose that the Legislature may deem most conducive to the common good.' "

People understood that they had a civic responsibility not to create artificial entities that could harm the body politic, interfere with the mechanisms of self-governance, and assault their sovereignty. They also understood that they did not elect their agents to positions in government to sell off the sovereignty of the people.

Here are a few examples of how different the rules were in the United States until the late 1800s. In many states, corporations were *prohibited* from owning other corporations, *prohibited* from donating to political candidates or charitable organizations, and *prohibited* from owning any land beyond what was necessary for the carrying out of their chartered duties. Boards of directors and stockholders were held *personally* liable for all harms and debts. The "limited liability corporation," as we know it today, did not exist.

> Dozens of new strategies are sprouting up across the United States and Canada that challenge illegitimate corporate authority and privilege.

Sadly, as we enter the twenty-first century, few Americans have any idea that such a history even existed in this country. Yet this is starting to change. Beginning in the early 1990s—thanks to the seminal work of Richard Grossman and his colleagues at the Program on Corporations, Law and Democracy (POCLAD)—Americans started to rethink *how* we go about challenging the harms that corporations get away with day in and day out. We began to rediscover the appropriate relationship between we the people and the fictitious subordinate creation we call the "corporation." And we began to reframe our analysis of the problem.

Yes, of course, clearcut logging and sweatshop labor and genetically engineered food are a big problem. But the much bigger problem is that we've allowed fictitious corporate "persons" to usurp our authority as citizens to make these and other critical societal decisions that affect all of us and the natural world.

If we no longer accepted critical societal decisions which affect all of us and the natural world, or pleaded with corporate leaders to cause a little less harm, what *would* we do? If we no longer celebrated as victories every brief delay in the corporate devastation of our world, what *would* we celebrate?

By the mid-1990s, new groups were sprouting up across the United States and Canada, and asking themselves these questions. Each was beginning to experiment with a different set of tools than anyone had used for a century. Groups like Democracy Unlimited in California, 180/Movement for Democracy and Education in Wisconsin, Friends of the Constitution in Nebraska, and Citizens Council on Corporate Issues in British Columbia, are all examples of this fledgling new movement.

Clearly, to ask people of every ideology to rethink how they respond to corporate harm is a very big task, so a number of groups are beginning with public education strategies. For example, in my community, six hundred residents came together for nine hours of town hall meetings last year to discuss the question, "Can we have democracy when large corporations wield so much power and wealth under law?" (Videotapes are available.)

Here are numerous examples of American and Canadian citizens educating and organizing themselves and others—no longer simply challenging individual corporate harms, but going after corporate privilege and illegitimate corporate authority. There is tremendous diversity in our goals and strategies, as one would expect in a fledgling new social movement.

Yes, it's still a small number of groups, but the number is beginning to grow rapidly, and there's no question that this growth represents a profound shift beginning to take place in the consciousness of citizens.

Consider these dozens of projects as a guide for you and your community. Contact the organizers. Learn from their mistakes, and replicate the projects that seem to work. There is no time to lose.

1. **Bold responses to corporations which chronically break the law**
   • The Wayne Township Ordinance (Mifflin County, PA) was enacted into law in 1998 by a 3–0 vote, and has since also passed in Thompson Township. It prohibits any corporation from doing business in the township (even if it is already located there) if it has a history of consistently violating any regulatory laws (environmental, labor, etc.), and further prohibits any corporation from doing business there if any of its current directors sits on other corporate boards that consistently violate regulatory law. Contact Community Environmental Legal Defense Fund (CELDF), 717-530-0931 or www.celdf.org

2. **Communities defending themselves against corporate power**
   • In November 1998, hundreds of campus organizers from across North America met at the Campus Democracy Convention and formed the 180/Movement for Democracy and Education. This chapter-based organization opposes the corporatization of education as well as other forms of institutionalized hierarchy and oppression, and calls for a 180-degree turn to assert democratic authority over their schools. Ongoing projects include: challenging the authority of corporate-controlled boards of regents, mobilizing opposition to the WTO, forcing administrators to stop purchasing from sweatshops, and exposing corporate-controlled research programs. Contact (608) 262-9036 or clearinghouse@tao.ca or http://corporations.org/democracy.

   • The Boulder Independent Business Alliance (BIBA) unites independent businesses to compete effectively against corporate chain stores. Recent work includes the Community Vitality Act currently under consideration by the Boulder City Council. BIBA is also helping other cities create IBAs. Contact (303) 402-1575 or info@boulder iba.org or www.boulder-iba.org.

3. **Prohibiting (or defining) corporate involvement in particular industries**

• New farming laws in Nebraska (Initiative 300, 1982), South Dakota (Amendment E, 1998), and Pennsylvania (1999) ban nonfamily-owned corporations from engaging in farming or ranching or owning farmland. Nebraska and South Dakota achieved their success through ballot initiatives that amended their state constitutions. Friends of the Constitution is a Nebraska coalition of eighteen farm, church, and environmental groups which joined together to defend and enforce Initiative 300. The governments of two Pennsylvania townships (Wells and Thompson) enacted similar ordinances. Several Pennsylvania townships are discussing similar legislation that would ban corporate logging or forest land ownership. Contact Dakota Rural Action, (605) 697-5204 or drural@brookings.net or www.worc.org/member.html#dra; in Nebraska, Nancy Thompson at FoC, (402) 494-9117 or nanthomp@pionet.net or www.i300.org; in Pennsylvania, Tom Linzey at Community Environmental Legal Defense Fund (CELDF), (717) 530-0931 or www.celdf.org.

4. **Revoking corporate charters**
• The New York Attorney General's office has shown surprising leadership recently in challenging corporate charters. The previous Republican Attorney General, Dennis Vacco, successfully revoked the charters of two nonprofit tax-exempt front groups for the tobacco corporations and seized and distributed their assets to two public institutions. The current Democratic Attorney General, Eliot Spitzer, proposed—in a preelection speech—a "death penalty" for corporations that cause serious harm, though he has failed to take any action after his election. Contact the Attorney General's office in Albany, NY, www.oag.state.ny.us.

• In 1998, the National Lawyers Guild (joined by thirty other groups and individuals) filed a 129-page legal petition to California's previous Republican Attorney General Dan Lungren requesting that he revoke the charter of Union Oil Company of California, UNOCAL, for its decades of lawbreaking and global harms. He responded with a terse nonexplanation. In 1999, with one hundred and fifty additional endorsing organizations and individuals, the petition was resubmitted to the newly elected Democratic Attorney General Bill Lockyer, who also promptly responded with a brief nonresponse. (A book including the petition and information about how to file such a document can be purchased for $12 from the Alliance for Democracy, 681 Main Street, Suite 16, Waltham, MA 02451.) Contact Robert Benson, (213) 736-1094 or heed@igc.org or www.heed.net.

5. **Rewriting state corporate codes**
   • In 1999, a small group of citizen activists wrote a model "Corporation Code" for the state of New Jersey that reins in illegitimate corporate privileges. Their choice of states was not a coincidence, as New Jersey was known as the "traitor state" at the turn of the century for overturning more than a century of legal tradition of citizen control over corporations via state legislatures. The draft document may be useful to anyone wishing to organize to amend their state's corporate codes. Contact Ward Morehouse, (212) 972-9877 or cipany@igc.org.

6. **Amending state constitutions**
   • Montana's Supreme Court, in a landmark ruling on October 20, 1999, found that the state (without showing a compelling state interest) cannot allow activities to continue that have the potential to poison the environment. Two environmental groups had challenged an exemption allowing mining activities to degrade rivers. This was the first time that the court tested a Montanan's constitutional "right to a clean and healthful environment" (Article II, Section 3, passed at their 1972 Constitutional Convention). The court stated, "Our constitution does not require that dead fish float on the surface of our state's rivers and streams before its farsighted environmental protections can be invoked." Contact Tom France at National Wildlife Federation Resource Center in Missoula, (406) 721-6705 or www.nwf.org.

7. **Challenging corporate personhood**
   • In 2000, the city council of a small community on California's north coast passed a Resolution on Corporate Personhood in the City of

Point Arena by a 4-to-1 vote. The resolution disavows the personhood status of corporations, and encourages public discussion on the role of corporations in public life. Contact Jan Edwards at Redwood Coast Alliance for Democracy, (707) 882-1818 or janedwards@mcn.org or www.iiipublishing.com/alliance.htm.

8. **Reclaiming our history, culture, and language**
    • "Citizens Over Corporations," a unique 52-page pamphlet on the history of corporate power and democratic movements in Ohio, was published in 1999 by the Ohio Committee on Corporations, Law and Democracy, a project of the Northeast Ohio American Friends Service Committee. (Send $3.50 to obtain a copy—checks to AFSC, 513 W. Exchange Street, Akron, OH 44302.) Pamphlets such as this need to be researched and written for every state in the union as the first step in designing campaigns to reclaim our authority over our corporate creations. Contact Greg Coleridge, (330) 253-7151 or afscole@aol.com.

    • "Measure F: The Arcata Advisory Initiative on Democracy and Corporations" won by fifty-eight percent of the vote in November 1998 in Arcata, California. It called for:
    1) two town hall meetings on the topic: "Can we have democracy when large corporations wield so much power and wealth under law?" These were attended by about six hundred residents, almost five percent of local voters; and
    2) the creation of a standing committee of the city council on "Democracy and Corporations" to begin reining in the authority and privileges of large corporations doing business in Arcata. Contact Democracy Unlimited, (707) 822-2242 or cienfuegos@igc.org or www.monitor.net/democracyunlimited.

    • As part of the Women's International League for Peace and Freedom's Challenge Corporate Power, Assert the People's Rights national campaign, six-session study groups are being formed around the country to "explore the history and roots of corporate power, examine global corporatization, decolonize our minds, and participate in democratic conversation." Copies of study materials are available. Contact Charmaine Sprengelmeyer, (215) 563-5527 or wilpf@wilpf.org or www.wilpf.org.

9. **Existing organizations reframing or expanding their work in order to more effectively challenge corporate authority**
   • In November 1998, the Labor Party's first Constitutional Convention unanimously passed a Workplace Bill of Rights which reframes the rights of workers to include worker (i.e., citizen) authority over their subordinate corporate institutions. Contact Ed Bruno, (617) 531-0901 or laborpne@aol.com.

   • The Northeast Ohio American Friends Service Committee is challenging state for-profit and not-for-profit corporate codes, looking at charter revocation, and unmasking federal and state regulatory agencies. Contact Greg Coleridge, (330) 253-7151 or afscole@aol.com.

Paul Cienfuegos is the cofounding director of Democracy Unlimited of Humboldt County based in Arcata, CA, and the coauthor of "Measure F: the Arcata Advisory Initiative on Democracy and Corporations." For information about the work of his organization or the workshops he leads ("First Steps in Dismantling Corporate Rule"), or to comment on this article, contact him at (707) 825-0740 or cienfuegos@igc.org. Paul also runs a social change bookstore with over two hundred titles on democracy and corporations (100fires.com). Paul wishes to sincerely thank Dean Ritz, Molly Moran, and Patrick Reinsborough for the substantial research assistance they provided for this article. Copyright Paul Cienfuegos 2000. This essay has been heavily edited for length. The full document—almost twice the length—is viewable on the Democracy Unlimited website www.monitor.net/democracyunlimited.

Follow the (Corporate) Money . . . and Shut It Down!

Randy Kehler

After the shutdown in Seattle, the World Trade Organization isn't likely to meet in the United States again any time soon. But the domestic institution that is responsible for trading away our democratic rights and sovereignty to unaccountable, antidemocratic, corporate-controlled global institutions continues to meet here almost daily. That's the U.S. Congress—in collaboration with the executive branch of the federal government, headquartered in Washington, D.C.

Why does our government put the interests of giant corporations over the rights of workers and communities, of children and the poor, of ordinary people who want a safe food supply, clean air, clean water, and a protected, sustainable environment?

To discover a—if not *the*—major reason for this, we have only to look at who's bankrolling the people we elect to office and their political parties: giant corporations, their political action committees (PACs), and their wealthy executives. In politics as in other areas of life, "the one who pays the piper calls the tune." Consider the following:

Major corporations donate **millions** in political contributions.

Corporate contributors receive **billions** in tax breaks, regulatory exemptions, and other government subsidies.

• Members of the Business Roundtable, a coalition of two hundred major corporations pushing for "permanent normal trade relations" (PNTR) with China, gave federal politicians and their political parties a whopping $58 million in political "contributions" in the first five months of 2000 alone. In May of 2000, not surprisingly, Congress finally granted PNTR to China—even though a Harris poll showed that seventy-nine percent of the American people said such status should not be given until China met human rights and labor rights standards.

• The health care industry—which includes pharmaceutical, health products, hospital, and nursing home corporations, as well as doctors and other health professionals—gave federal politicians and the two major political parties $49 million between January 1, 1999, and August 3, 2000. Is it any surprise that Congress can't seem to pass legislation opposed by this powerful industry—lower-priced U.S.-made drugs (including AIDS drugs), a prescription drug benefit for senior citizens on Medicare, and a patients' bill of rights?

What can we do about this obscene distortion of democracy? Two things.

First, we can follow the money—that is, find out and expose how much political money various corporate interests are contributing, who they're contributing it to, what they're getting in return, and what this is costing people and the environment.

And second, we can shut it down—that is, join with other groups whose goals are thwarted by corporate domination of our government and who are working to get corporate money out of the political finance system.

> *The purchase of democracy is a theft of freedom—a freedom that is essential to the protection of other basic human rights.*
> —Juliette Beck, organizer, Global Exchange

Following the money

1. Identify the industry (e.g., oil and gas) and/or corporations (e.g., Enron Corp) that are profiting from the problem your organization is trying to address (e.g., destruction of wildlife habitats and old growth forests).

2. Go to the Center for Responsive Politics website, www.opensecrets.org, and type in the name of that industry and those corporations to see how much they have given (Enron gave $1.8 million in 1999–2000), who the top recipients are (presidential candidate George W. Bush received $1.6 million from oil and gas companies in 1999–2000), and what the industry or corporation's political agenda is (e.g., the oil and gas industry wants to open more areas to drilling and pipelines).

3. Type in the names of particular politicians to see how much they have received (e.g., your own U.S. Representative and Senators), or the names of particular persons to see how much he or she has contributed to whom (e.g., CEOs or lobbyists who have been public spokespersons for the industry's point of view).

4. Find out what committees members of Congress sit

> *We cannot save the rainforest and support the rights of those remote peoples to maintain their forests, which serve as their supermarket and pharmacy, without PUBLIC GOVERNANCE as a helpful partner.*
> —Randy Hayes, president, Rainforest Action Network

> *Full public financing of elections is a structural adjustment, not a band-aid. It's a change that makes other changes possible.*
>
> —Jim Ace, trainer, Ruckus Society

on, since corporate donors target most of their contributions to those committees with jurisdiction over their industry (e.g., oil and gas corporations target the House and Senate energy and natural resources committees). This information is available on the Internet at www.house.gov or www.senate.gov.

5. If your own organization isn't already keeping track of this, contact a relevant citizen watchdog group in Washington, D.C., or elsewhere to find out about particular votes/actions (or blocked votes/actions) in Congress that affect the issue(s) you're working on.

6. Write up your findings in the form of a short report on how corporate political contributions make democracy impossible, prevent progress on the issues your organization is concerned with, and undermine the welfare of people and/or the environment.

7. Include in your report additional information showing how the current political finance system discriminates against nonwealthy people generally and people of color specifically (check out the website for the Fannie Lou Hamer Project, www.flhp.org)

8. Hold a press conference at the site of the corporation or donor to publicly release your report. Distribute a one-page summary that includes what people can do about it (e.g., join an upcoming action, write a letter of protest to the local newspaper, work for Clean Money/Clean Elections—see below).

9. Carry out a creative action that will dramatize the problem. For example, hang a huge banner, or price tag, in a highly visible place (like the side of a downtown building, from a water tower, between tall trees or lampposts), spelling out the political contributions "price" that, say, General Electric is paying to members of Congress in order to lower standards for PCB clean-up, and what this will cost human and other beings in the contaminated areas. Or organize a picket line *cum* guerilla theater (e.g., a senator auctioning off toxic dumping permits or child labor exemptions to the highest corporate-fat-cat bidders) outside corporate offices and/or stores (leafleting employees, shoppers, and passersby).

Shutting it down

Corporate financing of politicians, political parties, and their electoral campaigns blatantly violates widely held democratic values like "one person, one vote" and "government of, by, and for the *people*." Thus, corporate financing may be the most vulnerable part of the corporate juggernaut. For that reason, it should be a high priority for activist organizing. History has shown that piecemeal reforms of the political/electoral finance system don't work; despite the current restrictions on who can give how much to whom, the problem is as bad as ever, and getting worse.

> Sweeping campaign finance reform is "the one reform that can prevent the pollution and degradation of both our civic and natural environments."
> —Doris Haddock ("Granny D")

The only solution is to effectively abolish corporate (and other private-money) political contributions altogether by creating a comprehensive system based on full *public* financing for electoral campaigns, covering primary as well general elections. Such a system—called "Clean Money/Clean Elections"—has been passed by voters in Maine and Arizona for state elections and is already having amazing results. And there is a growing network of activists all over the country working to bring about this change for federal elections.

I see in the near future a crisis approaching that unnerves me and causes me to tremble for the safety of my country. . . . corporations have been enthroned and an era of corruption in high places will follow, and the money power of the country will endeavor to prolong its reign by working upon the prejudices of the people until all wealth is aggregated in a few hands and the Republic is destroyed.
—U.S. President Abraham Lincoln to Col. William F. Elkins, November 21, 1864, The Lincoln Encyclopedia, ed. Archer H. Shaw (New York: Macmillan, 1950)

With clean money/clean elections . . .

- Anyone capable of demonstrating a threshold level of public support can run for public office, regardless of their access to big money.
- Elections are no longer decided by who has the most money.
- Once in office, elected officials are no longer dependent on corporate and other big-money donors seeking legislative favors in return for their political contributions.

Check out Public Campaign's website www.publicampaign.org for information on who's working for Clean Money/Clean Elections and what people and organizations can do to help promote it.

Make no mistake about it—the abolition of corporate (and other private) financing of elections and related activities would constitute *a major, historic victory* for democracy and popular sovereignty. And, by altering the makeup and allegiances of Congress and the White House, it would make real reform possible in a host of other areas—from the rights of workers and local communities to the protection of public health and the environment, from sensible drug policies to nuclear and conventional disarmament, from fair taxation to safe food production.

For further information, contact the Alliance for Democracy: 681 Main Street, Waltham, MA, 02451 (781) 894-1179, peoplesall@aol.com, www.thealliancefordemocracy.org.

Democratizing Media

Linda Setchell

Almost all media that reach a large audience in the United States are owned by for-profit corporations—institutions that by law are obligated to put the profits of their investors ahead of all other considerations.

—Fairness and Accuracy In Reporting

Today, most U.S. media are owned by a handful of multinational corporations, and most them are tied to nonmedia industries. Their coverage is increasingly biased or censored when it comes to social and economic justice and the ecological well-being of the planet. It is in this context that the Independent Media Center (IMC) movement burst into the field of media to cover the 1999 Seattle World Trade Organization protest.

A month before Seattle made free trade a household topic of conversation, alternative media organizations, independent journalists, and activists conceived the idea of a space where independent journalists could edit and disseminate their coverage of the protests. They combined the existing media of print, photo, video, and audio with the democratic features of the internet to create www.indymedia.org, an interactive website that allows users to not only read, watch, or listen to stories, but to post their own works of media as well. During the Seattle WTO protests, the IMC website received over one million hits, more than CNN during the same five days.

Why was IMC so popular? It was the only source of accurate, up-to-the-minute coverage of events in Seattle. The major news networks, daily newspapers, and even national syndicated radio broadcasts failed to report the convergence of fifty thousand peaceful protestors or the use of military force to stop their actions. Instead of pictures of tear gas and armored tanks, the mainstream outlets focused their attention on a handful of broken windows and spray-painted storefronts.

After Seattle, the IMC concept spread rapidly. A second one was set up for Biodevastation 2000 in

Boston and a third followed shortly for the IMF–World Bank protest in Washington, D.C. Today over forty IMCs are located around the world. Most actually house media production offering media production workshops and mentoring programs. In Seattle, IMC volunteers train youth in a variety of media, while Boston IMC volunteers have created a series of workshops where community members learn how to produce pieces for community radio stations.

Many IMCs have evolved from covering protest actions to linking global and local issues. For example, the privatization of the prison industry in the United States has been linked to international free trade agreements, something that has yet to surface in mainstream media stories.

Many IMCs are also branching out beyond the Internet to disseminate their coverage in print publications, on radio shows, and via public access television. "IMC is not here to replace existing independent or alternative media outlets. Instead we are working to build connections between the existing independent media out-lets and to fill in the gaps," notes Kellan Elliot-McCrea, an IMC tech volunteer and longtime online activist. A major goal is to provide a consistent flow of non-corporate media to people who don't normally have access to alternative sources of information. Monthly print publications are coming out of New York City IMC and Seattle, while weekly radio broadcasts are being produced nationally here in the United States by IMC journalists from across the United States. Congo IMC works closely with Belgium IMC to disseminate information about Congolese issues that the mainstream press fails to cover in Belgium.

These accomplishments in a little over a year's time speak to the power of the burgeoning global justice movement worldwide. With its own system of information dissemination, the movement is beginning to reclaim power.

Linda Setchell helped found the Boston Indymedia Center in 2000. She is a grassroots environmental organizer for Clean Water Action.

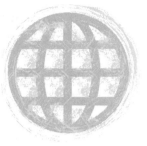

Mobilizing Consumers

The American consumer is a major player in the global economy. About a quarter of the world's purchasing power lives here, and access to it can make or break a developing economy. Especially critical is the garment industry, which developing nations can enter without much machinery, capital, or skilled labor.

"You are what you wear" is the garment industry's motto. In the 1990s, millions of U.S. consumers started deciding not to wear exploitation. The antisweatshop movement showed them the face behind the label and walked them up the supply chain to the person who sewed their clothes. Along the way consumers discovered the corporate framework that ties Third World workers to transnational capital, and where they fit in that framework.

As it grew, the antisweatshop movement took global justice into the mainstream. Corporations felt the heat and began to offer cosmetic reforms. Students refused to accept them and held out for truly independent human rights monitoring in garment factories abroad.

Any movement that has learned and accomplished this much has a lot of lessons for us. They are about broadening our movement; actually talking with people you don't know; and using reform campaigns as vehicles to transform the whole system.

Still, the antisweat movement faces challenges of its own, and they go to the core of its organizing assumptions:

- The limits of a human rights approach. The U.S. antisweat movement basically applies human rights principles to the global economy. In Central America, this approach has failed to win permanent improvements in workers' conditions (p. 199).

• The challenge of corporate regulation. The student antisweat movement created the Worker Rights Consortium to regulate corporate behavior overseas (p. 195). Yet students recognize that the Consortium may not even be able to monitor the two percent of apparel manufacturing destined for college campuses. What is the answer—union organizing? Government regulation? Rule changes in global institutions like the WTO? Can corporate behavior can be fundamentally reformed?

Or should we create new, noncorporate institutions like fair trade cooperatives? The antisweat movement is finally a solidarity movement that supports union organizing drives. In contrast, fair trade (p. 221) links producers and consumers as economic actors. The linking institutions—coffee growers' cooperatives, worker-owned distribution cooperatives, and fair trade networks—are the potential building blocks of a values-driven economy. They bypass corporations and model a just economy where ethical principles become economic ones.

—Mike Prokosch

Sustaining the Student Antisweatshop Movement:

Linking Workers' Struggles

Marion Traub-Werner

The challenge of this generation is figuring out how to transform the global economy. We aren't going to win this without institutional transformation. We have to be reaching out to middle America and telling a story that can be heard by rank and file unionists and church parish people. We have to build solid relationships with their institutions. And we have to work with the mainstream media which is the way we communicate. We have to be very good at that.

—Barbara Briggs, National Labor Committee

On more than two hundred campuses in the last three years, students have been protesting the conditions under which young people in other countries labor to produce our campus clothing. Students are smashing the corporate mirrors and exposing the reality of girls and women aged fourteen to twenty-four, making our clothes at poverty wages for fourteen hours a day.

Focusing on university-licensed products, students are demanding that universities adopt codes of conduct, publicly release the factory locations where university clothing is made, and require companies to pay workers making university clothing a living wage. They are also demanding that universities join a new initiative called the Worker Rights Consortium to improve working conditions in university contract shops. Students at the University of North Carolina won these demands. How might the antisweatshop movement evolve once its demands have been met?

"Question the contract"

The student antisweatshop movement in Chapel Hill began in the fall of 1997 when the university signed an exclusive eleven-million-dollar promotion contract with Nike. We began our campaign with the less-than-radical slogan "Question the Contract." We plastered the campus with flyers comparing workers' wages and celebrity payoffs for a Nike endorsement. The two central themes of the campaign—corporatization of the university and worker rights—attracted two different crowds. Faculty seemed more moved by the former and students by the latter. Since the students were most involved, we decided to focus the message of our campaign on sweatshops.

Nike's public relations machine responded to our challenge by sending a delegation of apologetic representatives, offering research grants to study the problem (under the name "The Rising Tide Program"), and distributing glossy packets on their social development efforts in Asia and Central America. Three professors organized a seminar on Nike, the university, and labor issues at which Phil Knight, Nike's CEO, made a surprise guest appearance. Knight explained how the needletrade (toys and clothes) was the first stage of development. He assured us that "once the roads were in" it was natural for companies like Nike to move on and make room for more capital-intensive industries. Newly industrializing nations continued along the road to capitalist bliss thanks to Nike's initial jump start.

With guest appearances by Phil Knight and former basketball coach Dean Smith, the Nike campaign on campus succeeded in grabbing national media attention, but we students were still at a loss for a demand. What did we want Nike and the university to do?

We started meeting with our fellow activists at Duke University. Until then, we had never ventured twenty minutes down the highway to confer with our comrades. Duke students and others introduced us to the Sweat-Free Campus campaign, an effort to push universities to adopt strong codes of conduct that set minimal

---

We don't have the institutional strength to take on the question of sweatshops across the board. So we've been doing symbolic cases where the story can be told, involving a significant U.S. company and workers who could use the help and stand up to the pressure, which is one factory in a hundred.

—Barbara Briggs, National Labor Committee

labor standards for the workers producing university-licensed products. By the end of the spring term in 1998, the university had set up a committee to recommend a course of action to the chancellor.

I served on the committee along with two other students. We descended into the crypt of university administration on a biweekly and weekly basis for a full year, bedeviled by the excruciatingly slow progress of nothing substantial. The university adopted a code of conduct but would not endorse a living wage. Universities around the country were signing on to a government-sponsored corporate initiative called the Fair Labor Association and the committee at UNC seemed poised to recommend the same action. Most importantly, the university had yet to require full public disclosure of factories making its licensed products.

By April 1999, after four successful sit-ins at other universities to win full public disclosure and a living wage, UNC students decided we could do the same. Fifteen students entered the university administration building a week and a half before the end of the semester. We knew we needed to win our demands before the

Two young Central American sweatshop workers find the labels they sewed . . . in a U.S. garment store. © *National Labor Committee*

summer started. The sit-in lasted four days and we received an outpouring of support from the greater community and from our fellow students. We demanded direct negotiations with the chancellor. By the third night, there were eighty of us occupying the building and we were really starting to stink the place up! Fearing that the sit-in might end in scandal, the chancellor finally agreed to our demands on the fourth day.

We lost ground during the summer when the university joined the Fair Labor Association. However, UNC later also joined the effort sponsored by labor rights activists, the Worker Rights Consortium. Students continue to be active on the sweatshop issue today on campus. They have also expanded their focus and joined with local labor struggles on and off campus, as well as antisweat community initiatives.

The campus antisweatshop movement and the national debate

Though university apparel represents less than two percent of apparel sales in the United States, the very visible debate raging on campuses over university apparel added fuel to the fire of the larger antisweatshop movement. The U.S. government, recognizing sweatshops as a blemish on its free trade agenda, had been working to put the public's mind at ease. While we were debating strong codes of conduct on campus, the U.S. government's Apparel Industry Partnership (AIP) had already released a code of conduct with standards so low that unions and prominent nongovernmental organizations left the AIP. The weakened AIP continued forward, setting up the Fair Labor Association to monitor factory conditions independently and eventually create a "No Sweat" label.

Publicly, students and universities continued debating ground-breaking issues like living wages and women's rights in codes of conduct through the spring semester of 1999. Privately, however, a select group of universities was being courted by the Fair Labor Association in a search for the legitimacy lost by the labor and human rights groups' pullout. The terms of the student antisweatshop debate shifted suddenly in March of 1999 when universities began to sign on to the Fair Labor Association. Under the FLA, companies can control which factories are monitored, who does the monitoring, when it is done, the

Rally for UNITE's municipal anti-sweat purchasing bill. © UNITE

methodology used, and the information gathered. The only information to be made public is to be highly sanitized.

Our loose network of campus groups, United Students Against Sweatshops (USAS), started an aggressive attack against the FLA and sped up work on its own code enforcement plan. The outcome was the Workers Rights Consortium (WRC). The WRC rests on the principle that workers and their advocates should be central to any effort to improve labor conditions. WRC monitoring will be run by local groups and respond mainly to worker complaints. The WRC will publicize information about factories and conditions to workers and their advocates. With the creation of this viable alternative, USAS groups around the country continue to organize for their universities to join the WRC. (For more information on the Worker Rights Consortium, check out www.workersrights.org.)

The limits of codes

With all this work on codes and monitoring, students are coming to understand their limits. Independent monitoring has had very mixed results even in single factories. In no way can it enforce labor standards in the hundreds of factories in any given region. As many have said, workers are the best monitors. But companies of course prefer voluntary codes of conduct and monitors to a union with a legally binding collective agreement or a functioning governmental labor department. In Asia, some companies have agreed to monitoring and then claimed they were not obliged to negotiate with the union.

Codes and monitoring have helped the student antisweatshop movement grow. Because of the campaign, students around the country have been thinking long and hard about what is a just workplace—a topic left out of the formal curriculum. Many students, including myself, have also gone through an important disillusionment process with codes. After laboring to getting them passed, we found that codes were not effective in improving working conditions. Most workers do not even know there is a code of conduct in their factory. When I asked Nike workers in the Dominican Republic what the code was, they guessed that it must be the little card hung on their sewing machines detailing machine maintenance and company rules.

As students, we have come to understand that codes and monitoring are merely two of many tools we need in this long and historic struggle for worker rights.

International solidarity

Cross-border solidarity requires a partnership of trust and respect between workers and their international allies. The antisweatshop movement has reached the mainstream U.S. public with the issues of child labor and ghastly labor practices like forced contraception. The most successful campaigns have usually highlighted the most brutal conditions. This focus, while receiving much media attention, has painted all workers as helpless victims. This image and language not only puts consumers in the position of savior rather than ally, but also reinforces exactly the young and docile image that global corporate garment corporations promote.

Living in Central America, I have seen a more complete reality. When I first arrived, I asked a cleaning woman I knew if she had ever worked in an apparel-for-export factory, commonly called a maquila. "I tried it once," she replied, "But I was too much of a crybaby. You have to be really tough to work there and I just couldn't take it." After interviewing women maquila organizers in Honduras and Guatemala, I understood what she meant. Some women and girls may indeed see themselves as victims with no options. But there are also many who see themselves as breadwinners and agents of their own destiny. They chose to work in the maquila. Some hope to improve their conditions through organizing. Many plan to work long enough to get the money for a *coyote* and head to the United States. These workers need to be at the table with us as we discuss the conditions under which they work and live and what we can do about them. As our grassroots campaigns continue, we need to focus on the diversity of maquila women's and girls' experiences and replace images of helpless victims with solid partnerships.

coyote (coy-yoh'-tay): a guide paid to smuggle immigrants across the Mexico–U.S. border.

Where does the movement go?

The student antisweatshop movement is now at a critical junction. How do we keep our movement going after the adoption of a code? How do we convert a code of conduct into real change in the apparel industry? How do we work in solidarity with workers in a way that is truly cooperative and not paternalistic? Most importantly, how do we build our leverage against corporations and on campuses long enough to help workers win real victories? Below, I suggest some guiding principles:

Stay focused on what we do best. The student antisweatshop movement is successful because students focus on educating and mobilizing other students on the issue. That is what we are good at. That is why companies are afraid of us. One lesson from the movement so far is that students should not let our message be bureaucratized. Our voice and our ability to influence other students is the one that can keep the issue focused on people, not paper.

Foster a national student-organizer community. Through regional and national organizing, students are developing networks with other campuses. Students have felt so empowered by those networks that some have gone to campuses with very little activism and jumpstarted campaigns by imparting their own experience and organizing tools to interested students. The student movement must keep developing the growing community of student and youth organizers not only through e-mail but also through gatherings specifically aimed at building youth power and leadership skills.

> The Marianas territory, exposed in the media as a sweatshop haven, "is a perfect petri dish of capitalism. It's like my Galapagos island."
>
> —Rep. Tom DeLay (R-TX), "A 'Petri Dish' in the Pacific," Juliet Eilperin, *Washington Post*, 26 July 2000, p. A10.

Develop international solidarity tools and push for them among U.S. labor unions. Students are ready to take our international solidarity to the next level. We want to support campaigns not conceived in a vacuum but rather initiated by workers and their allies. Students can't do this on our own. Students should be advocates of a more internationalist approach within the U.S. labor movement by aggressively supporting unions that take such an approach. We need to communicate our internationalist vision with other unions we partner with locally and nationally.

Expand and diversify our coalitions. Many students working on antisweatshop work understand the need to work in solidarity not just with working people abroad, but with folks at home. The United States Students Association and Jobs with Justice started a Student Labor Action Project in 1999 to help students connect to their local labor movement. This exciting initiative has already gone a long way in linking student antisweatshop activists to local unions and getting local unions to support antisweatshop campus work. As we embark on new campaigns or put our energies into existing one, students should prioritize campaigns that keep us connected to the larger community and active in building diverse coalitions in terms of race, gender, sexuality, and class.

Our power is in grassroots organizing on university campuses. We will be able to sustain ourselves if we focus on educating students and not being diverted in legalistic debates; if we encourage our peers to think beyond the image of helpless Third World women and push the labor movement to internationalize their interests; and if we work with local labor struggles. Together, we can build a solid national youth and student movement that turns the corporate agenda around.

Marion Traub-Werner currently works in Central America for STITCH and United Students Against Sweatshops, linking students, community activists, and labor organizers to organizing efforts in sweatshops in that region.

Central America Labor Solidarity: Lessons for Activists?

Stephen Coats

Globalization has burst into the national media and public conscious-ness since Seattle, but progressives know that globalization of national economies dates back a couple of centuries. Similarly, cross-border efforts to confront globalization date back a century or two. Most notably, in the nineteenth century European trade unionists founded the first international trade secretariats that still work to unite unions of similar industries in different countries.

Most of these early cross-border initiatives were confined to unions operating in the North. It has only been recently that cross-border efforts have been linked to the South involving actors outside the formal trade union structure. Many U.S. human rights, religious, and solidarity groups started cross-border labor solidarity work with South African workers in the struggle against apartheid.

> For a history of the West Coast, more Asia-focused anti-sweatshop movement, see Randy Shaw, *Reclaiming America: Nike, Clean Air, and the New National Activism* (Berkeley, CA: University of California Press, 1999).

In the 1990s, however, much of their focus shifted to Central America. Groups formed to fight U.S. Cold War policy, like the National Labor Committee for Democracy and Human Rights in El Salvador (NLC), ended up fighting for worker justice in the "new" neoliberal global economy. The U.S./Guatemala Labor Education Project (now the U.S./Labor in the Americas Project) began focusing exclusively on labor struggles in 1987 while other Central America solidarity groups gave labor an increasing role in their agendas. Now the student sweatshop movement, the Campaign for Labor Rights, Global Exchange, and others are providing new energy and leadership in the globalization struggle. A similar role is being played by the Maquila Solidarity Network in Canada, whose staff has been working on cross-border labor solidarity initiatives for a decade.

The most creative Central America labor support work is local, with such groups as the New York-based Coalition Against Sweatshops, the Cleveland-based Inter-Religious Task Force on Central America, the Minnesota Fair Trade Campaign, and many others adopting international labor solidarity campaigns and then developing their own organizing tactics to bring pressure to bear on the campaign target.

In short, we've got over ten years of experience of cross-border labor solidarity work between U.S. activists and Central America, where such work has taken place at a more extensive level than with any other region in the South.

Much good can be said about the labor solidarity work that has taken place with Central America over the past ten years. Specific campaigns have yielded path-breaking victories. The NLC campaign against The GAP in El Salvador led to the first independent monitoring of an apparel factory with respect to the application of a code of conduct. U.S./LEAP's campaign in support of Phillips-Van Heusen workers in Guatemala helped win the only collective bargaining agreement in Guatemala's maquiladora sector, and two years later U.S. sol-

The U.S. labor movement's engagement in Latin America has undergone a sea change with the election of John Sweeney as President of the AFL-CIO. The infamous American Institute for Free Labor Development (AIFLD) and its old guard has been replaced by the new American Center for International Labor Solidarity whose Latin American section is run by trade unionists who worked hard for AIFLD's demise. The Solidarity Center is now building genuine partnerships with workers in Central America who are organizing, without regard to ideological or U.S. foreign policy concerns. And the international trade secretariats have become increasingly engaged in Central America, financing organizing support work in the maquiladora sector, helping develop a strategic plan in the banana sector, and much more.

idarity helped workers at the Kimi factory in Honduras win another collective bargaining agreement.

More broadly, Central America labor activism helped develop the antisweatshop movement in the United States, especially on college campuses. It also helped transform the AFL-CIO's international work in the region. And Central American labor activism helped "persuade" U.S. corporations to accept the principle (if not the practice) that they are responsible for the treatment of workers not only at their own operations abroad but also at those of their suppliers. The most prominent illustrations of this new extension of what constitutes social responsibility for corporations have been the proliferation of codes of conduct and even a U.S. government-initiated "Apparel Industry Partnership," a direct if controversial response to the National Labor Committee's antisweatshop campaigns in Central America.

Finally, labor activism on Central America has been one of the streams feeding into the growing globalization movement that burst on the international media scene in Seattle.

However, these are advances in the North, not on the ground in Central America. While the level of violence against trade unionists in Central America has definitely declined, this is more a reflection of the general decline in human rights violations than anything else. Even in the maquila sector, which has received by far the lion's share of attention and support in the United States, there has been little progress outside of declines in child labor violations and physical abuse. Most of the complaints made by workers ten years ago remain valid today: long hours, forced overtime, poverty-level wages, recurring violations of labor law, and, in particular, the denial of the right to organize, a key focus of North-based work.

A number of maquila unions have been formed in Honduras and some remain in Nicaragua, without international support. Critics say that these unions are only nominally unions, with contracts that do nothing but recapitulate the national labor code requirements and that others are merely company unions intended to forestall independent unions.

Indeed, one can point to few advances in the right to organize in Central America's maquiladoras, at least where it has been supported by cross-border solidarity campaigns. Even our few victories have been short-lived. Phillips-Van Heusen closed its unionized facility in Guatemala in December 1998. Kimi closed in Honduras in May 2000 and shifted production to non-union plants in Guatemala. And while The Gap's subcontractor in El Salvador has improved factory conditions, the union has little power and no contract. In fact, no unions have won a contract in El Salvador despite numerous international campaigns. And now we see major reversals even in Nicaragua, where workers had made the most progress in unionizing their maquila sector.

Most U.S. and Northern groups who engage in cross border labor solidarity work put worker organizing at the top of their list of objectives. We all agree that advances in worker empowerment and self-determination should be the real measure of success although other goals are certainly legitimate and may be necessary preconditions (e.g., building a sweatshop movement in the North). But if worker organizing is indeed our ultimate measure, international solidarity work directed at the Central America maquiladora sector, where most of the attention in the North has been directed, has not yet realized its primary objective.

A few caveats before the lessons, however.

Obviously, apparel is not the only industry in Central America, although outside of the banana industry there is limited cross-border solidarity work in other sectors. Cross-border solidarity with banana workers is a completely different animal because the Central America banana industry is highly unionized. In fact, banana unions are the oldest and historically strongest private sector unions in Central America. Until recently, they have been so self-sufficient that they have rarely called for international solidarity, but this is changing as low-wage imports from nonunion Ecuador threaten the very existence of the Central American unions.

Public sector unions in Central America, which have received little attention in the North, have probably suffered the most in the past few years with privatization throwing tens of thousands of workers out of jobs and destroying some unions completely. While there have been regular calls for international solidarity, cross-border leverage from the United States is pretty much limited to fax and letter campaigns to national governments given the absence of goods exported to U.S. markets. While there have been a few modest successes in El Salvador, international solidarity work has generally failed to stem the tide of privatization in Central America.

Finally, it should be remembered that most of the worker organizing that goes on in the South goes on without international solidarity. Indeed, not all unions seek or want international support, even when it is available.

Lessons?

With these caveats, it's clearly risky if not dangerous to extrapolate global lessons from the experiences in one region of the world and one sector. Hence, these are put forth with a question mark. If our objectives are worker empowerment, i.e., organizing, our lessons seem to include:

1. Cross-border work must be grounded in partnership with organized labor on the ground in the South.

All the campaigns, tours, and media work in the world will do nothing to advance worker organizing in the South unless workers take advantage of the political space created in the consumer countries in the North. So far, the popular Nike campaign has not resulted in any advances for worker organizing in Central America, although Nike's college apparel comes from nearly a half-dozen factories in the region.

For workers to take advantage of the campaigns in the North, there must be a level of coordination, communication, and strategic planning that is all too often absent in our cross-border work. Admittedly, it's a lot easier to do in sectors that are organized, like bananas. In the Central American apparel sector, the absence of a solid, structured base, except in Nicaragua, makes it difficult to collaborate at a high enough level to be successful.

2. Such partnerships may be critical but they are also extremely difficult to develop and maintain. Obstacles, in no particular order, include:

- Language. An obvious but often overlooked issue is the basic ability to talk to each other across borders *fluently.*

- Culture. It took U.S./LEAP a while to figure out that Central American trade unionists would hardly ever tell us no to an idea we proposed. We mistakenly figured that if the head of a trade union central didn't like a proposed idea, he or she would say so. Now, we know that "yes" sometimes means "no."

- Trust. The long history of U.S. intervention in Central America continues. And while we think of ourselves as the good guys, we can be vulnerable to charges of protectionist impulses or "do-gooder imperialism." We're off-putting when we show up in a country and say we're here to save you. Trust takes a long time to build and constant work to maintain.

- Communication. Perfect Spanish, sensitivity to cultural differences, and the establishment of trust can't overcome the weak communication infrastructure in Central America. Bad phone lines, inconsistent servers, and the cost of travel throw up obstacles to maintaining the level of communication that is needed to carry out cross border work.

- Differing priorities for North and South. The priorities for a North-based consumer campaign ("Hey, I really need to get a good photo of a worker rally") may not be the priority of the trade union and worker rights supporters on the ground ("Sixteen more workers just got fired and need immediate legal assistance. Your photo will have to wait."). The differences may be legitimate, but can frustrate campaigns in the North that need a certain rhythm to be sustained.

- Lack of success to date. Central Americans may become more interested in developing effective cross-border solidarity partnerships once such partnerships have been shown to be successful. This is a chicken-egg issue, but so far, too much of our work in the North can be associated with closed factories and fired workers.

> Some have also questioned the wisdom of factory organizing, proposing an industrial union approach that has not yet been tested and, short of mass uprisings, requires more resources than currently committed to organizing.

- Local resource and capacity limitations. Central American unions, like most organizations in Central America, are poor and understaffed. For example, the coordinator and subcoordinator of the Coordination of Latin American Banana Worker Unions also head their respective national affiliates and have to field a dozen emergencies a day. Without technical or program staff to back them up, they have precious little time to devote to international solidarity efforts. The situation is even worse in the maquila sector. Until U.S. trade unions (the AFL-CIO and UNITE) and the International Textile Federation stepped in in the late 1990s, there were no paid organizers in the maquila sector in Central America.

- There is a lack of basic understanding of what types of leverage and support can be provided by activists in the North. Only the top leadership of the more active unions understand what corporate campaigns can do or cannot do; most workers and many leaders have little exposure to or experience with such key international tools as codes of conduct and worker rights conditions in U.S. trade programs.

3. **We're often divided internally. This is true both in the South, where trade unions are divided by ideology and personality, and in the North, where differences in tactics, strategies, personalities, and other agendas have kept us from optimizing our effectiveness. This lesson is hardly unique to cross-border work, but given the odds we're facing, it's particularly problematic.**

4. **Any victory is always in jeopardy. The closing of the Kimi factory in Honduras and the PVH plant in Guatemala, whose workers won collective bargaining agreements after years of struggle, good organizing, and extensive international support, raises the issue of the**

need to protect our victories. Even after a victory is won, the unions must continue to build their internal strength while technical support and international solidarity must be maintained.

5. The apparel industry, with its highly mobile capital (i.e., sewing machines), is notoriously difficult to organize anywhere in the world. United States unions have been unable to stop factory closings and the loss of hundreds of thousands of jobs in the apparel industry. Across the South, the vast majority of apparel factories are not organized. And even where they are, advances are often minimal. Few factories can afford to significantly increase wages in a highly competitive industry characterized by thousands of suppliers forced to offer the lower bids to giant North-based retailers. U.S./LEAP estimates that it cost Phillips-Van Heusen about an extra million dollars a year to operate its unionized factory in Guatemala where workers were paid decent wages for a regular 44-hour week, where overtime was paid and other benefits provided in accordance with the law.

6. In Central America, we must also take into account the impact of a long, violent, and generally successful history of repressing worker rights.

7. Finally, the other side is a lot stronger than we are. We're up against the most powerful forces in the world: transnational capital and our governments whose dominant interest is pushing free trade unencumbered by trade unions and worker rights.

Local lessons

Many of these (potential) lessons are for those who work nationally and internationally to develop cross-border relationships and campaigns. For local U.S. activists doing cross-border labor work, some of the lessons can be expressed in a set of questions that one might wish to review before taking up a cross-border labor campaign.

- What are the goals?

- Will worker organizing in the South be advanced in practice, not just in theory?

- Is the campaign reactive, without much prospect of changing the balance of power? For example, seeking to reinstate a handful of fired workers at a 2,000-worker factory is a valid and perhaps necessary goal but achieving it is unlikely to change power relations at the factory. Or is it proactive, with sufficient strength on the ground in the South that there is at least a chance of successful worker organizing?

- And is there a commitment to stick with the workers after they win, should victory be achieved?

This sobering litany of lessons, based on the general lack of success in advancing the ultimate objective of worker empowerment in Central America, should not keep us from being vastly encouraged by the rapid growth of the antisweatshop movement in the North, which has risen from nothing to the front pages of *The New York Times* in ten short years. The political space for organizing on the ground is increasing; now that space must be claimed and occupied.

Many of the steps toward claiming this space are outside our scope. Most of us in the North cannot increase the local capacity of unions in Central America or upgrade the communication infrastructure. However, we can and must:

- continue to build the broader globalization movement in the North (and across borders);

- build specific alliances not only within consuming nations in the North but also with student, human rights, labor, religious, and solidarity groups in the Asian countries that operate many of the maquilas in Central America (i.e., South Korea and Taiwan);

- link code of conduct campaigns and the implementation of codes to specific worker struggles and place support for worker organizing at the center of our demands;

- punish companies that cut and run when they close factories in response to union organizing, as well as reward those who do the right thing;

I would define globalization as the freedom for my group of companies to invest where it wants when it wants, to produce what it wants, to buy and sell where it wants, and support the fewest restrictions possible coming from labour laws and social conventions.

—Percy Barnevik, President of the ABB Industrial Group, quoted by Gerard Greenfield of the Canadian Auto Workers, "The Success of Being Dangerous."

- use Congressional action on trade legislation as opportunities to push for bilateral and international guarantees to respect the basic rights of workers, especially the right to organize;

- support the international trade secretariats that are uniquely positioned to provide technical support and leadership at a global level against specific industries; and

- minimize if not overcome divisions within our own ranks in order to optimize our effectiveness.

Perhaps our most important lesson, however, is that cross-border labor solidarity work between North and South is in its infancy, at least outside the formal trade union structure. It's only a decade old with respect to Central America, almost nonexistent with respect to South America and most of Africa, and just beginning with Asia. Capital, on the other hand, has been at the globalization game a long time. We're learning and we're building partnerships in the South but significant progress on the ground is going to take time, patience, and perseverance, if our experience in the Central America apparel sector is any guide. At U.S./LEAP, we learn each day how long the struggle is—and are inspired each day by the importance of the task and the growing opportunities for worker solidarity in the global economy.

Stephen Coats is the director of the U.S./Labor in the Americas Project (U.S./LEAP).

The Bangor Clean Clothes Campaign

Dennis Chinoy and Björn Skorpen Claeson

All of us have the chance to say that, where we live, corporations must be accountable to our community and respect our community values; that our shared sense of fairness and decency moves us to insist with one voice that sweatshop apparel in our community is not acceptable.

—Bangor Clean Clothes Campaign "Road Show"

The Bangor Clean Clothes Campaign was born in 1996. Its parent, Peace in Central America (PICA), was a solidarity organization that started resisting U.S. military aid to Nicaragua, Guatemala, and El Salvador in the early 1980s. When the shooting wars subsided, PICA, like many such groups across the country, began to explore in more depth the underlying political and economic agenda that had spawned U.S. involvement in these wars. And we considered how we might address ourselves to the persistent structures enforcing economic repression throughout the hemisphere.

We studied the debt crisis and the structural adjustment policies administered by the International Monetary Fund and the World Bank, the continued war on the poor even as the military wars were ending. We began to see that the same phenomena—wealth highly concentrated, social spending slashed, national economies hostage to corporate management—were a feature of life not only in Latin America but at home as well. Here, though, structural adjustment was not being enforced by guns or by lending institutions, but by public deception and scapegoating. Reaganism and the "Contract with America" that followed were making the country safe for corporations by persuading us that it was government itself, single welfare women, blacks, and immigrants that were somehow robbing us all blind.

How could we work against the corporate takeovers of national and world economies, and the atomizing consumer culture that supported it? PICA concluded that one key antidote was community-building at multiple levels: first, on a personal level, to nurture people making decisions together rather than individualistically, shopping-style;

second, in terms of local government, to affirm that communities have the right to specify what kind of corporate behavior is not compatible with local values; and third, internationally, to begin to create cross-border alliances as fledgling counterbalances to the globalized reach of transnational corporations.

Thinking along these lines, Peace in Central America morphed into Peace through Inter-American Community Action, retaining its acronym and history but retooling its mission. Its first project was the Bangor Clean Clothes Campaign.

The Bangor Clean Clothes Campaign was to be a community-based antisweatshop campaign. It would create a public consensus that clothes sold in Bangor should be made in accordance with internationally recognized standards of ethical production. This consensus would culminate in a city council resolution making that consensus official, a national first for a city government. The campaign would include an ambitious public education campaign, followed by a petition of area citizens and endorsements by a wide spectrum of community organizations. Then we could ask the city council to ratify a community consensus that already existed, rather than asking them to stick their necks out.

Past that, we weren't sure.

There were several rationales for the campaign:

- Foremost, if least explicit, a community has the right to insist that businesses which operate in a community abide by that community's values. The implication: If a community could decide to regulate corporate sweatshop practices, what else might it then decide it had a right to insist on?

- By linking Maine's quarter-century-long garment-industry job losses to corporate migrations south, we could raise a high-visibility issue in which the area had a clear economic stake.

- By showing that the fates of both United States and Third World workers were at the mercy of the same corporations, we could counter the image of the Third World poor "stealing our jobs" and lay the basis for cross-border alliances.

• Through a public education effort to publicize the unsavory practices of child labor and abusive working conditions, we could reclaim the mantle of "community values" for progressive social action. After years of liberals being browbeaten by the right, it would be refreshing to reclaim the mainstream flag.

• After years of being against things, we could offer our community a vision of positive collective action with practical as well as moral impact. The attraction to the Bangor City Council of being the first in the nation to take action was not inconsiderable.

• Finally, we hoped to create a model of community action that could be replicated elsewhere if successful. This offered the hope that networks of allied communities could greatly amplify consumer impact within a state like Maine, and nationally.

Petitions, roadshows, and resolutions

The first phase of the campaign took a year. Four months of planning preceded a Labor Day kickoff. The campaign was cosponsored by Bangor-area NOW, the Maine AFL-CIO, and the greater Bangor NAACP. Our U.S. representative John Baldacci spoke supportively at the kickoff event. The *Bangor Daily News* editorialized in favor of the campaign early on and at critical points.

We developed a slide presentation roadshow using slides of Salvadoran maquilas, testimony of maquila workers juxtaposed with that of displaced Maine workers, and interesting ways to present Nike profit margins. We gave presentations at schools, congregations, civic organizations, unions, the university, and social action groups. With these presentations we gathered petition signatures and petitioners as well.

We had community petitioning days and petition tables at every area precinct during the 1996 presidential election. By June 1997, nine months after the kickoff, we had 7,500 signatures from the Bangor area. They were not all Bangor citizens; they were all Bangor shoppers.

At the same time, with the roadshow as well as with personal contacts and visits, we solicited a spectrum of organizations to endorse the petition's call publicly: that the Bangor City Council affirm that "clothes for sale in Bangor should be made in accordance with internationally recognized standards of ethical production." Initially we signed up progressive organizations, a handful of socially responsible businesses, and religious groups. As the education campaign proceeded and as the list grew, we successfully approached more mainstream groups.

Strategically, we needed to specify the core criteria, from among numerous worthy contenders, that would describe clean clothes. We settled on four carefully worded statements regarding working conditions that didn't jeopardize children, that were free from physical, sexual, and emotional abuse, that provided wages that could secure an existence worthy of human dignity, and that insured freedom to organize. We drew the wording from International Labor Organization (ILO) standards and the United Nations (UN) Declaration of Universal Human Rights. We chose to omit specific minimum ages and wages. With these and many other decisions during the campaign, we attempted to craft a position that was sufficiently mainstream to be widely endorsed, but sufficiently meaningful to have impact.

From the outset, we initiated and maintained communication with the *Bangor Daily News* editorial page editor and with each Bangor City Council member. As the day approached for formal consideration of the resolution, we compiled for councilors a packet of materials regarding sweatshop production, job loss in Maine, relevant chapter and verse from ILO and UN documents, strategic letters of support, supportive editorials, and a paid newspaper ad of hundreds of individuals and seventy organizations.

We met with a city council subcommittee to specify that the resolution was not meant to hurt Bangor businesses but rather to create an atmosphere in which both consumers and retailers could relay a message to large clothing suppliers that effectively conveyed all of our commonly held values. We described a consumer-retailer partnership that the resolution would help promote. We offered the resolution that we had written.

After considerable discussion, the subcommittee was satisfied, and recommended to the Bangor City Council that the resolution pass. In June of 1997, the Clean Clothes Resolution was passed by the Bangor City Council, unanimously and enthusiastically. After working for this for a year, we still could hardly believe it had happened.

The resolution, of course, was not legally binding; area stores can still sell clothes made in sweatshops. But it did provide the moral mandate for the campaign to request local clothing retailers' participation. The challenge was to determine just what retailers could do that would seem compelling to the community, credible to the city council, and constructive to mainstream retailers. In short, what could they do that was both feasible and nontrivial?

The retailer/consumer pledge

We suggested a Clean Clothes pledge of mutual accountability: retailers work toward a Clean Clothes inventory, support selected national antisweatshop campaigns, and relay their concerns about sweatshops to their suppliers, while the Clean Clothes Campaign researches labor practices of store suppliers, provides educational materials for store personnel and customers, and promotes the stores to the wider community through publications and mainstream media. We knew that stores' commitment and level of activity would be in direct proportion to the moral and economic incentive they received from a community of shoppers. Six months after the Clean Clothes Resolution, we launched the Clean Clothes consumer/retailer partnership in a downtown public ceremony. Eleven stores, all locally owned, and some fifty individuals joined the partnership. City councilors gave their blessings, and U.S. Representative John Baldacci showed up unexpectedly to witness the event.

Almost three years after the beginning of the Clean Clothes retailer/consumer partnership, we have over thirty merchant members and some 1,500 individual members in over forty states. While the continuing challenge is translating member sign-up into member action, we have had some success. We have published three editions of the Clean Clothes Shopping Guide, providing shoppers with a view of the labor and human rights conditions behind the labels. It has been gratifying to hear retailers tell of shoppers coming through their doors, reading the guide.

The last three years we have organized Clean Clothes Fun Fairs in downtown Bangor to regale the public at large and have fun along with the seriousness of it all. A speaker of national repute (Charles Kernaghan, Jim Hightower) and a sweatshop fashion show featuring local athletes, a Franciscan brother, Bangor firefighters, and other local celebrities have become key components of a growing community antisweatshop tradition.

We have seeded new Clean Clothes Campaigns in southern and western Maine with coalitions of students, community members, labor, and religious people. The campaign has generated hundreds of articles in the local press, becoming part of public discourse in eastern Maine, and has also received national attention with articles in numerous newspapers and journals.

A city purchasing resolution

In 1999, we worked for four months negotiating an antisweatshop purchasing resolution with the city of Bangor. It seemed clear that a Clean Clothes city should walk the walk, holding themselves to the same ethical purchasing standards as they had earlier advocated for area retailers. We proposed a detailed supplier code of conduct, modeled on university codes and stronger municipal codes (including Pittsburgh's), and a lengthy working condition questionnaire. However, the city administration was not keen on the idea of being a keeper of public morals, and did not believe that the city should research vendors and bidders to learn about their labor practices or notify bidders that it is looking for companies with fair labor practices. A Citizen Advisory Committee to aid the city in making ethical purchases was completely out of the question.

It was only after we involved city councilors in the negotiation process that the administration's stance softened. We reached an agreement on a Clean Clothes purchasing resolution that requires the city to use a one-page questionnaire asking bidders to disclose names and addresses of manufacturing locations and working conditions, and, as far as possible, buy products made in accordance with the UN

Declaration of Universal Human Rights and ILO conventions. Some three months after the City adopted this antisweatshop purchasing resolution, the city administration publicly described the process of questioning companies about their working conditions as simply normal business practice. Everybody does it.

The City's antisweatshop purchasing resolution helped to re-energize the campaign and provide direction for area merchants. Once again, the City was in a position of moral leadership. If merchants' role in the campaign had been somewhat vague before—for example, how do they build up a Clean Clothes inventory?—the city resolution gave them something concrete to do: ask the questions about working conditions. We decided that a bottom-line criterion for participating merchants would be requesting apparel suppliers to fill out the Manufacturer's Working Conditions Public Disclosure form, the same form that the city uses. As a community, we can all express our concern and ask the questions—not just the city and clothing retailers, but any organization or business that purchases apparel.

At the time of writing, a radio station, a private school, and three restaurants have joined the campaign, along with twenty-five clothing merchants. That still leaves individual shoppers. We have urged shoppers to be vocal and to treat shopping as a form of civic participation and to tell stores about their concerns with sweatshop conditions. Yet there is still a missing piece of the puzzle. While the antisweatshop movement has been adept at telling people what not to buy, it has not been able to provide positive answers, telling people what they can buy in good conscience. We were worrying that by raising awareness of sweatshops and child labor without providing guidance on ethical shopping, we risked creating feelings of powerlessness and missing opportunities to capitalize on people's desire to do the right thing. At the same time, Clean Clothes retailers were telling us that the only way we would really have an impact in their stores would be to have a Clean Clothes label. Such a label would give shoppers something very easy to do: ask for the label.

The Clean Clothes label

The label is a community experiment. To qualify for the label, a

Resources available from the Clean Clothes Campaign
Model Clean Clothes resolution and petition.

- Model Clean Clothes antisweatshop purchasing ordinance
- Clean Clothes Organizing Guide
- Clean Clothes Shopping Guide
- Web-linked Clean Clothes Resource Center

Please contact the Bangor Clean Clothes Campaign at
PICA, 170 Park Street, Bangor, ME 04401, (207)947-4203;
info@pica.ws; www.pica.ws.

The Maine Clean Clothes Alliance includes the Bangor
Clean Clothes Campaign, the Clean Clothes Campaign of
Southern Maine, and Farmington Area Citizens to End
Sweatshops (FACES).

Clean Clothes Campaign of Southern Maine
27 Gorham Road, Suite G109
Scarborough, ME 04074
(207)883-0156
CCCSoMe@aol.com

Farmington Area Citizens to End Sweatshops (FACES)
P.O. Box 212
West Farmington, ME 04992
(207)778-2120
faces04938@yahoo.com
www.geocities.com/faces04938

company must publicly disclose manufacturing sites and working conditions; sign a detailed code of conduct certifying that the products were made under fair working conditions; pledge to allow union representatives and qualified human rights groups to talk with workers in a nonwork area, without a prior appointment, and without supervisors present in order to monitor working conditions; and sign a detailed union neutrality statement, ensuring that workers can make the decision to join a union free from any management harassment, threat, or retaliation. Local retailers, rather than the companies themselves, will attach the label. The idea is to find out how much consumer interest and pressure we can generate with the labels to provide incentive for the companies to live up to the pledges they make. And to provide union organizers and human rights organizations with a tool to help empower workers and hold the companies accountable to values they profess.

There is no question that community-based antisweatshop campaigns can have a major impact if we have the numbers. We recently spoke with a representative of a major women's clothing label that supplies a downtown Clean Clothes clothier. She told us that they were not quite ready for public disclosure of manufacturing facilities. The idea of "releasing proprietary information," she said, "feels funny." She admitted that this was a "pure business decision" and that the Bangor store simply wasn't significant enough to their bottom line. But, she added, if there were ten or twenty of these stores, all asking for disclosure, all saying that the workers behind the labels matter, that would make a difference. The message is clear: the corporations can be moved. We just need enough people, consumers and stores alike, involved.

Dennis Chinoy helped found the Clean Clothes Campaign and Björn Skorpen Claeson is PICA's staff director.

Projects of the Heart

Tony Vento

Cleveland's Inter-Religious Task Force is a fair trade force to reckon with. IRTF committees work against sweatshops, Third World debt, new "free trade" legislation, and the U.S. Army School of the Americas. The committees have chairpeople, regular monthly meetings with an educational component, and larger public meetings that are part of an organizing plan. IRTF's one hundred fifty volunteers put in thirteen thousand hours every year working to change the shape of the global economy. IRTF built a base that includes scores of social action committees, denominational social action offices, high school and college students, faculty, and staff.

Our strategy has two legs. First, we choose projects of the heart—projects that people can intuitively grasp, that make sense because of the basic justice issues involved, that tell real people's stories, that put a human face on the global economy. Second, we mobilize people around these projects when broader policy choices come up.

Fair Trade coffee was the door into many groups when we started. We soon added sweatshops, then debt two or three years ago. Each of these issues is important in itself, and it makes sense for the people involved. But they are also fantastic doorways into the understanding of economic globalization, mobilization, and action.

Take coffee. We go out to churches. We start by asking people, "Close your eyes. What do you think of when you hear *coffee?*" People think of the marketing images: Coffee Achievers, gourmet status coffee, Juan Valdez. We ask, "What do you know about Juan Valdez and his family's life?" Physically robust, dressed in beautiful handmade clothing, working in idyllic settings, a dash of machismo, the sexy edge—it's amazing, the world that is constructed in those ads. Then we talk about the reality of coffee workers: the pace of work, the families who work together, the eighty-pound sacks they have to carry, the clothes they really wear. Picking coffee in Juan Valdez's outfit would be like wearing a tuxedo to do gardening.

Why does this matter? Because coffee is the number two traded commodity in the global market. It is a luxury for us, but for the farmers and producing countries

A member of a Fair Trade coffee cooperative in Mexico sorting beans.

it is much more than that. Coffee is the history of these countries and of their relationship to the United States. We ask, what is the reality we're connected to by coffee, and what choices would we want to make?

Soon you've got a whole thing going. You problematize the ordinary everyday things that people have taken for granted here in the United States, and you use them to show people their place in the global economy.

Part of discussing their place has to be discovering their power. Before the discussion, it didn't matter what coffee you bought. We help people discover the power they already have without making heroic choices like quit-

> We take a multi-issue approach but with an entry point that is as clear, human, and compelling as possible.

ting their jobs and becoming full-time activists. We talk about those choices and we present a continuum of involvement, but we come back to what they can do to start as consumers, citizens, and members of communities: families, schools or colleges, churches.

You pick one important leverage point that cracks open the problematic of the everyday, and you go in depth with it, trusting that it will not just be important for the particular people it connects, but will show people a frame that applies to other areas of the global economy. We ask: What else does this make you think of?

By picking one point, one example, we can avoid what happens when you lay out the whole picture of the global economy and people say, "It's just too much." The education has to lead to action, or it's not even education. As Confucius said, "To know and not to do is not to know."

Once you've shown this is a systemic problem, everyone in the room needs to discover the passion of their heart and dig in on that in a mutual way. If this is really a system, like a shirt, if you pull on one thread, or if you repair one thread, it affects the whole system. There are certain strategic threads. You don't have to pull on all of them to unravel the shirt. Personally, you don't have to pull on more than one of them. But you need to find one to pull on, and the longer you can keep pulling, the better it'll be. Do it in a way that doesn't ignore the other people pulling on their threads. Do it in a way that has mutuality.

I like the Lilliput analogy in *Global Village or Global Pillage.* Around the world, thousands of us are throwing ropes over the giant to tie it down. You need to know that yours isn't the only rope, and that from one vantage point people don't see the whole giant. You need to take time and visit other places to see their ropes, making sure someone is holding onto your rope while you're gone. You don't have to feel guilty that you aren't doing all the other things.

To sum up, we walk on two legs. We choose projects of the heart, get people involved, and keep them connected with real suffering and real people for the long term. Do that with integrity. Don't just use the connection to make a political point, but stick with it so you change that particular reality. Because if this is a system there'll be systemic manifestations of the policy choices involved, and those help you understand the kind of community you're in and the power it has.

The second leg is, we let our members know when the iron is hot on policy issues. We tell people, "I don't know when, but don't be surprised if you get a legislative alert."

What have we built up using this approach? Cleveland is now the fourth largest market in the United States for Fair Trade coffee. That matters a great deal for the small coffee growers who now have a market. It shows us that international trade could look differently. In fact, it already does through our work. And in the surrounding community, it

> We're always sifting through the national networks' campaigns for material that fits what we're doing, and to see what's new coming up.

gives us more credibility to talk about free trade.

The most important lesson is to start where you are. We picked a good human connection where we could go in depth, give people an empowering connection, and plead with them to get involved.

Tony Vento is the ex-director of the Cleveland Inter-Religious Task Force.

Fair Trade Not Free Trade

Deborah James

In the post-Seattle climate, more people are demanding that corporations pay living wages to the workers who make their products. Most people in this country would rather buy a product produced under fair trade conditions than under sweatshop labor conditions. Fortunately, in the coffee industry, a Fair Trade alternative exists. And this is no small industry, considering that coffee is the world's second most valuable traded commodity, after petroleum. Over 130 million people in the United States are coffee drinkers; we consume over one-fifth of the world supply.

About half of the world's coffee is produced by small family farmers. Small farmers working without the benefit of an organized export cooperative typically have to sell to exploitative middlemen who generally pay them less than half of the export price. This export price is usually around $1 per pound, but it fluctuates wildly. Today this market is at a six-year low of about seventy cents per pound. This system of free trade in the coffee industry means farmers generally receive between thirty to fifty cents per pound of coffee that retails for around $10 per pound in gourmet coffee markets.

Fair Trade seeks to correct these imbalances by setting a minimum price of $1.26 per pound—a living wage. Rather than operating on a charity model, Fair Trade changes the entire business model to include fair wages for workers as an integral part of the business system. Fair Trade importers also must offer credit to coffee cooperatives at reasonable rates, which helps

Virginia Berman and Mark Swett of Equal Exchange hand samples of Fair Trade coffee to commuters in Canton, MA.

Equal Exchange

PRODECOOP, a Nicaraguan coffee cooperative, sold its first container of Fair Trade coffee to the worker-owned cooperative Equal Exchange in 1991. A right-wing government had come to power in Nicaragua in 1990 and began carrying out IMF-imposed structural adjustment plans. Small farmers working in the conventional market, at a time when world coffee prices were rock-bottom as they were the first half of the '90s, often lost their land. Producers who sold their coffee in the Fair Trade market, to Equal Exchange and to European fair traders, were able to defend their social and economic gains like health care and education against the fierce tide of privatization. Most importantly, as organized farmer cooperatives they were able to keep their land, and their dignity.

Beyond its pathbreaking role in fair trade coffee, Equal Exchange remains the largest fair trade coffee company in the United States, purchasing over 1.5 million pounds of coffee from seventeen cooperatives in ten countries in 2000. The company also promotes economic democracy within its own business. As a worker-owned cooperative, Equal Exchange has demonstrated the viability of engaging in the marketplace while treating fairly all of its diverse stakeholders—farmers, employees, investors, consumers, and the earth.

poor farmers get off the treadmill of debt. Fair Trade organizations develop long-term trading relationships and work directly with organized farmer cooperatives. Fair Trade also encourages sustainable farming techniques that are safer for the environment, wildlife, and the farmers. The Max Havelaar Foundation in Europe estimates that eighty to eighty-five percent of coffee produced by Fair Trade cooperatives is grown without pesticides. Supporting Fair Trade is a great campaign for groups interested in making links between ecology and labor, by demonstrating that what's good for the environment is good for workers as well.

Drink more Fair Trade coffee!

Fair Trade cooperatives last year collectively produced over sixty million pounds of coffee, yet were only able to sell half of that coffee at Fair Trade prices. That means there are over thirty million pounds available to the Fair Trade market. The big gap is in U.S. consumption. Over eighty roasters and importers have already signed on with TransFairUSA to offer Fair Trade Certified coffee, but that still represents a fraction of a percentage of the U.S. coffee market. We need to demonstrate to coffee companies that there is a serious consumer demand for Fair Trade coffee by organizing Fair Trade campaigns in every town together with campuses, churches, unions, farmers, and environmental and solidarity organizations. The following are ways in which national organizations and grassroots groups have been doing this.

Global Exchange began promoting Fair Trade Certification for coffee as an outgrowth of their ten-year commitment to supporting Fair Trade through their Bay Area craft stores and their

TransFairUSA

Established in 1998, TransFairUSA is the national monitoring organization that certifies importers and roasters here in the United States. Their goal is to encourage other coffee companies, including large mainstream ones, to pay farmers a living wage and to buy Fair Trade Certified coffee, so that all farmers eventually will receive the living wage they deserve. TransFairUSA is the U.S. member of an international network called the Fair Trade Labeling Organizations (FLO), which includes monitors from fourteen European countries as well as Canada and Japan. The International Fair Trade Registry includes over three hundred cooperatives in twenty different producer countries, representing over 550,000 farmers. In other countries, the national monitors also certify cocoa, honey, sugar, tea, and now bananas.

Members of the UCIRI cooperative in Mexico put the Fair Trade label on a bag of coffee.

support of the Fair Trade Federation. They now coordinate a national network of church, solidarity, and student groups to organize for Fair Trade in local neighborhoods. Several of these universities, churches, and city councils have passed Fair Trade Resolutions or Purchasing Restrictions. They also coordinated a national effort that convinced Starbucks to carry Fair Trade Certified coffee in all its 2,500 stores nationwide.

Oxfam, which has been active in the European Fair Trade movement for many years, recently began a U.S. campaign to promote Fair Trade coffee through their vast national network of campus groups. This campaign complements their support for Fair Trade coffee cooperatives that are working at a grassroots level to eradicate poverty.

Activists in Santa Cruz, California, got their city to pass a purchasing restriction limiting their city's coffee purchases to coffee that is Fair Trade Certified. At the city council meeting, activists played a video, *Santiago's Story*, by TransFairUSA, about Fair Trade from a farmer's perspective. A student spoke on the need for government and consumer support of Fair Trade Certification and Fair Trade Products. Then a coffee bar worker spoke about how he worked for four months on several coffee plantations last year. He spoke about his life on the plantation, how he worked twenty to thirty days without a day off, how he carried fifty-pound sacks on his back at the end of his workday (after which the hike to town took two to three hours). He described his adobe home—no inside plumbing, no electricity. He felt by speaking up he was helping friends and family in Mexico. At the end of the presentation, the council voted. All supported the Fair Trade Certified City Purchasing Policy.

Parishioners active with the San Francisco Archdiocese decided to take on the issue of Fair Trade coffee because of their long opposition to poverty and social control in Central America. They appreciated that the work complemented their campaign against sweatshops by offering a positive alternative and supporting a just economic system. Led initially by St. Ignatius Church, parishoners in four churches have taken turns edu-cating other parishes in their Diocese until all the churches serve Fair Trade coffee at their social hours. They have also gone door to door locally to convince local retailers to sell Fair Trade coffee. They are rewarded by seeing their coordinated efforts change their community.

These are just a few examples of organizations that have won positive changes. How did they do it? They educated the community showing the *Santiago's Story* video, having guest speakers, leafleting, and giving out free Fair Trade coffee samples. They organized diverse coalitions. They chose local targets: their church, their campus, a particular local company or café they thought would be interested. And they focused on achieving their goal within a specific period of time using local resources to highlight the real changes people can make by choosing Fair Trade.

If it weren't for the antisweat-shop movement and the anticorporate globalization movement, there would be much less awareness of the working conditions of poor people in developing countries and the need for a Fair Trade alternative. But those movements also need a Fair Trade partner to put forth the kind of vision we would like to see for the global economy—one based on justice and living wages for all, rather than corporate greed.

Fair Trade is only going to become powerful in volume if communities organize to ensure that local cafés and grocery stores sell it. But it's equally important to make sure that consumers across the country know why they should buy Fair Trade. The Fair Trade Certified label is your proof that the farmer got a fair deal. At least when it comes to our daily brew, there is finally an independently monitored alternative to sweatshops that sets a standard for Fair Trade in the global economy.

Deborah James is the Director of the Fair Trade Department of Global Exchange and a board member of the national Fair Trade Federation. She spearheaded the successful campaign last year to make Starbucks carry Fair Trade coffee and is currently coordinating a national public education campaign for Fair Trade Coffee.

By choosing Fair Trade coffee, we bring our purchasing decisions in line with the rest of our decisions about being an ethical person in the world and being responsible for the impact of our consumption choices. But equally important is our role as activists, in joining together with others to make changes in communities.

Changing the Rules of the Global Economy

Hasn't the U.S. globalization movement has put most of its creativity and nerve into changing the rules of the global economy? Its high-profile protests have targeted rule-makers like the World Trade Organization, the World Bank, and International Monetary Fund. Labor and its allies have fought Fast Track, which would change the rules and allow the administration to rush new trade treaties through Congress.

Look more closely. If the globalization movement had taken a fifth of the effort it devoted to protests in Seattle and D.C., and directed that effort toward Congress, Fast Track might be a distant dead memory.

Why doesn't the globalization movement focus on the U.S. government, which dominates the global rule-making institutions? Analysis, ideology, and attitude.

Analysis. Revolutionaries and reformists in the globalization movement agree that transnational corporations are running the global show. Why bother with the politicians on their payroll? *Let's name the real problem and go after it.*

Ideology. Many anarchists and others in the movement don't want to make government more powerful, especially the U.S. government. They're more interested in decentralizing. Rather than pushing government to rule corporations, *let's cut them down and build up a people-centered direct democracy.*

Attitude. Half of the country's eligible voters don't even vote, and the abstention gets higher the younger you go. *Lots of people just don't think real changes will come through the government.*

These are widespread attitudes and strong arguments. Before agreeing, though, let's remember our global and domestic allies who would suffer serious damage from passage of the Free Trade Area of the Americas. By putting creative, mass pressure on Washington, we can build the coalitions we need to transform the global economy.

—Mike Prokosch

The Indirect Action Network

Mike Dolan

The struggle against corporate globalization, as a matter of public policy, can be described as a tug-of-war between big business on one side and civil society on the other, with policy makers and opinion leaders (political elites and the mainstream media) in the middle. The various constituencies of the Fair Trade movement in this country are coordinated so that they can exert the maximum collective grassroots muscle to pull elected officials and media away from their slavish devotion to the corporate agenda. That operational coordination is achieved by a structured national coalition. Maybe you've heard of it.

The Citizens Trade Campaign (CTC) came together during the mother of all trade policy fights—the debate over the North American Free Trade Agreement

> The WTO is the place where governments collude in private against their domestic pressure groups.
> —Anonymous WTO official, *Financial Times*, April 30, 1998.

(NAFTA) in the U.S. Congress in 1992 and 1993. Folks today think Seattle was the first time that Teamsters and Turtles got together, but the truth is that a powerful "blue-green" alliance was forming a decade ago when the Bush administration was negotiating NAFTA. The original institutional members of the CTC include the Teamsters, Steelworkers, United Auto Workers, UNITE, Friends of the Earth, National Farmers Union, United Food and Commercial Workers, National Family Farm Coalition, Americans for Democratic Action, the Methodist Board of Church and Society—and my organization, Public Citizen, founded by Ralph Nader over twenty-seven years ago.

Other allies and affiliates of the CTC over the years have included the Sierra Club, ACT UP, Clean Water Action, International Campaign for Tibet, and the Free China Movement. The newest CTC coalition member is the MAGI—Ministers Against Global Injustice, a national network of African-American pastors who worked together in opposition to the NAFTA for Africa bill.

The basic strategy of the CTC is to target swing members of Congress from two ends—the Hill and the field. When trade legislation is pending, public interest lobbyists link up in D.C. and swarm the halls of Congress. Then they pass important intelligence and insights about undecided members to the great and good grassroots. The field organizers, meanwhile, bring together activists from different sectors to put pressure on those same members when they come home, and submit their impressions back to the CTC lobbyists on Capitol Hill.

From the first, we have surprised members of Congress (and their staffs) with the breadth of the coalition that visits to talk trade policy. "Did my scheduler make a mistake and double-book this meeting?" the member might say, as he looks about his district office conference room at the various sectors represented. "What issue might bring all of you and your disparate concerns to me at the same moment?"

The issue is Fair Trade. It is the central policy debate of globalization, which is the most profound political and economic issue of our time. At stake are the basic premises and direction of U.S. participation in the global economy. The

CTC has been in the vanguard of the progressive movement in this debate from the first. Today, there are CTC affiliates throughout the country, organized as state Fair Trade campaigns and coalitions. To find out more—and the coordinates of the activist base nearest you—call the CTC at (202) 778-3313 or go to its website at www.tradewatch.org.

Mike Dolan is the west coast field director of the Citizens Trade Campaign.

FTAA: Stopping NAFTA Expansion by Fighting Privatization

Mike Prokosch

The greatest single threat to the multilateral trading system is the absence of public support.

—U.S. Trade Representative Charlene Barshefsky, The Globe and Mail, *Toronto, September 10, 1999.*

Public opinion polls since 1995 consistently show that two-thirds to four-fifths of U.S. residents don't want new trading agreements without worker rights and environmental standards. That is a vital base of support for our movement and an immense barrier to the expansion of corporate globalization.

The event that did the most to create this overwhelming consensus was NAFTA. Many experiences drew the globalization movement's many constituencies together, but the one that transformed broad public opinion was the campaign against NAFTA in the early 1990s and the experience of NAFTA's actual effect after it passed.

Now think about a NAFTA for the entire hemisphere, which Washington is pushing on millions of people who saw what NAFTA did and don't want any more of it. Think of starting to organize against this with a movement that is already mobilized and visible.

The Free Trade Area of the Americas is that unpopular NAFTA expansion. The FTAA threatens every corner of our lives. It would lock thirty-four nations into a corporate-dominated framework that will be very difficult to undo. The FTAA hits the United

> Free trade is another form of structural adjustment.
>
> —Maude Barlow

States much more directly than the WTO, IMF, or World Bank: It is about this country and this hemisphere. It is also an organizer's dream. With negotiations due to finish by 2005, it offers a three-year opportunity to build long-lasting "Seattle coalitions" state by state across the United States.

Organizing that dream into a reality means identifying the material interest pieces, the pieces of the FTAA that hurt my job, my family, and my community. One of those pieces is privatization.

Leading with race, class, and gender

Almost everywhere you turn in the United States, a public good is being privatized, defunded, or deregulated. Women, children, workers, and people of color are the hardest hit when public hospitals are closed, welfare recipients are forced to displace union workers, and states shift money from public schools to private jails.

Just as privatization in the U.S. started well before the FTAA was imagined, the deindustrialization of the United States started well before NAFTA. What NAFTA did was change the rules, making it safer and easier for corporations to invest internationally. It locked in a new investor rights regime which it is very difficult to reverse.

The FTAA would do to public services what NAFTA did to industrial jobs in the United States. It would change the rules to favor transnational corporations and cut down the unions in their way. Under the FTAA, education and water would become trillion-dollar "markets" where you must pay to play.

A campaign against the FTAA and for democratically controlled services could:

- connect global activists with the people of color and working-class people who lose access when services are privatized.

A people's alternative to the FTAA

Some of the hemisphere's largest social movements have joined to oppose the FTAA and propose a more just alternative.

The Hemispheric Social Alliance (HSA) includes national networks of trade union, environmental, peasant, women's, indigenous, human rights, and development organizations. Continental networks like the Interamerican Regional Organization of Workers (ORIT) and the Latin American Coordinator of Campesino Organizations (CLOC) also belong. Their counterproposal, "Alternatives for the Americas: Building a People's Hemispheric Agreement," can be downloaded from www.web.ca/~comfront/alts4americas/eng/eng.html.

For more information contact the Alliance for Responsible Trade's domestic coordinator Tom Hansen at (773)583-7728 or msn@mexicosolidarity.org, or its international coordinator Karen Hansen-Kuhn at (202)898-1566 or khk@dgap.org.

- connect local and global activists with the teachers and others who could lose their unions when services are privatized.

- inside the labor movement, extend global awareness from the already-hit industrial unions to the public sector and service unions that are next on the corporate target list.

- connect us with Latin America, where fights against privatization are the leading edge of resistance to globalization. A campaign against privatization could create a mass, hemispheric, and successful movement against the FTAA.
- unite work against the FTAA, the WTO (whose General Agreement on Trade in Services mirrors the FTAA services agreement), the World Bank, and IMF, whose structural adjustment programs brought privatization to Latin America.

- challenge property-first libertarianism and change U.S. consciousness by asking, what should we own in common and what rights should be guaranteed everyone?

The globalization movement needs a long-term campaign to provide local organizing hooks, and to identify a common frame that

Stop Wasting America's Money on Privatization

"The structural adjustment policies of the IMF and World Bank harm working families throughout the globe. . . . What the Bank and IMF call "structural adjustment" abroad, they call privatization, downsizing, and contracting out here in America."
—Bobby L. Harnage, National President, American Federation of Government Employees (AFGE)

In the past decade, hundreds of thousands of government employees have lost their jobs. The jobs did not vanish, however. Many of them went to private contractors and according to AFGE, the result has been wasted federal money, less oversight.

Last year AFGE launched the SWAMP Campaign, which stands for Stop Wasting America's Money on Privatization. SWAMP fights against privatization of public services because it abuses workers and exploits taxpayers. The future of America should be in the hands of workers that serve the public, not multinational corporations that serve only themselves, and are accountable to no country and no government but only to their own bottom line.

AFGE represents six hundred thousand federal workers across the nation, with many in California, Texas, and Washington D.C. Many local AFGE unions may want to join community organizations and fight against privatization. If you're interested in making this link, call (202)737-8700 and ask for the SWAMP campaign, or check the SWAMP webpage, www.afge.org\swamp\index.htm.

unites local with labor and global work. This campaign would be broad enough to encompass hundreds of local fights, but focused enough to give logic to our collaboration.

Lessons for the World Bank Bond Boycott

Zahara J. Heckscher

Learning from the history of the antiapartheid movement:

1. *Know that young people can change history.* In 1986, Nelson Mandela was in prison. Black people could not vote and lived in a virtual police state. The South African government was using military force to brutally suppress pro-democracy activists. Anyone who said that within six years Mandela would be elected president in a mostly peaceful election would have been seen as a dreamer or a lunatic. Students in the United States helped make this impossible dream a reality by raising awareness about apartheid, forcing their universities to sell stock in companies that operated in South Africa, and helping to get economic sanctions imposed against South Africa. Students in England, Australia, Canada, and France used similar tactics. Combined with heroic efforts of students and others in South Africa, this economic pressure helped end the apartheid regime. In the same vein, now we can help transform or abolish the World Bank.

2. *Think long-term.* The U.S. antiapartheid movement began around 1960, when George Hauser and others founded the American Committee on Africa. Martin Luther King encouraged a U.S. boycott of South Africa in the 1960s. In the '70s, following the massacre of students in Soweto in South Africa, students around the world began campaigning for their universities to divest from corporations doing business in that country. These efforts laid the groundwork for a vibrant student antiapartheid movement in the 1980s. While we all hope that transforming or abolishing the World Bank won't take decades, we should know that the struggle may be a long one. We must take temporary setbacks in stride, and not let them discourage us in our long-term struggle for global justice.

3.   *Remember* that, as Frederick Douglass said, "Power concedes nothing without a demand." The World Bank is supported by billions of dollars, many strong-armed governments, and hundreds of multinational corporations that benefit from structural adjustment. These institutions will not give up their evil ways because they have a sudden change of heart. Apartheid did not end because President Botha woke up in a good mood one day. Apartheid ended because activists inside and outside South Africa exerted massive political, social, and economic pressure on the regime. Demand does not just mean rowdy demonstrations; it can also include peaceful meetings, creative nonviolence, legislative action, and economic boycotts.

> *They no longer use bullets and ropes. They use the World Bank and the International Monetary Fund.*
> —Rev. Jesse L. Jackson, quoted in B. Rich, "50 Years of World Bank Outrages," *Third World Resurgence 49* (January 1994):p. 25.

4.   *Educate yourself and others.* The divestment movement was successful not only in generating economic pressure against apartheid, but also in creating a broad-based movement through education. Likewise, the World Bank Bond Boycott has much more value than the mere selling of bonds. If student activists use effective educational techniques, the boycott can help thousands of people see through the Bank's public relations image to the reality of its destructive impact. In addition, by educating yourself, you can become a more effective activist. Don't think that education about economic institutions has to be boring. Liven it up with debates, dramatizations, and participatory workshops (see contacts at end). Check out the creative anti-World Bank websites. Choose to write term papers about issues related to the World Bank, so you can get credit while you learn.

5.   *Don't listen* to those who say "The issue is too complicated; you just don't understand." The rich old gray men in suits told us that line about apartheid, too. Yes, apartheid was complicated. Yes, the World Bank is complicated. Slavery was complicated, too, but these complications did not diminish the fact that it was wrong. While it is extremely important to educate yourself about the World Bank, don't let yourself suffer from information paralysis. In other words, don't believe that you must know

World Bank Bond Boycott

Global institutions like the World Bank may seem too big and distant for us to change. In reality, the tools to stop the Bank are in our hands.

The World Bank is a bank. Banks have to get their money somewhere. If most of their depositors close their accounts and withdraw they money, they choke off the bank's lifeblood, and the bank collapses.

The World Bank gets eighty percent of its money by selling bonds to cities, states, universities, unions, churches, and pension and mutual funds. Four out of every five dollars that the World Bank uses to destroy South Africa's health care system, or build oil pipelines through African forests, or underwrite gold mines that spill cyanide into rivers in Guyana, come from our colleges, city governments, churches, unions, and our pension or mutual funds that are buying World Bank bonds.

This is how we can choke off the World Bank. Across the country people are going to their city governments and university administrations and asking them to promise that they

every detailed factoid about the Bank before you can take action to change it.

6. *Make links with groups overseas.* The U.S. antiapartheid movement had strong links with South African activists, and these activists played a critical role in educating students here. Their reports from the front lines inspired and enlivened the divestment movement. For example, Dennis Brutus, a South African former political prisoner, met law student Randall Robinson during a speaking tour of the United States. Inspired in part by that meeting, Robinson became a leader in the U.S. antiapartheid movement, eventually initiating a year of sit-in protests at the South African embassy. Students today should be sure to organize events on campus with speakers from the developing world who can convey firsthand information about how the World Bank impacts their countries. This type of event can provide essential sparks to keep the movement alive, and inspiration for the next generation of social justice activists.

will not buy any World Bank bonds. San Francisco, Oakland, Berkeley, the Communication Workers of America, the United Electrical workers union, and several churches have passed resolutions supporting the World Bank boycott.

The Bond Boycott campaign was dreamed up by Haitian activists who were fighting World Bank programs in their country and joined by activists in the United States, Africa, and Ecuador. Nine out of ten countries represented on the boycott board are in the global South.

Passing a Bond Boycott resolution is not difficult. We are not asking them to sell the bonds they have. We are just asking them not to buy any more. This will gradually cut off new buyers for Bank bonds and tighten a noose around the Bank's neck—an international noose, because this is an international campaign.

For detailed steps for starting a campaign plus excellent handouts and supporting materials, contact World Bank Bond Boycott at (202)299-0020, check out www.worldbankboycott.org or send e-mail to bankboycott@econjustice.net.

7. *Make links with local issues.* The most effective student groups understood that institutional racism existed far beyond South Africa's borders. They supported antiracist actions at their schools as well as local community organizations. Likewise, it's important to be aware of how the structural adjustment programs of the World Bank have parallels in our own country from cuts in education to lack of affordable health care and housing. Furthermore, World Bank policies overseas lower wages in the United States, and create environmental problems for the whole planet. Seek allies among local education, labor, and environmental groups; support their events, and encourage them to get involved in your campaigns.

8. *Internal group power dynamics and processes matter.* The most painful part of the student antiapartheid movement was the racial divide within the movement. White students did not understand that for a black student, getting arrested might have more serious implications than it does for a white

student due to institutional racism in the criminal justice system. The consensus process that predominantly white organizations used was seen as overly cumbersome by some African-American students. White students tried to get African-American students to join their actions, but rarely went to black student organizations to support their actions. If the World Bank bond boycott is to be effective, and truly multiracial, predominantly white organizations must be willing to support organizations of students of color, even if the issues they work on are not directly related to the boycott. White students must also be committed to look inside themselves at ways they have internalized the racism of our society.

9. *Think about what you are for, not just what you are against.* The South African struggle was guided by a vision of a free and democratic South Africa, as articulated by the Freedom Charter (a great subject for a research project). Spend time discussing what the world could look like if oppressive institutions like the World Bank were transformed. Bring in workshop facilitators or guest speakers who can help guide the process and share ideas from the struggle in other countries.

10. *Think strategically.* Sometimes the antiapartheid movement seemed to go from action to action without a long-term plan. Make sure your organization's goals are clear. For example, get your university to sign a statement that it will not purchase World Bank bonds; then share your success with other campuses and participate in a congressional campaign to cut off World Bank funding. Once your goals are clear, create a plan that will target your actions to what is most likely to reach your goal. Be sure to include a variety of types of actions so all people who want to be involved can do so at a level they feel comfortable with.

11. *Find allies.* In the antiapartheid movement, progressive faculty, administrators, student government representatives, media contacts, and trustees were critical partners in getting universities to divest. Find out who your friends are and work with them.

The struggle to change the World Bank will be immensely difficult. Like apartheid, global corporatism is an ugly, powerful monster that will not easily be killed. But the alternative to this struggle is to let our planet, people, culture, and environment be destroyed. The future is ours. Let's fight for it.

Zahara J. Heckscher is a graduate student at American University who has been active in both the antiapartheid and anti-World Bank movements. She is available to lead workshops about "Lessons From the Anti-Apartheid Movement," "Beyond April 16: Next Steps in the Campaign Against Corporate Globalism," and "Alternatives to the Peace Corps: How to Live Your Dream of Volunteering Overseas." Heckscher can be reached at (202)387-4109 or peacepeace1@hotmail.com.

The Maine Ethical Purchasing Campaign

Björn Skorpen Claeson

In June 2000, Maine's Legislature voted to use the state's tax money to support jobs with dignity for sweatshop workers, help vendors become more accountable for their products, and level the playing field for ethical Maine businesses and workers that shouldn't have to compete for state contracts against corporations that abuse sweatshop and child labor.

The bill is the crest of a wave that has swept through the state since 1997, when the city of Bangor passed the nation's first Clean Clothes Resolution (page 209). In 1998, Bangor activists helped a faith-based group near Portland form the Clean Clothes Campaign of Southern Maine. Then, in the wake of the 1999 protests against the World Trade Organization in Seattle, students, faculty, and residents organized Farmington Area Citizens to End Sweatshops (FACES). Their first action was to make University of Maine-Farmington a sweat-free campus.

In summer 2000, these campaigns joined labor, faith-based and other concerned organizations in a Maine Clean Clothes Alliance. Church groups started their own Clean Clothes projects. Student groups led discussions, organized, and met with legislators. Neighbors came together for house parties, talking about the harm that sweatshops do to their world, what they can do in their communities, and how they can make their voices heard in the state legislature. Local apparel and footwear workers organized on the shop floor to tell legislators how important the bill could be to their livelihood. And high school youth organized youth and local constituencies, in one case bringing together thirty people to meet with a key legislator.

Over fifty Maine organizations and unions expressed their support for the antisweatshop purchasing law. Over sixty Maine businesses said it was the right thing to do and that complying with the law would impose no cumbersome burden on them.

The Maine Anti-Sweatshop Purchasing Law passed by a two-to-one margin in the House, unanimously in the Senate, and on June

International Right to Know Campaign

Should toxic chemicals and repressive labor practices be exported to developing countries after they have been banned here? A dozen U.S. organizations are saying "no!" They support new legislation that would require U.S. corporations operating overseas to:

- report *toxic pollutants* they release into the air, land, and water.
- report the amount of *natural resources they extract*, process, or purchase abroad.
- report when they have applied for the right to increase *pollutant emissions* from an overseas facility.
- report serious work-related *injuries and deaths*.
- inform workers about *hazardous chemicals in the workplace*.
- report on their *labor rights policies* and any *complaints* against them, and post the ILO Declaration of Fundamental Principles and Rights at work in every domestic and foreign facility.

20, 2001, the Maine legislature passed a budget that includes the groundbreaking antisweatshop law.

The first of its kind for a state, the law requires businesses seeking contracts to sell footwear, apparel, and textiles to the Maine state government to sign an affidavit that to the best of their knowledge products they supply to the state were not made in a sweatshop as defined by the Purchasing Code of Conduct. The law includes a provision against cutting and running, ensuring that the state of Maine and local state vendors will not take the easy way out—simply canceling contracts with offending suppliers—but instead will push suppliers to negotiate with their workers and respect labor rights.

Decency vs. the WTO

It may seem obvious that we

- disclose *security arrangements* with state or private police, military, and paramilitary forces.
- report on their *human rights policy*, and *complaints* received from communities, and any *human rights lawsuits* against them.
- disclose the *name and location* of all their overseas facilities, plus their subcontractors' and subsidiaries' facilities.

The International Right to Know legislation would also required covered businesses to maintain detailed records of this information, allow government prosecution of individuals and businesses that fail to comply, and allow private citizens and organizations to sue violators and collect damages.

To lend your support to the campaign, contact national field organizer David Waskow at Friends of the Earth, (202)783-7400, x108, dwaskow@foe.org.

should be able to decide how our government spends public money. Up until recently, government procurement has been a matter of national or local prerogative. And that's very important. As the largest purchasers of goods and services in the world, governments can do a great deal of good.

Governments can create jobs and strengthen local economies by giving preference to local businesses or specifying minimum local content requirements. They can reduce environmental damage by purchasing recycled materials. Governments can assist women-owned, minority-owned, and veteran-owned businesses. Governments can also help improve working conditions for sweatshop workers around the world with fair labor purchasing standards.

This is all about impressing our values, human values, on the economy. But there is now a move in the World Trade Organization and in the negotiations for the Free Trade Area of the Americas to place government procurement under a free trade regime. The goal is to give transnational corporations access to one of the world's biggest markets—government contracts.

An FTAA draft agenda calls for all government procurement to follow the principle of nondiscrimination. This means that only the end product counts, not the way it was made. Like goods must be treated in a like manner, no matter who made them or in what labor or environmental conditions. Foreign companies must be treated at least as well as domestic ones. Every country is entitled to the best treatment that other countries get, no matter their human rights record. Supplier qualifications must be limited to those essential for a supplier to fulfill the terms of the contract.

No longer could governments buy preferentially from local vendors or environmentally responsible vendors or fair labor vendors or vendors that pay a living wage. No longer would government purchasing be subject to democratic decision-making.

Ultimately, the Maine Ethical Purchasing Campaign says *no* to the WTO, *yes* to democracy, *yes* to humanity. If trade agreements tell us we cannot have an Ethical Purchasing Law, thousands of Mainers will be ready to take another step.

Practical Tips

Great ideas and organizing strategies are the most important ingredients of resistance to the current global economy, and they are the main focus of this book. But organizers also need basic tools. This section includes advice for using the Internet, publicizing your work, researching a new campaign, raising money, and dealing with state repression.

This section is by no means complete, but it will give newer activists some basics and refresh experienced organizers. The *Yellow Pages* section lists contact information for many different issue organizations.

Internet Organizing

Brandon Wright

The world business community uses information technology to coordinate activities quickly and efficiently, and to avoid restrictions placed on them by governmental and nongovernmental organizations. Activists around the world need to start connecting, communicating, and collaborating with the same tools that their adversaries have mastered.

It does not take deep pockets to do this. Organizations have a number of freely available tools at their disposal including free storage space, server space, e-mail accounts, and ISP (Internet Service Provider) accounts.

Global activists can use information technology every day in two areas of their work: communication and research.

Communication

While every organization is unique, their work often overlaps. Organizations that are fighting for the same cause should try to network whenever possible and not duplicate their work. E-mail, listservs, and newsgroups are excellent ways to stay connected and informed, but a free web-based service named Yahoogroups is now available.

Many activists and organizations abroad lack cheap and reliable phone service, electricity, and computers.

At http://groups.yahoo.com/, a Yahoogroup can be created by entering each person's e-mail address. They will then receive an e-mail asking if they want to be part of the Yahoogroup, and they pick out an individual password to access the group. Your Yahoogroup is the equivalent of a 24-hour online meeting room. Here are some of the features:

- Your Yahoogroup is given one e-mail address. Instead of pasting your entire address book into your e-mail, you can send a message to one address and it will go out to everyone in your group.

- The message archive stores every message that your group has sent, creating a valuable vault of information which comes in handy more often than you might think.

- Each group receives twenty megabytes of free storage space. This means your Yahoogroup can act as a server. If a report or database needs work, you can upload it to your Yahoogroup. Any group member can then download it, make the necessary changes, and upload it back to the Yahoogroup.

- The calendar option allows you to set up events and meetings with automatic e-mail reminders to keep everyone in your group on the same page.

- Each Yahoogroup has its own private chat room if you need to schedule an online meeting.

Research

The Internet can also be used as a massive library for almost any type of research. Most government agencies have websites, and a good place to start your research is at the website of the agency that regulates the topic you're looking for. Most university research departments have websites as well. Use them to your advantage; a lot of the research you need to do has probably been touched upon before. For the financially well supported organization, Lexis-Nexus is one of the best research pay-sites. Failing that, most public libraries have online searches where you can look for material online and even access some articles. A good web page to begin with is the California Digital Library at www.dbs.cdlib.org. This web page is accessible outside California; it contains information from news sources throughout the world. There are websites like this in every region, and the time spent finding them is usually much less than the time spent researching without them.

Security

Every form of communication has its drawbacks. Before discussing classified information via e-mail, look at a good key-based cryptography program. There are free programs to protect your e-mail, such as GnuPG. A good place to begin is: http://hotwired.lycos.com/webmonkey/backend/security/tutorials/tutorial1.html.

This website explains different types of cryptography and offers free tutorials to get you started, as well as links to websites where you can download encryption programs.

Make sure to keep your online organizing up to date, secure, and backed up. Don't use passwords straight out of the dictionary, or potential crackers can figure them out with their password-cracking software. Try using alphanumeric passwords.

In the wake of September 11, the FBI is increasing Internet surveillance and acquiring tools to read encrypted messages. For the latest information on privacy issues go to the cyber-liberties page at http://www.aclu.org, or to the Electronic Privacy Information Center, http://www.epic.org. To be really safe, find out what could be held against you and don't discuss it electronically, any more than you would on the phone.

Internet organizing has its limits. The organization that relies solely on technology will get burned when a server goes down or its office gets a virus. Emotion and emphasis cannot be transmitted through an e-mail; nothing replaces face-to-face collaboration. However, these free tools give organizations a way to supplement personal contacts and direct action with information and collaborations that would otherwise be impossible.

The digital divide

Information technology is not equally available to everybody. Whites in the United States are nearly three times as likely to have a computer at home as Latinos and blacks. This digital divide is growing at both the household and institutional level.

Many community-based organizations (CBOs) cannot afford technological renovation. Yet this lack of information technology makes them less effective in the battles they wage. This continual cycle keeps many CBOs from enjoying and benefiting from the technological boom. This cycle is a perfect example of the digital divide, a problematic social implication of technology that exists wherever technology is found.

Somehow, CBOs must embrace this technology and use it to collaborate and unite with similar groups internationally. The bridge that traverses the digital divide will be built upon partnerships among global organizers.

Brandon Wright works with the Center for Global, International, and Regional Studies at the University of California-Santa Cruz, and serves as the Instructional Coordinator for the Global Information Internship Program (www2.ucsc.edu/giip). If your organization needs IT (information technology) development, you can contact Brandon at bwright@cats.ucsc.edu.

Internal Communication: Beyond E-Mail

Betsy Leondar-Wright

Voluntary groups are only as strong as the flow of communication among them. Some activist groups rely heavily on e-mail for communication among members. There are three limitations to this cyber-reliance:

- Most Americans don't have regular access to e-mail. If you don't reach unwired people, you will disproportionately exclude low-income people, African-Americans, and Latino people.

- Many busy activists get such high volume of e-mail that they react to one more message, even from a group they care about, as just spam (junk e-mail).

- For urgent messages, e-mails can be too slow to reach members who don't check their e-mail daily.

If e-mail is your primary mode of communication, but some group members don't have e-mail accounts, designate someone to print out all messages and send them to those members.

In addition, these simple, old-fashioned communication methods can strengthen your group, but are too often forgotten.

Member list

It's simple, it's obvious, and it's surprising how many groups don't do it. Type up the contact information for everyone who has attended one or more meetings. Give the list to everyone on the list. Update whenever new people join.

Reminder calls

People are far more likely to become and stay active in a group if they get personalized phone calls about their involvement, asking them to play particular roles, checking in on how it's going, and inviting them warmly to the next meeting or event. These calls are time-consuming, but they work.

Many core groups shrink by attrition because they neglect to follow up with people who miss a meeting. The people in the room set up the next date and then forget to tell missing members, who are then more likely to miss more meetings. Part of every "Next meeting" agenda item should be listing active members not present and dividing up who will call each of them.

Phone tree

For urgent alerts, like legislative news or a changed meeting place, a phone tree can reach all active members fast without burdening any one person with making all the calls.

The person at the top of the tree should be the easiest to reach and the most reliable. The next layer or two should also be reachable day and evening, and firm commitments should be made to pass on messages within an hour. Hard-to-reach people should be at the bottom of the tree.

Any group member with urgent news should call the top of the tree, who calls the second layer and so on.

For very urgent news that must reach everyone, the message can include a request that the bottom of each branch call the top person to say that the message reached them.

These principles of internal communication also apply to outreach. It's possible to organize an event or a campaign using e-mail listservs as the primary recruitment tool, but the results will be weaker in both diversity and depth of commitment. There's no substitute for talking with people one-on-one in a customized way that answers their concerns and plays to their strengths and enthusiasms. Make some outreach phone calls, knock on some doors, have some one-on-one e-mail conversations, walk up to some strangers at events, and the dialogues you have will pay off in greater numbers of more diverse people getting more deeply involved in your organization.

Betsy Leondar-Wright is a founding member of United for a Fair Economy and is its Communications Director. She is coauthor of Shifting Fortunes: The Perils of the Growing American Wealth Gap, published by UFE in 1999. Before working at UFE, she directed a state human services advocacy coalition and an affordable housing group.

Getting into the Mainstream Media

Betsy Leondar-Wright

Media coverage will advance all your other goals. The people you contact directly will be more likely to get involved if they've heard of your group and your issues in the media. To maximize your media coverage, incorporate media strategy discussions into all your organizational planning sessions.

Make sure the media outlets you target include a broad range:
- Radio and TV talk shows
- Radio news
- Television news
- Newspaper news stories
- Feature articles and interviews
- Columnists
- Op-eds, letters to the editor, and guest columns
- Magazine articles

- Online publications
- Alternative and independent media

Your media strategy needs to vary by the media climate you are in, which may be cold or hot or somewhere in between.

In a cold media climate

A cold climate is when there is little or no discussion of your issue in the local or national media. It is very common to have a cold climate about global issues in your local media, as their focus is usually local news.

Your goal in this climate is to push your issue into public awareness. Tips on overcoming this chilly atmosphere:

- Make it incredibly easy for journalists to talk with representatives of your group. Don't ask them to come to your events, and don't hold press conferences. Give them high-quality and persuasive materials and offer to talk about them on the phone or in person where they are.

- Focus on independent and progressive journalists, and on radio public affairs shows, which are often the easiest media coverage to get. Approach columnists, who have more latitude than reporters in what to cover.

- Do creative actions that are so dramatic and unusual that journalists will feel drawn to covering it as news even if the issue does not interest them. Expect to get just one photograph or five seconds of TV visuals, and make sure that one visual communicates your core message. Find a five-word or shorter slogan that makes sense to people who have never head of your issue. Put it on banners and signs in clear black and white so that it is readable at a hundred paces. Turn signs toward any cameras.

- Look for very local angles based on the affiliations of your group leaders. Neighborhood, hometown, college, and alumni papers might cover a local person doing something interesting.

- Use news hooks: world-wide events that the media will be covering anyway, such as holidays, government decisions, crises, and information releases. Connect your story with the news hook in your press materials and press calls.

• Ask prominent community leaders to speak up about your issue, for example by authoring an op-ed column for the local paper.

In a hot media climate

A hot media climate is when issues related to yours are being debated in the media frequently, and when opinion journalists (columnists, talk show hosts, etc.) are vehemently taking sides. Since the Seattle WTO protests, the climate for global trade issues has heated up, especially in major cities on the East and West Coasts.

Your goals in this climate are to get your viewpoint into bigger, more mainstream media, to have your group leaders be quoted regularly as the respected representatives of your viewpoint, and to prevent damaging and distorted coverage. Tips on reaching these goals:

• Send out regular press releases as the story unfolds, with new facts and quotes.

• Aim high. Send your releases to the biggest and most mainstream outlets, in a wider geographical range, as well as to the press list you created in colder times.

• Work hard at establishing the credibility of your group. This includes carefully choosing spokespeople who will communicate well to your new broader audience, and removing all the movement jargon from the materials you send to the press. Releasing a study or report full of carefully researched new information, if possible including people with credentials and a member of your group as coauthors, is a good way to get credibility with journalists.

• Don't get sidetracked from your core issues by negative spin in the media, whether it's gossip about a group member or a debate about who was violent, protestors or police. Continually look for ways to make the news stories focus on the content of your issue.

Of the six steps in a publicity campaign . . .

1. Develop your story. For news media, your opinions are not enough; you have to *do* something—hold a hearing, release a study, do a direct action, meet with a congressperson, give an award.

2. Build your press list. Call media outlets to ask for contact names, e-mail address, phone and fax numbers, and so on.

3. Choose and prepare your spokespeople.

4. Write the press release and other materials.

5. Mail, fax, or e-mail your materials to journalists.

6. Make pitch calls to journalists to ask them to cover your story.

. . . . number six is the most important.

Most news stories happen because someone made a phone call to a journalist. That someone could be you.

Media resources
Ryan, Charlotte. *Prime Time Activism*. Boston: South End Press, 1990.
Salzman, Jason. *Making the News*. Boulder, CO: Westview Press, 1998.

How to write and use a press release

—adapted from Jason Salzman

What is a press release?

- Informs reporters about your event, report, or issue.

• More detailed than the advisory, which is like a press release but is sent well in advance. Should tell all the information a reporter needs to write their piece.

• Envision, then write the press release as the news story *you* would want to see written.

• Send it out the morning of, or the day before, the event.

Elements

• Headline. This will make or break a news release—include the most important information in the headline, and make it punchy. The headline can be up to four lines if necessary, including a subhead, if used, but keep it short (and remember to use a large font).

• Important information should jump off the page—most reporters will only spend ten seconds looking at a release.

• Spend seventy-five percent of your time writing the headline and the first paragraph.

• Use the inverted pyramid style of news writing. Make your most important points early in the release and work your way down.

• Keep sentences and paragraphs short. No more than three sentences per paragraph.

• Include a colorful quote from a spokesperson in the second or third paragraph.

• Include a short summary of your organization in the last paragraph.

• Mention "Photo Opportunity" if there is one. Be sure to send a copy of the release to the photo desk.

Form

- In the top left corner, type "For Immediate Release."

- Below "For Immediate Release," type the date.

- Contact Information: In the top right corner, type names and phone numbers of two contacts. Make sure these contacts can be easily reached by phone. Include the contact's home phone number, if appropriate.

- Type "###" at the end of your release. This is how journalists mark the end of a news copy.

- Type "MORE" at the end of page one if your release is two pages, and put a contact phone number and short headline in the upper-right hand corner of subsequent pages.

- Print your release on your organization's letterhead.

How to distribute it

- A release should be sent out the morning of, or the day before your event. In some cases, you may want to send an embargoed copy to select reporters ahead of time, meaning that the information is confidential until the date you specify.

- Generally, send a release to only one reporter per outlet, but sending to columnists and editorial board members at the same outlet is okay.

- If your release announces an event, send it to the daybooks. A daybook lists news events scheduled to take place in the region on that day. Someone from each major outlet reviews the daybooks each morning.

- **Always** make follow up calls after you send the release. If your release is announcing an event, make the calls the morning before your event is scheduled.

- Have a copy of the release ready to be faxed when you make the calls.

Adapted from Jason Salzman's Making the News and SPIN Project materials.

Building a New Group

Mike Prokosch

You've got a group—three, four, five people who want to do something about globalization. Here is a model to build toward. You can't create all these pieces at the start, but as you grow, add pieces to this organizing spiral. It will help you attract more people and hold onto them because they are growing politically and becoming more effective.

The Organizing Spiral

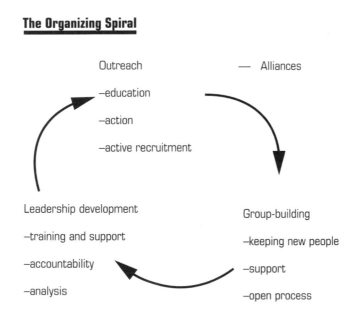

Outreach — Alliances
–education
–action
–active recruitment

Leadership development
–training and support
–accountability
–analysis

Group-building
–keeping new people
–support
–open process

The Outreach Phase: Education

Education is essential because it builds a base of support for your work. Most students on campus and most people in your community will never join your sit-in, but it makes a big difference whether they support you or whether they think you're jerks. One of our movement's greatest strengths is that two-thirds of the people in the United States think there shouldn't be any new trade agreements unless they respect worker rights and the environment. That puts limits on what the government and corporations can do and how they can do it. It also gives us a starting point to build from.

Our two-thirds support didn't magically appear. It came from a decade of education that led to Seattle. Much of that education, in turn, came out of the campaign against NAFTA in the early 1990s. The moral: Education and action form a small spiral within the larger organizing spiral. You bring people the information, help them discover what the issues are, ask them to take action, gain visibility, and once you have visibility more people will want to be educated. So:

- Well before an action, hold a teach-in that says to your community, "There is a problem, here's who caused it, and here's what we need to do about it." At the teach-in, recruit intensively: Get everyone's name on a clipboard when they walk in, actually talk to people and mark the most interested names, make a pitch for your action, and get the names of the people who raise their hands (or better, pull them together immediately to start planning and bonding).

- Hold smaller teach-outs in house parties, congregations, libraries, union halls, or dorms. Look at the Popular Education section for some effective workshops which you can adapt.

- Educate your own group on more advanced topics—and invite the public; you can pick up new members this way.

Action

Education isn't the starting point for everybody. Action can also be the place where new people first meet your group and decide to get involved.

Since direct action training is fairly common these days, let's just say that

- action is only one point in the organizing cycle, and

- you should follow up after an action by immediately contacting the new people who showed up or expressed some sort of interest.

Active recruitment

Besides direct action and recruiting at educational events, tabling is another great way to get more members. Set up a table and ask people to sign a petition, write a letter, make a phone call, take some step that builds your action or campaign. But when people come up, don't just shove a pen at them. Talk with them. You'll find the people who are really interested, you'll make a personal connection, and you'll invite them to your next meeting—which should be about action, not just talk.

Once you have three or four new interested people, *follow up immediately.* Call them and remind them about the meeting. Set up a new members' orientation. Meet for coffee. Show that you're interested in them and take them seriously. Find out what they're interested in and talk about how that fits into your group. *Do not wait* to follow up because when people first discover you, they are at the peak of their interest. You need to take them at that high point and move them into your group. You do that by making a personal connection.

The Group-Building Phase: Keeping new people

Recognizing that newcomers are new helps you set up a system for welcoming them and making your group more equal. You can use a buddy system where existing group members pair up with new people, explain the group's culture, and help them integrate socially. You can have fifteen-minute orientations for new people at the start of your meetings. You can have a new members' brochure that explains your goals, principles, processes, phone numbers and e-mails.

If you are deliberate about bringing in new people, your group will remain open even while you are getting stronger and more unified.

Open process

Consensus decision-making has many strengths. Done well, it:

- builds unity in a group;

- includes everyone in decisions;

- builds self-confidence and stronger activists;

- builds equality; and

- gets you to "yes" without consuming all your group's time.

However, consensus can be done badly too. Like any decision-making method, it can be abused so that a few strong personalities push others around. Just calling what you are doing "consensus" or following a few rules doesn't guarantee good results. If consensus isn't working, here are some other models to try:

- Majority vote for ordinary business. This works well in a small group.

- Representative democracy for coalitions and large groups, like spokescouncils.

- Consensus for high-risk situations like people risking arrest and for small, values-based groups to use on core decisions like their mission statements.

So step back every so often and see if your decision-making process realizes the values you started with. If it doesn't, change it. Borrow from other processes, like voting or representative democracy, and see if they work better. Your decision-making process is a tool, not a religion. Approach it critically, look at other models, and put together the one that works best for your group—without obsessing on it. Pretty good is good enough. You've got things to do in the outside world.

The Leadership Development Phase: Support

This is a sensitive topic in our new movement, but leaders emerge in any group. They are the people with the skills, vision, or determination to inspire others and help them find the place to participate. We don't need a movement that lacks these people. We need a movement where all can become leaders in their own particular ways.

The key is support. Everyone in your group should have the support to become an exciting speaker, creative performer, stunning analyst, or a detail-oriented event organizer.

Few of us grow alone. It's scary going out on a new limb. One of your group's jobs is to recognize when someone is ready to do it. That means:

- an open culture and process;

- skills-sharing within the group; and

- going outside the group for skills and training you can't provide.

It is good to provide these in a systematic way and not just wait for unskilled people to ask. (By asking, they risk looking stupid.) When you are doing an action or a new project, identify the skills it will require and set up a training for everybody in the group.

Accountability, aka getting things done

"We'll all do it" means "nobody will remember to do it." If you are personally responsible, you're likelier to remember to do it, and so is everyone else. Here is one model called Collective Leadership with Individual Responsibility. That means:

- *Everyone makes decisions together.* You meet to plan a new project; everyone shapes it and sets the goals.

- *You identify exactly who will carry out each piece of the plan.* Don't walk out of the room until you have divided up the work and you know who is doing each piece.

- *You provide the support people need to do their tasks.* Look around and see if you will need a training in fundraising, tabling, or running meetings. Pair new people with more experienced activists. Don't yell at the people who didn't carry out their task; identify the support they need to do their job and figure out how to get it to them.

- *There is a coordinator.* Someone in the group regularly calls the people who took on tasks. S/he asks how they are doing, in detail. If tasks aren't getting done, s/he helps them develop a plan for getting them done on time. S/he looks for places where they need support and makes sure they get it.

- *There is regular, collective evaluation.* Every so often, or at the end of a project, the whole group reviews what did and didn't get done. The group holds people accountable but it supports them at every step; it learns from mistakes.

Try this method and watch people grow. For more details, see the CISPES organizing guide listed below.

Analysis

Unity is essential for a group to last. What unites you? Among other things, a common analysis of what's wrong, who's responsible, and what it will take to change it. Analysis will help you:

- describe what you're fighting and figure out how to fight it intelligently.

- see who else is fighting it and thus find strong allies. (They're not just anybody, they're the people who recognize the same enemy.)

- become more articulate in speaking about your political work and more critical in thinking about it.

- build unity in your group that is based on principles, not just friendships or the sense of a movement.

- choose what your group will work on and what it won't.

Where do you get analysis? By reading, discussing, and going to hear people who sound as if they've figured it out. You can make it a group project where different people check out analyses from different sources, come back together, compare notes, and see what *you* think. One thing our movement does have is plenty of analysis. However, you may have to look to find people who integrate race and gender into their analysis of the global economy.

An Ambitious Step: Building alliances

As strong as your group is, it won't win alone if you are going up against big adversaries like the government and transnational corporations.

You probably want to build up your group before you start looking for allies. Alliance-building is a long process of building trust and working relationships with people who may be very different from you in class, race, culture, and worldview. Before you take that on, know who you (as a group) are. Then you can figure out what you have in common with potential allies.

Though it's a long process, it starts with a human step: go talk to someone. Meet with a few contacts or leaders in the group you are approaching. Tell them what you are organizing, ask what they are doing, and see if there is a good reason to work together. Don't expect them to get on board your project just because you are on the right side or doing the right thing. Think about supporting what they are doing—their picket line, their letter-writing campaign for affordable housing. Think about what you could add to that, and ask them if they want you to do it. Follow their lead.

Why spend so much time building up a group?

There's a myth in this country, and it separates us from our strength. The myth is: to win, you have to have the majority actively with you. The winner is the one who gets more than fifty percent of the vote.

Call us for organizing advice!

Jia Ching Chen, National Network Organizer
JustAct: Youth ACTion for Global JUSTice
333 Valencia Street, Suite 101, San Francisco, CA 94103
(415)431-4204 x208
www.justact.org.
Jia Ching is an organizer with JustAct: Youth ACTion for Global JUSTice. He has experience organizing direct actions around the country and working with the youth movement in the San Francisco Bay Area to fight police brutality and the prison industrial complex.

Antonia Juhasz, Program Director
International Forum on Globalization
Building 1062, Fort Cronkhite, Sausalito, CA 94965
(415)229-9357
Antonia has worked for many years to educate the public on how international trade and investment agreements affect such local concerns as environment, women's issues, small business, and labor. She is very skilled at breaking down globalization initiatives, such as the MAI, World Trade Organization, World Bank and IMF, into issues that everyday people understand and can organize around. Antonia is now directing programs at the International Forum on Globalization related to international trade and finance.

Robert Naiman, Senior Policy Analyst
Center for Economic and Policy Research
1015 18th Street NW, Suite 200
Washington, D.C. 20036
(202)293-5380 x212
naiman@cepr.net www.cepr.net.
Bob can answer questions about the International Monetary Fund, World Bank, World Bank bonds, World Trade Organization, NAFTA, Trade and Labor Rights, Globalization and Economic Growth.

Rachel Neumann, New York City, rachelbeatrice@yahoo.com.
Rachel has been involved in activist politics for twenty
years, building alliances among young people across cultural, racial, and economic differences. She trains people
in creative action planning and decision-making, community
building, antioppression work, nonviolence, and legal support. Currently, Rachel is working both nationally and
locally to strengthen and reveal the connections between
struggles for justice at the local, national, and international levels. She has worked with the New York City Direct
Action Network, New York City Chiapas Coalition, Reclaim
the Streets, the New York People's Law Collective, Student
Liberation Action Movement, and Teachers & Writers.

Mike Prokosch, United for a Fair Economy
37 Temple Place, Boston, MA 02111
(617)423-2148 x24
mprokosch@ufenet.org www.ufenet.org
Mike learned to organize with CISPES, the Committee in Solidarity with the People of El Salvador. He can help solve
organizational problems and think through campaigns that
will help build local organization. He also develops participatory education workshops like "Globalization for Beginners" and "FTAA for Beginners" and trains workshop leaders.

Larry Weiss, Resource Center of the Americas
3019 Minnehaha Avenue, Minneapolis, MN 55406
(612)276-0788 x19
www.americas.org
Larry's experience is in developing local coalitions between
labor and other social justice sectors that focus on the various aspects of corporate globalization (maquilas/sweat-
shops, structural adjustment, trade agreements), and in
connecting national and international networks and campaigns.

See **www.globalroots.net** for articles on building a local-
global movement.

This is *not* how social change happens. During the 1960s, most Americans never sat in at lunch counters or marched against the Vietnam War. But the civil rights and antiwar movements abolished legal segregation and stopped U.S. military intervention overseas for fifteen years. Social scientists say that sucessful movements tend to have about two percent of the population active and a majority passive supporters.

Who are the two percent? Determined people like you. What they have are strong groups that provide

- analysis

- skills

- support

- education to the people around them

- organization of actions that reached out for more support

- active recruitment

- alliance building

You don't have to do all this

Start with the steps that seem most useful to you, and use this model as a template. Set it against what you are doing every so often (when you are doing evaluations every quarter or half year) and see if it identifies a missing piece which is limiting your growth.

Resources

One short handbook that walks you through this organizing spiral is "Building Solidarity, Building Committees," $5 from CISPES, P. O. Box 1801 New York, NY 10159. You can also check out the longer Organizing Guides on page 284.

Researching Global Corporations and Institutions

Whether you're organizing a short-term campaign or building a long-term movement, research is essential. It will:

- tell you who's behind specific, destructive global policies . . . and whom to pressure to change them.

- identify corporate targets for a local campaign.

- identify allies. (They're the people who are being hurt by the same corporation or policy as you!)

"But I don't know how to do research," you may say. Don't let that stop you. Many friendly organizations stand ready to help you find targets and map out campaigns. Here are a few.

Corporate Dirt Archives, www.corporations.org
Extensive information about various transnational corporations, organized by industry and issue. If you can't find what you want, see their wonderful "Researching Corporations" link that is full of advice and more links for digging up the dirt about a particular corporation.

Corporate Watch, www.corpwatch.org, (415)561-6568.
This web page is full of resources that will help you research corporate activity, plus fact sheets on the IMF, World Bank, and Structural Adjustment Programs (SAPs). Follow the link "Research Corporations" for a step-by-step guide to researching a corporation. Corporate Watch does not provide users with customized research on a particular company, industry, or issue; for that, go to "Affiliate Organizations," which lists groups that help the public with research. "Globalization and Corporate Rule" lists material on the WTO, World Bank, IMF, UN and Corporations, and Global Financial Crisis. Corporate Watch's sponsor is the Transnational Action and Research Center (TRAC).

Dirty Money, www.ewg.org/dirtymoney/
"See for yourself how money from corporations and coalitions affect environmental decision makers." Search by politician, environmental problem, company, or state.

Research for Action Web Site Library, www.igc.apc.org/datacenter /ir/websearch.html
The ImpactResearch team provides the on-call research that social justice organizations need to develop effective campaign strategies. They also provide research training and consultation to justice organizers and activists. Services are free to most no- and low-budget organizations and coalitions working on social justice, economic justice and environmental justice issues, principally in the United States. Justice organizations with resources pay for work on a sliding scale. ImpactResearch: A Program of the DataCenter, 1904 Franklin Street, Suite 900, Oakland, CA 94612, (510)835-4692, datacenter@datacenter.org

Spotlight on Corporations, www.essentialaction.org/spotlight, (202)234-9665
Essential Action's Spotlight on Corporations publishes data on corporate wrongdoing.

The Corporate Consensus: A Guide to the Institutions of Global Power
George Draffan, www.endgame.org, (541)468-2028
A 100-page guide to the institutions driving corporate globalization and governance (the WTO, Business Round Table, Trilateral Commission . . .). Analyzes how corporates acquire power and how they use it. Profiles global trade instituions with their phone numbers, addresses, next meetings, members, soft money contributions, etc. The cost is $5 including shipping, or $3 per copy for bulk orders (forty-nine or more). Checks to League of Wilderness Defenders, HCR-82, Fossil, OR 97830.

The Campaigner's Guide to Financial Markets: Effective Lobbying of Companies and Financial Institutions, cornerhouse@gn.apc.org
Nicholas Hildyard and Mark Mansley, The Corner House, UK

A 204-page guide that analyzes financial markets and their pressure points, with detailed advice for researchers and campaigners. $30 for nonprofit groups, $90 for companies and institutions, zipped PDF files (782KB) free. United States checks accepted, payable to Corner House Research, no credit cards. The Corner House, PO Box 3137, Station Road, Sturminster Newton, Dorset DT10 1YJ, UK, tel. +44 (0)1258 473795.

Long-Range Planning

These two planning methods from Deborah Barndt and Saul Eisen can help you figure out how to reach your long-term goals. They require time and focus. Planning requires reflection and full discussion; it does not work well under pressure for immediate action.

Naming the moment

The process of political analysis for action, or *naming the moment*, moves through four phases.

Phase 1—*Identifying ourselves and our interests*
Who are "we" and how do we see the world?
How has our view been shaped by our race, gender, class, age, sector, religion, etc.?
How do we define our constituency? Are we of, with, or for the people most affected by the issue(s) we work on?
What do we believe about the current structure of the United States? about what it could be? about how we get there?

Phase 2—*Naming the issues/struggles*
What current issue/struggle is most critical to the interests of our group?
What are the opposing interests (contradictions) around the issue?
What are we fighting for in working on this issue, in the short term and in the long term?
What's the history of struggle on this issue? What have been the critical moments of the past?

Phase 3—*Assessing the forces*
Who's with us and against us on this issue (in economic, political, and ideological terms)?
What are their short-term and long-term interests?
What are their expressed and their real interests?
What are the strengths and weaknesses of both sides?
What about the uncommitted?
What actors do we need more information about?

What's the overall balance of forces?
Who's winning and who's losing and why?

Phase 4—Planning for action
How have the forces shifted from the past to the present? What future shifts can we anticipate?
What free space do we have to move in?
How do we build on our strengths and address our weaknesses?
Whom should we be forming alliances with in the short term and the long term?
What actions could we take?
What are the constraints and possibilities of each?
Who will do what and when?

Naming the Moment: Political Analysis for Action by Deborah Barndt is available from the Jesuit Centre for Social Faith and Justice, 947 Queen Street E., Toronto, ON, M4M 1J9, Canada.

Force field analysis

Use this model once you have already analyzed your situation and decided on a major goal. Often that goal is very ambitious and not immediately attainable. Force field analysis can help you find useful intermediate goals which will help you move toward the major goal.

It helps to look at the forces which are helping you reach the goal, and those which are hindering or pushing in the opposite direction.

1.   It is best to work in groups of three to five people who share a common goal and work in the same situation.

2.   Ask the group to draw the following diagram on newsprint, defining briefly the *present situation* and the *major goal.* They should write one summary statement about each of these along the vertical lines.

3.   Then ask the group to list the helping forces on the left side, drawing longer or shorter arrows to indicate the strength of the forces that are pushing the present situation toward the goal. On the right-hand side, list the hindering forces which prevent change or reduce its

Helping forces ➡ **Present situation** ⬅ Hindering forces   **GOAL**

power. Again use shorter or longer arrows to indicate the strength of these forces.

4.   Explain that one can move toward the goal *either* by increasing the helping forces *or* by weakening the hindering forces. Sometimes the more pressure that comes from the helping forces, the more resistance develops in the hindering forces. In such cases, it is often best to start be reducing the hindering forces.

5.   Now ask the group to choose *either* one of the helping forces which they could strengthen *or* one of the hindering forces which they could reduce or weaken.

6.   You can take this force as the new situation and ask the group to identify its goal in regard to working with this force. Repeat the process—draw a new diagram listing the helping and hindering forces that work toward your new subgoal. This process can be repeated two or three times with clear subgoals, till you completely work out your step-by-step strategy to reach your major goal.

Time: two or more hours.
Materials: newsprint, markers, and tape.
A Problem Solving Program by Saul Eisen comes from NTL, 1201 16th Street, NW, Washington, D.C. 20036.

You Stand Up to Corporate Globalization . . .

But You're Afraid to Ask for Money?

Pam Rogers

Fundraising is organizing. When you learn to fundraise effectively, you are learning the organizer's two most basic skills: motivating people to take action and strongly asking them to do it.

Fundraising is not about getting money out of people. It is about giving them the opportunity to help change the world. Your donors aren't moneybags. They are thinking people whom you can convince to care about your cause. (If they don't, you won't get money out of them.) Don't just ask them for money. Ask them to take political action—call Congress, join a protest. Involve them in your campaigns, because that builds their personal commitment.

Let's look at a typical personal visit. It is one of the most basic organizing techniques, and it's the same whether you ask a new person to join your organization, to donate money, or both.

The personal visit

• *Get to know* your "prospect," the person who could become a donor/activist. Make friends. Find out what you have in common.

• Describe the *problem* you are confronting: a global corporate polluter, a new trade treaty in Congress, an INS crackdown on immigrants. To describe it you can lay out an analysis, tell a story about someone who's getting hurt, or describe how you got involved and why you care. Personal stories can be strongest, but use the approach that will work for the person you are talking to. Whatever approach you use, convey the *urgency* of the problem you're facing.

• Describe your *solution.* How will you stop this urgent problem? How will that solve the larger pattern of corporate domination, environmental destruction, and global injustice that we are facing?

• *Ask* for exactly what you want. Ask for a definite amount of money and say what that amount will accomplish. AND/OR ask your prospect to do one definite thing and say why.

- *Shut up.* Let the person make up his or her own mind. Maybe you will get less than what you asked for, but you don't know that till he or she answers.

- *Close the deal.* Collect the check, or arrange when you will. Promise to call the day before the protest to make sure he or she remembers and shows up.

Personal visits take time. But they pay off many times over. Once you have visited a donor (or an activist), you can call and renew their support of money or time. Having met you, donors are more likely to take your call. They can imagine your face while you're talking. The personal bond you made during your first visit will strengthen your pitch when you get to the asking for money.

People give to causes. But they also give to people. And they join organizations and become active not just when the politics click, but when the personal connections do.

Once you have signed on a new donor

- Ask again. Renew all your donors at least twice a year.

- Keep in touch. Periodically send all your donors an update.

- Give them ways to get involved. If you're holding a protest or teach-in, send a flyer and handwrite a short note so they are personally invited.

- Share your successes. When you are coming off some stellar event and you are still jazzed, call your donors and let them hear the triumph in your voice. If you're going to be on TV, call and tell them so they can tune in. If you're in the paper, photocopy the article/photo and mail it to your donors. Include a return envelope even if you don't ask for a new donation. You'll be surprised!

Everyone asks and everyone gives

If all donors are potential activists, all activists are potential donors. During your regular meetings, pass a hat for people to donate. Sure, members have donated their time, but who is going to pay for the leaflets for next Saturday or the snacks that kept the group going for another hour of great discussion?

Regular fundraising is a good idea for three reasons:

• People start to recognize that fundraising is a normal part of life, and their anxiety about fundraising drops.

• If you're going to be asking other people for money, you should give first. It gives you the right to ask. You're not asking them to do anything you haven't.

• Everyone can practice giving the pitch. The pitch explains why people should give. A good pitch appeals to both your head and your heart. It is passionate. And it's personal. If you're the one who has to give the pitch at the next meeting, think of why *you* are doing this work, and take it from there.

Everyone gives and everyone asks. The biggest mistake many movement organizations make is to charge just one person or one committee with raising the bucks. If everyone asks, everyone gets to confront a social taboo, summon up their commitment, and work through their fear. Once you go out on a limb and see it doesn't break off, you'll go further out next time. *Fundraising builds strong activists.*

Faith-based organizations have this fundraising thing down. They ask every week and they make you feel good about your gift. Copy them!

Five simple ways to raise money

• The old-fashioned bake sale or garage sale. It's a good time to spread the word about your organization's work. Set up in a place with a lot of foot traffic.

• Organize an event, such as a talent show (or a talent-less show), an open-mike poetry or stand-up comedy night. Your sister used to date the lead singer from some current cool band. Plead with her to ask if they will do a concert for you! At the event, make a pitch for the next action you are organizing, sign people up, talk to them that night, and call them before the action to get them there.

• Designate a phone bank night when everyone in your group calls everyone on your list, plus their friends, asking for a donation. Also ask them to take action.

• Organize a house party where people come and hear about your work and are asked for money collectively.

• Have your group brainstorm the most successful fundraising event each person ever attended. Decide which will work the best for your group and adapt it.

Remember: The best fundraising brings people into your group, encourages them to become part of the effort, and is fun.

Tips for asking effectively

• Be clear about the goals of your group and how you are working to reach them.

• Ask for something tangible. "Five dollars pays for x number of leaflets, $10 covers the cost of a giant puppet, and $25 buys a seat on the bus for the rally in D.C. for someone who can't afford it!"

• Have a vision. Just exactly what are you asking people to support?

• Have a budget. Determine how much money you need and let people know what it is. You can always have a bare-bones budget and a this-would-be-really-great-if-we-raise-this-much-money budget.

• Set up a bank account and keep meticulous records of what comes in and what goes out.

• Practice the pitch with your group. Practice asking for specific amounts of money.

- Remind people of all the dumb things we spend money on. The money we are raising now is for justice! Make fundraising a joyful activity. People will respond to your enthusiasm.

- *Do not be afraid of asking for big gifts.* There might be people in your group now who could write out a check to the organization for $500 or $5,000 but they don't want people to know that they have access to that kind of money or they are afraid that their relationship with the group will change. If you know people like this, you can certainly ask them for a donation and figure out with them how to guarantee their confidentiality if that is important. Or, your group may know someone in the community who could contribute large amounts. Visit them and invite them to one of your events. As they get to know the work, ask them for a gift.

Dancing with the IRS

If your organization is going to grow and hire staff, you will need to figure out some sort of incorporation. (The group will need to pay payroll taxes, etc.) Incorporating with your state is quick, easy, and cheap. But if your organization wants to receive grants from foundations and/or wants to make sure that donors can deduct their contributions from their taxes, you will need to file papers with the Internal Revenue Service to become a "charitable" group. If your group meets the requirements, it will receive a 501(c)3 tax status which will allow you to do the above.

A number of progressive social change foundations are willing to fund small groups that have not incorporated or don't have their 501(c)3 status. They can funnel the money through a larger organization that is willing to treat the smaller group like its project. This is legal and it saves you a lot of expense and hassle if you can find the right mother or father organization. Look for a medium to large progressive organization, preferably one doing similar work to your own.

Pam Rogers directs the fundraising program at United for a Fair Economy. She is the coauthor of Robin Hood Was Right, *a guide to responsible philanthropy.*

Fundraising resources

Chardon Press publishes and distributes an entire catalog of fundraising resources. www.chardonpress.com, P.O. Box 11607, Berkeley, CA 94712, (510)704-8714. Their catalog features:

Grantsmanship Center Magazine is published four times per year and is free to nonprofit organizations. P.O. Box 17220, Los Angeles, CA 90017, (213)482-9860.

Kim Klein, *Fundraising for Social Change.* Learn about asking for money, personal solicitation, researching prospects for large gifts, direct mail fundraising, fundraising by telephone, special events, and more.

Kim Klein, ed., *The Grassroots Fundraising Journal.* Published six times a year, it includes timely articles on a range of fundraising topics.

RESIST's "Finding Funding: A Beginner's Guide to Foundation Research" is available in print or on their web page. www.resistinc.org, 259 Elm Street, Suite 201, Somerville, MA 02144-2950, (617)623-5110, resistinc@igc.apc.org

Andy Robinson, *Grassroots Grants.* This book focuses on proposal writing and foundation grantseeking.

Mal Warwick, *How to Write Successful Fundraising Letters,* Strathmoor Press, 2550 Ninth Street, Suite 103, Berkeley, CA 94710-2516, (800)388-3348.

Encountering and Countering Political Repression

Chip Berlet

The protests in Washington and Philadelphia in April and August 2000 were a shock for many activists. Police illegally raided convergence centers and destroyed puppets—and got away with it. They beat, teargassed, and illegally detained hundreds of nonviolent protesters. Government security forces monitored organizers before the demonstrations, released false information to the media, and framed protesters for crimes they didn't commit. This article tells you what to do about it.

When you're trying to wash the tear gas out of your eyes with a bottle of spring water, it's the wrong time to learn about political repression. So reading this section now has a practical value.

Surveillance, infiltration, harassment, media demonization, disruption, police misconduct, excessive use of force, and other repressive techniques have been used to stifle dissent in the United States since it was founded. Repression appears whenever social and political movements threaten the status quo and challenge the unequal distribution of power and wealth. Every progressive movement has faced political repression, and every progressive movement has—and will—sweep it aside. The sooner activists learn the basics, the faster political repression can be successfully countered.

Brian Glick has outlined the four main repressive techniques used during the FBI's illegal Counterintelligence Program (COINTELPRO): Infiltration, Psychological Warfare from the Outside, Harassment Through the Legal System, and Extralegal Force and Violence. After activists exposed COINTELPRO and it was terminated, many of the surveillance and disruption activities previously employed by the FBI were shifted into a network of right-wing "countersubversive" institutions and groups in the private sector.

> If there is no struggle, there is no progress. . . .
> Those who profess to favor freedom, and yet depreciate
> agitation . . . want crops without plowing up the
> ground. They want rain without thunder and lightning,
> they want the ocean without the awful roar of its many
> waters. . . . Power concedes nothing without a demand.
> It never did—and it never will. . . . The limits of
> tyrants are prescribed by the endurance of those whom
> they oppress.
>
> —Frederick Douglass (1857)

Ross Gelbspan showed how clandestine right-wing groups coordinated attacks on the movement against U.S. intervention in Central America while law enforcement and intelligence agencies looked the other way.

At the same time the FBI and other public law enforcement agencies sought to regain authority for spying on dissent by reframing it as leading to criminal activity or as a cover for terrorist violence. In Philadelphia the public and private countersubversion networks worked together. The search warrant used to justify a police raid on the headquarters for the protestors planning demonstrations against the Republican Party convention in the summer of 2000 included false allegations from the Maldon Institute, part of a right-wing intelligence network dating back to the 1960s. (For more on Maldon, see: http://www.publiceye.org/liberty/Maldon.htm.)

Demonstrations

Most activists will face political repression in the streets in the form of police using excessive force such as kicking and beating demonstrators, indiscriminate and dangerous use of tear gas, mass arrests, and roughing up those arrested. Street Law 101 starts with the idea that it is pointless to argue constitutional rights with someone about to hit you with a heavy wooden baton. The National Lawyers Guild has written several guides on the law and exercising your rights of political protest. Read these guides before taking to the streets. (See http://www.publiceye.org/liberty/Security_for_Activists.htm)

> The four main techniques of political repression used during the 1960s and 1970s
> by Brian Glick, author, **The War at Home** [excerpt used by permission of author]
>
> 1. **Infiltration**: Agents and informers did not merely spy on political activists. Their main purpose was to discredit and disrupt. Their very presence served to undermine trust and scare off potential supporters. The FBI and police exploited this fear to smear genuine activists as agents.
>
> 2. **Psychological warfare from the outside**: The FBI and police used myriad other dirty tricks to undermine progressive movements. They planted false media stories and published bogus leaflets and other publications in the name of targeted groups. They forged correspondence, sent anonymous letters, and made anonymous telephone calls. They spread misinformation about meetings and events, set up pseudo movement groups run by government agents, and manipulated or strong-armed parents, employers, landlords, school officials, and others to cause trouble for activists.

Arrests

Legal repression can include indiscriminate arrests, bogus charges, high bails, long detention before arraignment, abuse in jail, and punitive sentencing. Take these factors seriously in making your plans.

Choose your leaders wisely and democratically, and then defend and protect them. Train others to step forward if leaders are arrested, and arrange beforehand for legal support for all those who are detained.

Be aware that some people, especially those with family caretaking responsibility or medical issues, need to avoid arrest. Find ways for

3. **Harassment through the legal system**: The FBI and police abused the legal system to harass dissidents and make them appear to be criminals. Officers of the law gave perjured testimony and presented fabricated evidence as a pretext for false arrests and wrongful imprisonment. They discriminatorily enforced tax laws and other government regulations and used conspicuous surveillance, "investigative" interviews, and grand jury subpoenas in an effort to intimidate activists and silence their supporters.

4. **Extralegal force and violence**: The FBI and police threatened, instigated, and themselves conducted break-ins, vandalism, assaults, and beatings. The object was to frighten dissidents and disrupt their movements. In the case of radical Black and Puerto Rican activists (and later Native Americans), these attacks—including political assassinations—were so extensive, vicious, and calculated that they can accurately be termed a form of official "terrorism."

Copyright 2000 Brian Glick. A longer overview is at http://www.publiceye.org/liberty/War_at_Home/Glick_Overview.html.

them to participate in your demonstrations with a reduced level of risk. Hand out poems and song sheets to those who plan to engage in nonviolent civil disobedience, and sing in jail to keep spirits high.

Divide and Conquer

Don't let your critics or establishment figures divide your coalition by targeting people or groups with unpopular ideas. The following familiar refrain is old and tired: "If only your group didn't include (fill in the blank: anarchists, communists, feminists, gays and lesbians, vegans, witches, atheists) you would be more effective." Baloney. It's a

Washington D.C., February 2000. © *Diane Greene Lent*

trick. Allow one slice and the blade of division keeps cutting. Set your group's principles of unity in a democratic fashion, and then welcome as participants all who abide by those rules.

Disruptive Behavior

It really doesn't matter why someone becomes disruptive or acts like a provocateur, the point is that every group has a right to establish principles of unity that include acceptable limits on behavior. If your group is devoted to nonviolence, then a person who continuously suggests trashing store windows probably is in the wrong group. Spend time struggling with them over the principles your group has established. If they are still unwilling to change their behavior, ask them to leave. Don't agent-bait people who are disruptive or who act suspiciously. Scurrilous rumors weaken a group's sense of trust and loyalty. Deal with behavior, not intent—because intent is often not easy to ascertain.

Paranoia

OK, sometimes they *are* out to get you. Obsessing over the details is

Common Sense Security

Sheila O'Donnell

As our movements have become stronger and more sophisticated, the techniques of the state, corporations, and right-wing groups have also become more sophisticated. We have seen government agents, corporate security, and right-wing intelligence networks share information as well as an ideology.

Caution and common sense security measures in the face of the concerted efforts to stop us are therefore both prudent and necessary.

Spend a few minutes to assess your work from a security point of view: understand your vulnerabilities; assess your allies and your adversaries as objectively as possible; do not underestimate the opposition. Try to assess your organizational and personal strengths and weaknesses. Do not take chances. Plan for the worst; work and hope for the best.

Trust your instincts and resist when possible. One of the biggest blocks to resistance is the failure to recognize that we are under attack. None of this advice is intended to frighten but to create an awareness of the problems. Knowledge of the strategies and tactics of your adversaries will strengthen your movement.

Cover yourself; it's a tough world out there.

Web advice for common sense security:

http://www.publiceye.org/liberty/Security_for_
Activists.htm

pointless. Repression happens. Take reasonable precautions and move on. Don't let bogus experts divert you from your goals with scary talk about wiretaps and infiltrators. This is a form of self-aggrandizing, disruptive behavior. Clicks, buzzing, and electrical fluctuations on a phone line are symptoms of either bad phone service or a bug, and the most experienced and honest experts with thousands of dollars worth of equipment will tell you they can't really tell the difference unless they physically find a bug. (For more information, see http://www.publiceye.org/liberty/Whatbugs.html.)

Bottom line

The goal of political repression is to stop you from being an effective activist. By educating yourself and working in a team with others as part of a larger movement, you can overcome these schemes to protect power, privilege, and preserve the status quo.

Chip Berlet, senior analyst at Political Research Associates, worked as a political organizer from 1967 to 1987 with civil rights, anti-Vietnam War, labor union, antifascist, and other groups. He specialized in demonstration and rally logistics, media, and security. He has written extensively on political repression, worked as a paralegal on lawsuits against government intelligence abuse, and was a cofounder of Police Misconduct and Civil Rights Law Report.

Further Reading

Churchill, Ward, and Jim Vander Wall. *Agents of Repression: The FBI's Secret Wars Against the Black Panther Party and the American Indian Movement.* Cambridge, MA: South End Press, 1988.

Churchill, Ward, and Jim Vander Wall. *COINTELPRO Papers: Documents from the FBI's Secret Wars Against Dissent in the United States.* Cambridge, MA: South End Press, 1989.

Donner, Frank. *The Age of Surveillance: The Aims & Methods of America's Political Intelligence System.* New York: Alfred Knopf, 1980.

Donner, Frank. *Protectors of Privilege: Red Squads and Political Repression in Urban America,* Berkeley, CA: University of California, 1991.

Feldman, Jonathan. *Universities in the Business of Repression: The Acad-*

emic-Military-Industrial Complex and Central America. Cambridge, MA: South End Press, 1989.

Gelbspan, Ross. *Break-Ins, Death Threats and the FBI: The Covert War Against the Central America Movement.* Cambridge, MA: South End Press, 1991.

Glick, Brian. *The War at Home: Covert Action Against U.S. Activists and What We Can Do About It.* Cambridge, MA: South End Press, 1989.

Herman, Edward, and Gerry O'Sullivan. *The Terrorism Industry: The Experts and Institutions That Shape View of Terror.* New York: Pantheon, 1990.

Karp, Walter. *Liberty Under Siege: American Politics 1976–1988.* New York: Henry Holt & Co, 1988.

Keller, William W. *The Liberals and J. Edgar Hoover.* Princeton, NJ:Princeton University Press, 1989.

Marx, Gary T. *Under Cover: Police Surveillance in America.* Berkeley, CA: Twentieth Century Fund/University of California Press, 1988.

Schultz, Bud, and Ruth Schultz. *It Did Happen Here: Recollections of Political Repression in America.* Berkeley, CA: University of California Press, 1989.

Waging War on Dissent, a report by the Seattle National Lawyers Guild and WTO Legal, www.seattle.indymedia.org.

After the Haymarket bomb explosion in 1884, urban police expanded their surveillance over the street life of the poor, who had once enjoyed remarkably free use of public spaces. To be able to use what had once been open to them, lower-class men found themselves increasingly at odds with the law and also found it more difficult to make political statements in public.

—Robert W. Wiebe, *Self-Rule: A Cultural History of American Democracy.* (Chicago, 1995), 136–137, as quoted in James Green, *Taking History to Heart* (Amherst, 2000), 106.

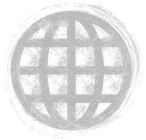

A Movement
Yellow Pages

Applied Research Center publishes reports on institutional racism and racial justice organizing including "Eracisms," a profile of several antiracist organizations. Their magazine *ColorLines* documents organizing and activism that is antiracist and radical, based primarily in communities of color. www.arc.org, (510)653-3415, 4096 Piedmont Avenue, PMB 319, Oakland, CA 94611-5221, colorlines@arc.org.

Institute for MultiRacial Justice publishes *Shades of Power,* an excellent antiracist organizing magazine. www.arc.org/C_Lines/ArcColorlines.html, 3311 Mission Street #170, San Francisco, CA 94110, i4mrj@aol.com

Center for Third World Organizing trains people of color in community organizing. www.ctwo.org, 1218 E. 21st Street, Oakland, CA 94606, (510) 533-7583, ctwo@ctwo.org

Challenging White Supremacy Workshop focuses on building an antiracist movement against global capitalism. 2440 16th Street, PMB 25, San Francisco, CA 94103, (415)647-0921, cws@igc.org.

Colours of Resistance is a grassroots network developing multiracial, antiracist politics in the movement against global capitalism. It produces a magazine, a website, and published articles, shares ideas through an e-mail discussion list, and facilitates workshops and events. www.tao.ca/~colours, c/o Shakti Women of Colour Collective, QPIRG at McGill, 3647 University Street, 3rd Floor, Montréal, QC, H3A 2B3, Canada, colours@tao.ca.

People's Institute for Survival and Beyond is an antiracist training center based in New Orleans that does trainings all over the country. http://eric-web.tc.columbia.edu/directories/anti-bias/pisb.html, 1444 N Johnson Street, New Orleans, LA 70116-1767, (504)944-2354.

Planting Seeds Community Awareness Project has an extensive list of antiracist resources as well as antiracist workshops. http://www.tao.ca/~plantingseeds, PO Box 33368, Austin, TX 78764, (512)326-5632, plantingseeds@tao.ca

Books on Race and Gender
Aguilar-San Juan, Karin, ed. *The State of Asian America: Activism and Resistance in the 1990s.* Cambridge, MA: South End Press, 1994.
Allen, Robert *Reluctant Reformers: Racism and Social Reform Movements in the United States.* Washington, D.C.: Howard University Press, 1974.
Jaimes, M. Annette, ed. *The State of Native America: Genocide, Colonization, and Resistance.* Cambridge, MA: South End Press, 1992.
Martinez, Elizabeth 'Betita'. *De Colores Means All Of Us: Latina Views for a Multi-Colored Century.* Cambridge, MA: South End Press, 1998.
Mies, Maria. *Patriarchy and Accumulation on a World Scale: Women in the International Division of Labor.* New York: Zed Books, 1986.
Naples, Nancy, ed. *Community Activism and Feminist Politics: Organizing Across Race, Class and Gender.* New York: Routledge, 1998.
Payne, Charles M. *I've Got the Light of Freedom: The Organizing Tradition and the Mississippi Freedom Struggle.* Berkeley, CA: University of California Press, 1995.
Potts, Lydia. *The World Labour Market: A History of Migration.* New York: Zed Books, 1990.
Salomon, Larry R. *Roots of Justice: Stories of Organizing in Communities of Color.* Chardon Press, 1998.
Roediger, David R., ed. *Black on White: Black Writers on What it Means to Be White.* New York: Schocken Books, 1998.

Challenging Corporate Authority
These organizations' primary mission is to challenge corporate authority and corporate privilege, and reclaim democracy from corporate persons, rather than focusing on particular corporate harms or industries. For a look at their strategies see "Paradigm Shift," p. 173.

180/MDE (180/Movement for Democracy and Education), http://corporations.org/democracy, Madison, WI, (608)262-9036, clearinghouse@tao.ca.**Alliance for Democracy**, www.afd-online.org, Waltham, MA, (781)894-1179, peoplesall@aol.com.

Citizens Council on Corporate Issues, www.corporateissues.org, c/o Gil Yaron, Vancouver, BC, Canada, (604)734-1815, ccci@corporateissues.org.

Democracy Unlimited of Humboldt County, www.monitor.net/ democracyunlimited, c/o Paul Cienfuegos, Arcata, CA, (707)822-2242, cienfuegos@igc.org.

POCLAD (Program on Corporations, Law and Democracy), www.poclad.org, c/o Mary Zepernick, South Yarmouth, MA, (508)398-1145, people@poclad.org.

Polaris Institute, www.polarisinstitute.org, c/o Tony Clarke, Ottawa, Ontario, Canada, (613)746-8374, tclarke@web.net.

Reclaim Democracy! www.reclaimdemocracy.org, Boulder, CO, (303)402-0105, info@reclaimdemocracy.org.

Workgroup on Citizen Authority (of the Jeannette Rankin Peace Center), www.jrpc.org, c/o Dean Ritz, 519 So. Higgins, Missoula, MT 59801, (406)543-3955, democracy@jrpc.org.

Climate Change

The Heat Is On, a book that nails transnational oil and coal corporations for changing the world's climate, has a website, www.heatisonline.org, with a comprehensive directory of science sites, political action organizations, and technical solutions groups.

Greenpeace targets corporations and governments for their refusal to cut fossil fuel use and greenhouse gas emissions. www.greenpeaceusa.org, 702 H Street NW, Washington, D.C. 20001, (800)326-0959.

Public Interest Research Groups advocate clean power, clean air, clean cars, and clean energy as the solutions to global warming. Contact your state PIRG through http://pirg.org/index.html, U.S. PIRG, 218 D Street, SE, Washington, D.C. 20003, (202)546-9707, uspirg@pirg.org.

Union of Concerned Scientists is an excellent source of scientific information on global warming. www.ucsusa.org, 2 Brattle Square, Cambridge, MA 02238, (617)547-5552, ucs@ucsusa.org.

See also Sierra Club.

Creative Action

The Activist Cookbook. $17 +s/h from United for a Fair Economy, www.ufenet.org, 37 Temple Place, Boston, MA 02124, (617)423-2148, info@ufenet.org.

68 Ways to Make Really Big Puppets by Puppeteers' Coop. $4 from Bread and Puppets' Catalogue, 753 Old Heights Road, Glover, VT 05839.

Drums and Demonstrations. $4 from Super Sonic Samba School, http://ssss.console.net, 3345 Gregory Street, San Diego, CA 92104, (619)281-1066.

Puppet Cookbook. $25 from In the Heart of the Beast, 1500 East Lake Street, Minneapolis, MN 55407, (612)721-2535.

Wise Fool Basics. $10–15 from Wise Fool, www.zeitgeist.net/wfca/wise-fool.htm, 2633 Etna Street, Berkeley, CA 94704, 415-905-5958.

Cross-Border Organizing

The **UE-FAT Strategic Organizing Alliance** supports democratic, independent unions in Mexico. United Electrical Workers, http://www.igc.apc.org/unitedelect/#, One Gateway Center, Suite 1400, Pittsburgh, PA 15222-1416, (412)471-8919, ueintl@igc.apc.org.

American Friends Service Committee's Mexico-U.S. Border Program, and its Immigration Program, issue reports and organize on both sides of the border with offices from Texas to the Pacific Ocean. www.afsc.org, 1501 Cherry Street, Philadelphia, PA 19102, (215)241-7000, afscinfo@afsc.org.

Coalition for Justice in the Maquiladoras is a trinational coalition pressuring corporations for safe workplaces, a safe environment, and a fair standard of living in the assembly industry. http://enchantedwebsites.com/maquiladora/cjm.html, 3120 West Ashby, San Antonio, TX 78228, (210)732-8957.

Cross Border Links collects contact info for organizations in the United States, Mexico, and Canada that work on cross-border issues. www.irc-online.org/cbl/.

Democratic Economy

Center for a New American Dream: "More fun, less stuff!" Cut consumption in our lives. www.newdream.org, 6930 Carroll Avenue Suite 900, Takoma Park, MD 20912, (877)68 DREAM, newdream@newdream.org

Communities by Choice is a virtual community of people who want to see their communities develop sustainably, with resources to help people make sustainable decisions. www.CommunitiesbyChoice.org.

Equal Exchange is a worker-owned co-op offering consumers gourmet coffee direct from farmer co-ops using sustainable methods in Latin America, Africa, and Asia. www.equalexchange.com, 251 Revere Street, Canton, MA 02021, (781)830-0303, info@equalexchange.com.

Ithaca Hours circulates local currency which stays in the community and builds an accountable economy. www.ithacahours.org, HOUR Town, Box 6578, Ithaca, NY 14851, (607)272-4330, hours@lightlink.com.

Rural Coalition is an cross-border alliance of over ninety community-based groups in the United States and Mexico who share skills, strategies, and resources. Among many other projects, they set up a web-based super-market so food co-ops can purchase directly from agricultural co-ops. www.farmworkers.org, 1411 K Street NW, Suite 901, Washington, D.C. 20005, (202)628-7160, ruralco@ruralco.org.

Development Advocacy

The Development Group for Alternative Policies (DGAP) works with citizens' organizations overseas to ensure that their priorities inform decisions made in the North. www.developmentgap.org, 927 15th Street NW, 4th Floor, Washington, D.C. 20005, (202)898-1566, dgap@developmentgap.org.

Grassroots International provides funding, education, and political sup-port to its progressive partners in Africa, the Middle East, Latin America, and the Caribbean. www.grassrootsonline.org, 179 Boylston Street 4th Floor, Boston, MA 02130-4520, (617)524-1400.

Oxfam America works with with poor communities around the world to solve hunger, poverty, and social injustice. www.oxfamamerica.org, 26 West Street, Boston, MA 02111-1206, (800)77-OXFAM, info@oxfamamerica.org.

Direct Action

Direct Action Network has DANs around the country and a national coordinating spokescouncil called Continental DAN. www.directaction-network.org.

Donnelly/Colt Graphix is a source for every left-wing bumper sticker, poster, or mug as well as the *Handbook for Nonviolent Action*. Box 188, Hampton, CT 06247, (860)455-9621.

Peoples Global Action is a worldwide network of direct-democracy, anti-authoritarian groups including some of the world's largest mass movements. **PGA/North America** can be reached through the Tampa Bay Action Group, (727)896-TBAG, oneworldnow@att.net, or the Anti-Capitalist Convergence, (514)526-8946, clac@tao.ca.

Ruckus Society trains environmental and human rights activists in nonviolent civil disobedience skills, often in training camps before major direct actions. Their website contains excellent manuals for planning direct actions, working with the media, making and hanging banners, and more. www.ruckus.org, 2180A Dwight Way, Berkeley, CA 94704, (510)848-9565.

Training for Change is a strategy and training center for nonviolent direct action. Check out George Lakey's article, "Mass Action Since Seattle: 7 Ways to Make Our Protests More Powerful." www.trainingfor-change.org, 4719 Springfield Avenue, Philadelphia, PA 19143-3514, (215)729-7458, peacelearn@igc.org.

War Resisters League leads nonviolent trainings and publishes the standard text, *Handbook for Nonviolent Action*. 339 Lafayette Street, NY, NY 10012, (212)228-0450, wrl@igc.org.

Environment

ACERCA supports indigenous peoples and environments in southern Mexico and Central America, using those as a lens on the global economy. www.acerca.org, P.O. Box 57, Burlington, VT 05402, (802)863-0571, acerca@sover.net.

Earth First! uses direct action against corporate power that exploits the environment. Order their journal or *Ecodefense: A Guide to Monkeywrenching* by writing to Earth First! Journal, P.O. Box 1415, Eugene, OR 97440.

Friends of the Earth documents and opposes environmental destruction by transnational corporations, the World Bank, and IMF. They advocate the "democratic reform of international trade institutions." www.foe.org/internatinal, 1025 Vermont Avenue NW, Washington, D.C. 20005, (877)843-8687, foe@foe.org.

International Rivers Network shows how global finance (especially the World Bank) is affecting water and aquatic ecosystems, and campaigns against the Bank and private commercial banks that promote inappropriate river development projects. (510)848-1155, irn@irn.org.

LightHawk uses small aircraft to expose the destruction of watersheds, deserts, rivers, and forests by industrial-scale timber cutting, off-road vehicle use and road building, and mining in North and Central America. www.lighthawk.org, P.O. Box 29231, San Francisco, CA 94129, sfo@lighthawk.org.

Native Forest Network. See ACERCA (above) for eastern North America office. For western North America, P.O. Box 8251, Missoula, MT, (406)542-7343, nfn@wildrockies.org.

Project Underground exposes environmental and human rights abuses committed by the mining and oil industries, and supports communities opposing them. www.moles.org, 1916A MLK Jr. Way, Berkeley, CA 94704, (510)705-8981, project_underground@moles.org.

Rainforest Action Network protects tropical rainforests and the human rights of those living in and around those forests. www.ran.org, 221 Pine Street Suite 500, San Francisco, CA 94104, (415)398-4404, rainforest@ran.org. To get involved in RAN's Citigroup campaign contact Ilyse Hogue (ihogue@ran.org), Patrick Reinsborough (organize@ran.org) or Beka Economopolous (beka@ran.org), or call (800)989-7246.

Silicon Valley Toxics Coalition works to improve the environmental health and safety practices of the electronics industry in California and the Asia-Pacific Basin. www.svtc.org, 760 N. First Street, San Jose, CA 95112, (408)287-6707, svtc@svtc.org.

Sierra Club's Responsible Trade Campaign opposes anti-environmental trade treaties and institutions like the WTO and FTAA. www.sierraclub.org, 408 C Street NE, Washington, D.C. 20002, (202)547-1141, dan.seligman@sierraclub.org.

The Video Project distributes environmental videos about the fate of our planet. www.videoproject.net, (800)475-2638, video@videoproject.net. *See also Greenpeace, Student Environmental Action Coalition, Sierra Student Coalition*

Environmental Justice

Environmental Justice Fund is a national membership organization that helps build the capacity of its member groups by expanding their funding and enhancing programs. 310 8th Street, Suite 100, Oakland, CA 94607, (510)267-1881, ejfund@ejfund.org.

Economic Environmental Justice Project Deepak Pateriya, dpateriya@igc.org, 1715 W Florence Avenue, 2d floor, Los Angeles, CA 90047.

South African Exchange Program for Environmental Justice focuses on the effects of toxics and the deteriorating environment in South Africa, and bridges communities in the United States with their counterparts in South Africa around environmental justice. www.saepej.org, 555 Amory Street, Boston, MA 02130, (617)522-0604, rdixit@mindspring.com .

Southwest Network on Environmental and Economic Justice seeks binational, grassroots solutions to environmental problems on both sides of the U.S.-Mexico border. www.irc-online.org/cbl/fairtrade/ na/sneej.html, 117 Seventh Street NW, Albuquerque, NM 87102, (505)242-0416.

Indigenous Environmental Network protects Mother Earth and indigenous rights from contamination and exploitation by strengthing respect for traditional teachings and natural laws www.ienearth.org, P.O. Box 485, Bemidji, MN 56601, (218)751-4967, ien@igc.org.

Farming, Food, and Health
CATA, El Comité de Apoyo a los Trabajadores Agrícolas, helps organize farmworkers in Pennsylvania, New Jersey, and Puerto Rico to improve their living and working conditions. P.O. Box 510, Glassboro, NJ 08028, (856)881-2507, catanc@aol.com.

Corporate Agriculture Research Project and its weekly e-mail magazine, *The Agribusiness Examiner*, monitor corporate agribusiness and supports alternative, democratically controlled food systems. www.ea1.com/CARP/, P.O. Box 2201, Everett, WA 98203-0201, (425)258-5345, avkrebs@earthlink.net.

Farm Labor Organizing Committee is a union of midwestern farmworkers based in Ohio. www.iupui.edu/~floc/, 1221 Broadway Street, Toledo, OH 43609, (419)243-3456.

INFACT, best known for its groundbreaking Nestlé and GE boycott campaigns, is taking on the global tobacco industry. www.infact.org, 46 Plympton Street, Boston, MA 02118, (617)695-2525.

Institute for Food and Development Policy/Food First highlights root causes and value-based solutions to hunger and poverty around the world, with a commitment to establishing food as a fundamental human right. www.foodfirst.org, 398 60th Street, Oakland, CA 94618, (510)564-4400 foodfirst@foodfirst.org.

Institute for Agriculture and Trade Policy builds international networks of farmers and consumers for a sustainable world agriculture and trade policy. www.iatp.org, 2105 1st Avenue South, Minneapolis, MN 55404, (612)870-0453, info@iatp.org.

National Family Farm Coalition brings together farmers and others from thirty-three states to strengthen and preserve family farms. www.nffc.net, 110 Maryland Avenue NE, Suite 307, Washington, D.C. 20002, (202)543-5675, nffc@nffc.net.

National Farmers' Union is a general farm organization with a membership of nearly three hundred thousand farm and ranch families throughout the United States. www.nfu.org.

Pesticide Action Network North America links a hundred organizations and thousands of individuals to replace pesticides with ecologically sound alternatives. www.panna.org, 49 Powell Street, Suite 500, San Francisco, CA 94102, panna@panna.org.

Books on food and farming
Boucher, Douglas M., ed. *Hunger in a Bountiful World.* Oakland, CA: Food First Books, 1999.

Henderson, Elizabeth and Robyn Van En. *Sharing the Harvest: Community Supported Agriculture in America.* March 1998. Currently back ordered with Fedco Seed Catalog, P.O. Box 520, Waterville, ME 04903-0520. How-to manual, examples of successes, historical background, chapter on "CSA in the global supermarket."

Lappe, Frances Moore, Joseph Collins, and Peter Rosset., *World Hunger: Twelve Myths.* New York: Grove Press, 1998.

Morris, David. *Hogging the Market.* Minneapolis, MN: Institute for Local Self-Reliance, 1999, www.inmotionmagazine.com/hogging.html.

Shiva, Vandana. *Stolen Harvest: The Hijacking of the Global Food Supply.* Cambridge, MA: South End Press, 2000.

UC Cooperative Extension. *Community Supported Agriculture, Making the Connection.* Guidebook for farmers. $25 + $5 S/H. Available from UC Cooperative Extension, attn: CSA Handbook, 11477 E. Avenue, Auburn, CA 95603.

General

Alliance for Democracy opposes corporate globalization with campaigns against the General Agreement on Trade in Services (GATS), against corporatization of the United Nations, and for local alternatives. www.afd-online.org, Waltham, MA, (202)244-0561, rcaplan@igc.org or (617)266-8687, dlewit@igc.org.

Political Research Associates analyzes those organizations, leaders, ideas, and activities of the U.S. political right that undermine democracy and diversity. www.publiceye.org, 1310 Broadway, Suite 201, Somerville, MA 02144, (617)666-5300.

Tennessee Industrial Renewal Network is a forty-member coalition of labor, community, religious, environmental, and student groups working for fair trade and economic justice. 1515 E. Magnolia Avenue, Suite 408, Knoxville, TN 37917, (423)524-4424, tirn@igc.org.

Genetic Engineering

Council for Responsible Genetics monitors new genetic technologies in human genetics, commercial biotechnology and the environment. www.gene-watch.org, 5 Upland Road, Suite 3, Cambridge, MA 02140, (617)868-0870, crg@gene-watch.org.

GE Food Alert Campaign is seven organizations committed to testing and labeling genetically engineered food. www.gefoodalert.org, 3435 Wilshire Boulevard #380, Los Angeles, CA 90010, (213)251-3680, gefoodalert@emediacy.org.

NERAGE (New England Resistance Against Genetic Engineering) and other RAGEs combat genetic engineering, especially of food. www.bckweb.com/nerage/links.

See also Friends of the Earth and Greenpeace.

Global South movements

Focus on the South works with NGOs and people's organizations in Asia-Pacific and other regions. Its electronic bulletin *Focus-on-Trade* analyzes regional and world trade and finance. www.focusweb.org, c/o CU.S.RI, Wisit Prachuabmoh Building, Chulalongkorn University, Phayathai Road., Bangkok 10330, Thailand, 66-2-2187363-5, admin@focusweb.org.

Brazil's **Landless Workers Movement** is the largest social movement in Latin America and one of the most successful grassroots movements in the world. www.mstbrazil.org. Friends of the MST can be reached at Global Exchange, 2017 Mission Street #303, San Francisco, CA 94110, fmst-request@globalexchange.org (put "subscribe" in the body of the message).

Third World Network provides a platform for Southern interests in global meetings and institutions, books and magazines including *Third World Resurgence*. www.twnside.org.sg/twr.htm, 228 Macalister Road, 10400 Penang, Malaysia, 60-4- 2266728, twn@igc.apc.org.

Human Rights

Amnesty International campaigns worldwide for all the human rights in the Universal Declaration of Human Rights. Their ground-breaking collaboration with the *Sierra Club,* **Defending Those Who Give the Earth a Voice**, produced a campaign booklet entitled "Environmentalists Under Fire." www.amnesty.org, 322 8th Avenue, New York, NY 10001, (212)807-8400.

Derechos Human Rights is an Internet-based human rights organization with affiliates around the world, e-mailing lists, and an Internet human rights journal. www.derechos.org, P.O. Box 43299, Oakland, CA 94624-0299, (510)483-4005, hr@derechos.org.

Human Rights Watch investigates human rights violations, holds abusers accountable, and challenges governments to respect international human rights law. www.hrw.org, 350 Fifth Avenue 34th Floor, New York, NY 10118-3299, (212)290-4700, hrwnyc@hrw.org.

Peace Brigades International (PBI) offers unarmed protective accompaniment to people, organizations, and communities threatened with violence and human rights abuses. www.igc.apc.org/pbi/usa.html, 1904 Franklin Street Suite 505, Oakland, CA 94612, (510)663-2362, pbiusa@igc.org.

Immigration

BIOS, Border Information and Outreach Service, has a great list of border organizations and websites at http://www.irc-online.org/bios/internet/links_a.html#A. BIOS also publishes *Borderlines* with monthly in-depth analysis of one particular border issue in the U.S./Mexico relationship. (505)842-8288, borderlines@irc-online.org.

National Immigration Forum builds public support for policies that welcome immigrants and refugees to our country. www.immigrationforum.org, 220 I Street NE, Suite 220, Washington, D.C. 20002-4362, (202)544-0004.

National Network for Immigrant and Refugee Rights (NNIRR) works for a just immigration and refugee policy in the United States and defends the rights of all immigrants and refugees, regardless of immigration status. www.nnirr.org/nnirr, 310 8th Street Suite 307, Oakland, CA 94607, (510)465-1984.

See also American Friends Service Committee.

Information on Globalization

Bretton Woods Project's bimonthly *Update* critiques key IMF and World Bank initiatives. www.brettonwoodsproject.org.

Bank Information Center produces detailed, useful "Toolkits for Activists" which describe the structure, functions, policies, and procedures of the IMF, World Bank, and regional development banks. www.bicusa.org, 733 15th Street NW, Suite 1126, Washington, D.C. 20005, (202)737-7752, info@bicusa.org.

Center for Economic and Policy Research provides economic analysis and media work to back up global campaigns. www.cepr.net, (202)293-5380 x212, naiman@cepr.net.

Citizens' Guide to Trade, Environment and Sustainability explains how the world trade system works and how it affects us all. Covers free trade institutions and negotiations, case studies of trade disputes, social and environmental impacts of free trade, long-term changes and next steps. www.foei.org/activist_guide/tradeweb/.

Coalition for Global Solidarity and Social Development has a website with articles, reports, and documents about globalization, the IMF, WTO,

and World Bank, among other progressive issues. www.globalsolidarity.
npaid.org.

Global Trade Watch has the lowdown on NAFTA, the WTO, MAI, and
upcoming trade legislation. www.tradewatch.org, 215 Pennsylvania
Avenue SE, Washington, D.C. 20003, (202)546-4996,
Global Update-Seattle has a newswire on globalization updated daily by
readers. www.globalupdate.org

Institute for Policy Studies researches and publishes accessible informa-
tion on the global economy including the *Field Guide to the Global
Economy.* www.ips-dc.org, 733 15th Street NW, Suite 1020, Washington
D.C., 20005, (202)234-9382.

Interhemispheric Resource Center is a well organized, extensive web
resource for foreign policy information, with *Foreign Policy in Focus*, the
online "Progressive Response," and a "world in numbers" link with useful
statistical information. www.irc-online.org. *See also BIOS and Cross Border
Links under Immigration and Cross Border Organizing.*

International Forum on Globalization offers publications and conferences on globalization and the international financial institutions.
www.ifg.org, 1062 Fort Cronkhite, Sausalito, CA 94965, (415)229-9350,
ifg@ifg.org.

Mexico Solidarity Network has updates, urgent actions, links, and trips
to Chiapas and Mexico. www.mexicosolidarity.org, 4834 N. Springfield,
Chicago, IL 60625, (773)583-7728, msn@mexicosolidarity.org.

1WorldCommunication offers updates, documentaries, and resources
from resistance movements around the world. www.1worldcommunica-
tion.org, (413)323-7629.

Resource Center of the Americas has publications and workshops about
issues, movements, and protests throughout North, South, and Central
America. www.americas.org, 3019 Minnehaha Avenue S., Minneapolis,
MN 55406, (612)276-0788.

Transnational Action and Research Center (TRAC) is a very strong
research and campaign support project that publishes *Corporate Watch*,
designs campaigns, and maintains a website full of useful links to organization and information sources. www.corpwatch.org, trac@corpwatch.org.

Hundreds of U.S. organizations support unions, political movements, and human rights in specific countries. We can only list a few globally focused networks.

Alliance for Global Justice supports national protests and campaigns against the WTO, FTAA, IMF, World Bank, and other institutions of corporate globalization. (202)544-9355, 1247 E Street SE, Washington, D.C. 20003.

Center for Economic Justice strengthens international grassroots movements against corporate-driven globalization and promotes just alternatives via the World Bank Bonds Boycott (p. 000) and the South-North Exchange. www.econjustice.net, 144 Harvard Drive, SE, Albuquerque, NM 87106, (505)232-3100, info@econjustice.net.

50 Years Is Enough: U.S. Network for Global Economic Justice is a coalition dedicated to the profound transformation of the World Bank and the IMF. www.50years.org, 1247 E Street SE, Washington, D.C. 20003, (202)IMF-BANK, wb50years@igc.org.

Global Exchange offers focused campaigns, "Reality Tours" to the global South, and an excellent website with fact sheets, articles, and links to other organizations. www.globalexchange.org, (415)255-7296, 2017 Mission Street #303, San Francisco, CA 94110, (415)255-7296, info@globalexchange.org.

Hemispheric Social Alliance is a South-driven network of unions and grassroots groups whose "Alternatives for the Americas" lays out a people's alternative to the Free Trade Area of the Americas (FTAA). For their U.S. affiliate, the Alliance for Responsible Trade, contact www.art-us.org, (773)583-7728, msn@mexicosolidarity.org (Tom Hansen, Domestic Coordinator).

People's Global Action links worldwide resistance against global capitalism. www.nadir.org/nadir/initiativ/agp/en/, info@agp.org.

Witness for Peace is a nonviolent, faith-based organization supporting peace, justice, and sustainable economies in the Americas by changing U.S. policies and corporate practices. www.w4peace.org, 1229 15th Street NW, Washington, D.C. 20005, (202)588-1471, witness@witnessforpeace.org.

Labor Solidarity

Alliance for Sustainable Jobs and the Environment (ASJE) started with an alliance between northwest loggers and labor, and is seeking to expand. www.asje.org, 1125 SE Madison, Portland, OR 97214, (503)736-9777, asje@asje.org.

Jobs with Justice is a national campaign for workers' rights which helps connect labor and other forces in the globalization movement. 501 3rd Street NW, Washington, D.C. 20001-2797, (202)434-1106, jobswjustice@jwj.org.

Labor Notes is the voice of union activists who want to "put the movement back in the labor movement." Subscribe to their monthly magazine. www.labornotes.org, 7435 Michigan Avenue, Detroit, MI 48210, (313)842-6262, labornotes@labornotes.org.

United Farm Workers (UFW) represents workers who have a direct experience of globalization. www.ufw.org, P.O. Box 62, Keene, CA 93531.

United Steelworkers (USWA) is in the forefront of the union fight against free trade, and has allied with United Students Against Sweatshops. www.uswa.org, 5 Gateway Center, Pittsburgh, PA 15222, (412)562-2560.

U.S./LEAP works with U.S. religious, human rights, and trade union groups to support workers' rights in Central America. www.usleap.org, P.O. Box 268-290, Chicago, IL 60626, (773)262-6502.

See also Cross-Border Solidarity, Sweatshops

Listservs

50 Years Is Enough. Action alerts, news, and updates on the World Bank and IMF. subscribe50years@yahoo.com.

STOP-IMF. Open, moderated listserv (not a discussion group) which posts newsclips, reports, news releases, updates, urgent actions, and analyses on topics relating to the (IMF), structural adjustment, and Third World debt. Averages two messages a day. E-mail rob@essential.org and write "subscribe stop-imf" in the subject line.

Focus on Trade, the monthly electronic newsletter of Focus on the Global South, covers trade, finance, politics, and international relations from a

Southern perspective. For those interested in the South critique and campaigns on the IMF and the World Bank. admin@focusweb.org.

Focus on the Corporation distributes a weekly column by Russell Mokhiber, editor of *Corporate Crime Reporter*, and Robert Weissman, editor of *Multinational Monitor* magazine. Sharp-edged critique of corporate actions, plans, abuses, and trends. E-mail rob@essential.org and write "subscribe corp-focus" in the subject line.

GATS. "You say you're ill? I see a market!" The new frontier of corporate expansion is to turn human services into profit opportunities. This listserv tracks the WTO's ongoing negotiation of the General Agreement on Trade in Services (GATS). E-mail rcaplan@igc.org and indicate which you lists you want to join: General, Water, Education, Prisons, or Health.

More listservs. For a longer list, e-mail Neil Watkins neil@econjustice.net.

Media

Adbusters magazine is the flagship publication of the culture-jamming movement and the sponsor of Buy Nothing Day. http://adbusters.org, 1243 West 7th Avenue, Vancouver, BC V6H 1B7 Canada, (800)663-1243, adbusters@adbusters.org.

Citizens for Independent Public Broadcasting is a national membership organization working for independently funded, accountable, truly public system. It supports chapters with a training manual, video, and a national clearinghouse for organizing. www.cipbonline.org, 1029 Vermont Avenue NW, Suite 800, Washington, D.C. 20005, (202)638-6880, cipb@cais.com.

FAIR, Fairness and Accuracy in Media monitors media bias and censorship with its magazine, *Extra!*, its weekly radio program, Counterspin, Action Alerts to an international activist network, a Women's Desk and Racism Watch Desk. www.fair.org, 130 W. 25th Street, New York, NY 10001, (212)633-6700, fair@fair.org.

Independent Media Centers are a global democratic collective of independent media organizations and journalists offering grassroots, noncorporate coverage of protests and, increasingly, community organizing. www.indymedia.org, general@indymedia.org.

National Radio Project produces and distributes high quality public affairs and news programs (including its daily Live Wire Independent News and weekly "Making Contact") with diverse perspectives and opinions not typically heard in the mass media. www.radioproject.org, 1714 Franklin Street Suite 311, Oakland, CA 94612, (510)251-1332.

Organizing guides

Alinksy, Saul. *Rules for Radicals.* New York: Random House, 1971. The classic Industrial Areas Foundation (IAF) community organizing guide.

Ayvazian, Andrea. "Organizational Development: The Seven Deadly Sins." Peace Development Fund, P.O. Box 270, Amherst, MA 01004, 1986, 22 pp. Describes obstacles like founder's disease, burnout, and growth without a plan.

Bobo, Kimberly, Jacquelyn A. Kendall, and Steve Max. *Organizing for Social Change.* Santa Ana, CA: Seven Locks Press, 1990. The standard organizing text from the Midwest Academy. Basic principles of direct action organizing, choosing issues, developing strategies, and tactics, finding the right organizational model, designing actions, fundraising, building coalitions, recruiting volunteers, using computers, developing leaders, running meetings, using the media, working with community boards, working with religious groups, working with unions, and more.

Delgado, Gary. *Beyond the Politics of Place.* Oakland, CA: Applied Research Center, 1994. A critique of Alinsky-style community organizing with particular emphasis on organizing in communities of color.

Kahn, Si. *Organizing: A Guide for Grassroots Leaders.* New York: McGraw-Hill, 1982. General guide including how to get started, plan strategy, conduct meetings, research, train, communicate, and work with media. Also addresses issues of culture in organizing.

Rogers, Mary Beth. *Cold Anger.* Denton, TX: University of North Texas Press, 1990. The story of Ernesto Cortes and the IAF model of community organizing.

Staples, Lee. *Roots to Power.* Westport, CT: Praeger Publishers, 1984. Professional community organizing textbook with chapters on organizing philosophy and process, issues and strategy, developing and carrying out action plans, organization and leadership development, research, negotiations, media, and lobbying.

Sweeney, Megan. "Women Change the Face of Organizing." *The Neigh-*

borhood World. (February/March 1993): 3. Discusses women's style of cooperation, coalition-building, and inclusiveness.

T'Shaka, Oba. *The Art of Leadership*. Richmond, CA: Pan Afrikan Publishers, 1990. Volume I defines the leadership and organizing traditions of Africans and African-Americans, and describes ways to build organization. Volume II includes a major story of the Black Church, an explanation of FBI and CIA disruption tactics, and more. An appendix lists political education materials.

Williams, Eugene. "Talking with Myself." Regional Council of Neighborhood Organizations, 5600 City Avenue, Philadelphia, PA 19131-1395, 1992, 6 pp. Uses a question-and-answer format to critique deficiencies in white-dominated organizing training centers, particularly as they address issues of race and culture.

Peace
Asia-Pacific Center for Justice and Peace promotes economic justice, political freedom and genuine security, and links grassroots groups in Asia, the Pacific, and the United States www.apcjp.org, 110 Maryland Avenue NE, Suite 504, Washington, D.C. 20002, (202)543-1094, apcjp@igc.org.

Peace Action is a membership organization working to abolish nuclear weapons, redirect excessive Pentagon spending to domestic investment, end global weapon sales, and resolve international conflicts peacefully. www.peace-action.org, 1819 H Street NW, #420, Washington, D.C. 20006, (202)862-9740.

SOA Watch seeks to close the U.S. Army's School of the Americas and end the training of human rights abusers funded by U.S. tax dollars. For information or their new video, contact www.soaw.org, P.O. Box 4566, Washington, D.C. 20017, (202)234-3440, soawatch@knight-hub.com.

See also American Friends Service Committee, Institute for Policy Studies (U.S. bases).

Popular Education
Alternative Women in Development/New York brings a feminist analysis, incorporating gender, race, and class, to workshops about women in the global North and South. It is networking with women and women's groups who advocate a similar analysis. Carol Barton, Alt-WID/NY, 12 Dongan Place #206, New York, NY 10040, (212)304-9106, cbarton@igc.org or elmira Nazombe, 160 Ryders Lane, New Brunswick NJ 08901, (732)932-1180, elmira@rci.rutgers.edu.

American Friends Service Committee conducts economic literacy and popular education work in several cities and states. AFSC's Praxis Project, 59 E. Van Buren Street, Suite 1400, Chicago, IL 60605, (312)427-2533, praxisafsc.igc.org.

Cantera—Popular Education and Communication Center, www.oneworld.org/cantera/education/index.html.

Catalyst Centre for Popular Education, www.catalystcentre.ca/ orginfo.htm.

Center for Popular Economics demystifies economics, provides alternatives to mainstream and conservative analyses, and leads annual week-long Summer Institutes on the U.S. and international economies. www.ctr-popec.org, P.O. Box 785, Amherst, MA 01004, (413)545-0743, thm@econs.umass.edu.

ELAN, the Economic Literacy Action Network, includes several of these popular education groups and publishes the *Unpacking Globalization Tool Kit* with samples of several groups' workshops. $24 + shipping from Highlander Center.

Global Source provides global programs, curricula, lesson plans and consultations for K–12 educators. For a complete online catalog sorted by age appropriateness, contact www.GlobalSourceNetwork.org, P.O. Box 30094, Seattle, WA 98103, (206)781-8060, info@GlobalSourceNetwork.org.

Highlander Research and Education Center supports economic justice and democracy groups in the Southeast. It develops and shares popular education and participatory research ideas and materials. www.hrec.org, 1959 Highlander Way, New Market, TN 37820, (865)933-3443, swilliams@highlandercenter.org.

Project South: Institute for the Elimination of Poverty & Genocide develops popular political and economic education and action research to understand and transform our society. www.peacenet.org/projectsouth/, 9 Gammon Avenue SW, Atlanta, GA 30315, (404)622-0602.

United for a Fair Economy trains volunteers to lead workshops workshops like The Growing Divide (between the rich and the rest of us), Globalization for Beginners, Challenging Corporate Rule, and The Racial Wealth Divide. UFE also supports a national trainers' network and develops creative actions like Billionaires for Bush or Gore (www.billion-airesforbushorgore.org). www.ufenet.org, 37 Temple Place, Boston, MA 02111, (617)423-2148, info@ufenet.org.

Women of Color Resource Center has produced *Women's Education in the Global Economy* (WEdGE), an interactive workbook for community-based, educational, and workers organizations ($25). www.coloredgirls.org , (510)848-9272, 2288 Fulton Street, Suite 203, Berkeley, CA 94704, chisme@igc.org.

See also Resource Center of the Americas.

Prison activism

Prison Activist Resource Center (PARC) has information, resources, and books about the prison industrial complex. www.prisonactivist.org, P.O. Box 339, Berkeley, CA 94701, (510)893-4648.

Prison Moratorium Project's (No) Punishment for Profit and Not With Our Money! campaigns work with students and labor against private prisons. www.nomoreprisons.org, PMP c/o DSA, 180 Varick Street 12th Floor, New York, NY 10014, (646)486-6715.

Critical Resistance has campaign information, contacts for national conferences, resources, and links to other organizations. www.criticalresistance.org, 1212 Broadway, Suite 1400, Oakland, CA 94612, (510)444-0484, critresist@aol.com.

Religious

Jubilee is a global movement for the cancellation of poor countries' international debt. The Jubilee USA Network is at www.j2000usa.org, (202)783-3566, 222 East Capitol Street NE, Washington, D.C. 20003-1036, coord@J2000U.S.A.org and Jubilee South is at http://jubileesouth.net, lidy@fdc.org.hp or donna@aidc.org.za.

NETWORK is a national Catholic social justice lobby. www.igc.org/network, 801 Pennsylvania Avenue SE, Suite 460, Washington, D.C. 20003, (202)547-5556, network@networklobby.org.

Quixote Center is a faith-based, social justice center working with people in Haiti, Nicaragua, and the United States who have few resources for their struggles. www.quixote.org, P.O. Box 5206, Hyattsville, MD 20782, (301)699-0042, quixote@quixote.org.

Unitarian Universalists for a Just Economic Community works on local and regional initiatives for systemic economic change. 110 Arlington Street, Boston, MA 02116, (617)542-0634, uujec@uujec.org.

Reproductive Rights

Planned Parenthood's International Program works for reproductive choice in U.S. policy worldwide. www.plannedparenthood.org, 810 Seventh Avenue, New York, NY 10019, (212)541-7800, communications@ppfa.org.

Population Action International supports voluntary family planning and other reproductive health services via U.S. policy and by working with organizations in developed and developing countries. www.populationaction.org, 1300 19th Street NW, 2nd Floor, Washington, D.C. 20036, (202)557-3400, pai@popact.org.

Sweatshops

Campaign for Labor Rights mobilizes grassroots activists to end sweatshop abuses and child labor in the United States and abroad. Its **Labor Defense Network** responds rapidly and effectively when workers are repressed. www.summersault.com/~agj/clr/, 1247 E Street SE, Washington, D.C. 20003.

The Clean Clothes Campaign is applying community values to the global economy. www.bairnet.org/organizations/pica, 170 Park Street, Bangor ME 04401, (207)947-4203. info@pica.ws.

International Labor Rights Fund helps protect global workers' rights with campaigns like Rugmark and Foul Ball. www.laborrights.org, 733 15th Street NW, Suite 920, Washington, D.C. 20005, (202)347-4100, laborrights@igc.org.

National Labor Committee exposes sweatshops in the media and supports the antisweatshop movement with campaigns, videos, other materials, and research. www.nlcnet.org, 275 7th Avenue, 15th Floor, New York, NY 10001, (212)242-3002.

National Mobilization Against Sweatshops is fighting for the forty-hour workweek and eight-hour day, and fundamentally transforming the sweatshop system for all. www.nmass.org, P.O. Box 130293, New York, NY 10013-0995, (718)633-9757, nmass@yahoo.com.

Responsible Shopping Guide and ways to make your city a Fair Trade

Zone, plus links to websites for more information. Global Exchange, www.globalexchange.org/ftzone, (415)255-7296.

STITCH is a network of women labor organizers and activists who directly support women's efforts to organize in Central America through training exchanges between U.S. and Central American organizers, through delegations, and through a documentation project that collects women's testimonies about their experiences organizing in Central America. The first testimonies appear in *Women Behind the Labels* ($5 from STITCH c/o Hannah Frisch, hf52@aol.com). www.afgj.org/stitch, 4933 S. Dorchester, Chicago, IL 60615, (773)924-5057.

UNITE, the U.S. garment workers' union, is supporting high school and college antisweatshop campaigns and legislation to ensure that city workers' uniforms are made in union shops instead of sweatshops. www.uniteunion.org/sweatshops, 1710 Broadway, New York, NY 10019, (212)265-7000.

U.S. Dept. of Labor No Sweat Program's web page has "Garment Enforcement Reports" which show contractors with violations of the Fair Labor Standards Act and list manufacturers they are known to have done business with. www.dol.gov/dol/esa/public/nosweat/nosweat.htm.

United Students Against Sweatshops (USAS) coordinates anti-sweat groups on two hundred U.S. campuses and supports the Worker Rights Consortium. www.usas.org, 1413 K Street NW, 9th Floor, Washington, D.C. 20005, (202)NO-SWEAT.

Worker Rights Consortium supports and verifies compliance with anti-sweat codes of conduct developed by colleges and universities across the country. www.workersrights.org, c/o Lafayette Avenue Presbyterian Church, 85 South Oxford Street, Brooklyn, NY 11217, (202)778-6354, wrc@workersrights.org.

Also see Coalition for Justice in the Maquiladoras.

For background info on immigration, sweatshops, U.S. labor, and how they are affected by globalization go to www.sweatshopwatch.org. This page has numerous links to other sites.

Videos
This is What Democracy Looks Like, 2000, 70 minutes. Captures the raw

energy of the WTO protests and the launching of a movement. Big Noise Films, P.O. Box 842, Cambridge, MA 02238, (617)515-4249, www.big-noisefilms.com.

It's Our Water, Damn It!, 2000, 35 minutes. Extraordinary footage of the fight against the privatization of the water in Cochabamba, Bolivia. 1 World Communication, (413)323-7629, www.1worldcommunication.org.

The following videos can all be borrowed from the American Friends Service Committee for a small donation, plus shipping. www.afsc.org/nero/bigcat/globecon.htm, 2161 Mass. Avenue, Cambridge, MA 02140, (617)497-5273, pshannon@afsc.org.

Showdown in Seattle: 5 Days that Shook the WTO, 2000, 60 minutes. Lively and well edited, especially strong on the issues that brought thousands of people to Seattle.

Global Village or Global Pillage? 1999, 27 minutes. An overview of the global economy and the possibilities for changing it, focusing on "the race to the bottom," with success stories.

Deadly Embrace: Nicaragua, the World Bank, and the IMF, 1999, 30 minutes. Structural adjustment and Washington's war on Nicaragua. Powerful; humanizes globalization.

Banking on Life and Debt, 1995, 28 minutes. How the lending practices of the World Bank and the IMF have contributed to poverty in developing countries like Brazil, Ghana, and the Philippines.

Coffee: The People Behind Our Everyday Cup, 1993, 40 mins. How our drinking habits drive the lives of Central American coffee workers.

Ties that Bind: Stories Behind the Immigration Controversy, 1996, 56 minutes. NAFTA and multinational corporations, U.S. immigration policy and the reality of crossing the border illegally, and how immigrants built the United States.

Arms for the Poor, 1998, 25 minutes. How the U.S. military industrial complex impoverishes and represses the developing world at taxpayers' expense.

Women

Center of Concern's International Gender and Trade Network uses research, advocacy, and economic literacy to promote equitable, social, and sustainable trade. www.genderandtrade.net, 1225 Otis Street NE, Washington, D.C. 20017, (202) 635-2757 x135, secretariat@coc.org.

East Asia-U.S. Women's Network Against Militarism opposes military violence against women, the environment, and society. 353 30th Street, San Francisco, CA 94131, (415)550-7947, gwyn@igc.org.

International Gender and Trade Network coordinates research and economic literacy among seven regional networks of gender advocates. www.genderandtrade.net or for weekly electronic updates, e-mail secretariat@coc.org and ask to be added to the "genderandtrade" listserv.

WEDO, Women's Environmental and Development Organization, seeks social, political, economic, and environmental justice for all through the empowerment of women. www.wedo.org, 355 Lexington Avenue, 3rd Floor, New York, NY 10017, (212)973-0325, wedo@igc.org.

Women's International League for Peace and Freedom is a grassroots advocate for women's empowerment worldwide. 1213 Race Street, Philadelphia, PA 19107-1691, (215)563-7110, wilpf@wilpf.org.

Women's EDGE is an advocacy coalition protecting human rights and promoting equality for women in the global economy. www.womensedge.org, 1825 Connecticut Avenue NW, Suite 800, Washington, D.C. 20009, (202)884-8396, info@womensedge.org.

See also Popular Education

Youth

180 Movement for Democracy in Education uses radical education and organizing to to transform our schools and communities into truly democratic spaces. www.corporations.org/democracy/, 731 State Street, Madison, WI 53703, (608)262-9036, clearinghouse@tao.ca.

JustAct—Youth ACTion for Global JUSTice works to develop in young people a life-long commitment to social and economic justice around the world. Its educational projects enable young people to critically analyze their lived social reality and its network links students and youth to grassroots movements working for equitable, sustainable, and self-reliant communities, locally and globally. www.justact.org, 333 Valencia Street Suite 101, San Francisco, CA 94103, (415)431-4204, colin@justact.org.

Sierra Student Coalition is a student-run network which trains activists and organizes national campaigns. www.ssc.org, P.O. Box 2402, Providence, RI 02906, (888)JOIN-SSC, ssc-info@ssc.org.

Student Alliance to Reform Corporations (STARC) challenges corporate power and works for democratic accountability. www.corpreform.org.

Student Environmental Action Coalition (SEAC) aims to uproot environmental injustices locally and globally. www.seac.org, (215)222-4711, ncc@seac.org.

Also see United Students Against Sweatshops

Glossary

Alternatives—Economic policies that benefit wide segments of the population rather than only corporations and stockholders. An example would be trade policies that contribute to workers' rights and protect the environment while simultaneously addressing nations' economic concerns.

Alternatives for the Americas—The name of a document written by citizens' organizations from dozens of countries in the Western hemisphere. It is part of an international grassroots effort to influence or derail the Free Trade Area of the Americas negotiations currently being held with little popular input.

Bretton Woods—The site, in New Hampshire, of the discussions which led to the creation of the World Bank, the International Monetary Fund (IMF), and the GATT.

Cross-Border Organizing—Efforts by workers and communities from different countries to work together to achieve common objectives.

Debt (see *Third World Debt*)

Dumping—Selling products abroad at prices below the cost of production in the home country. Exporters who do this seek to gain market share by wiping out their competitors.

Fair Trade—A movement that values environmental protection, higher standards of living for workers, and human rights. Fair trade also refers to goods produced under decent working conditions for fair wages, using methods that are not harmful to the environment.

Fast Track—Legislation that can limit each chamber of Congress to twenty hours of debate on a trade agreement, force a vote within sixty days, and ban amendments, thus choking off democratic input.

Foreign Direct Investment—Investment that results in a physical presence in a foreign country, for example, when a company builds a production facility in another country or has a stake in a business or natural resource overseas.

Free Trade or Liberalized Trade—Cross-border trade without tariffs or other government regulations on imports including health and environmental policies (see *Trade Barriers*). Supporters claim that free trade brings consumers low-cost goods, that local producers become more competitive, and that new jobs are created when foreign companies move in. Critics say free trade forces local producers out of business when they can't compete with transnational corporations. Cheap grains also force family farmers off their land and undermine food security. Furthermore, free trade creates pressure on local governments to lower environmental, labor and other regulatory standards in order to attract and keep foreign investment.

FTAA (Free Trade Area of the Americas)—A free trade agreement under negotiation since 1994 by North and South American governments, as well as those of Central America and the Caribbean. It would be like NAFTA for the entire Western hemisphere with the exception of Cuba. Proponents hope it will be ratified by 2005. Citizens' organizations from many countries are trying to influence the negotiations, but do not receive the access to negotiations that corporations receive. (see *NAFTA* and *Alternatives for the Americas*.)

GATT (General Agreement on Tariffs and Trade)—An international agreement and organization founded in 1948 to regulate trade across national borders. The GATT has been renegotiated through eight different rounds. Trade liberalization through the reduction of tariffs and nontariff "barriers to trade," such as agricultural subsidies and government regulations, has been its primary objective. Should countries fail to abide by the terms of GATT, sanctions may be applied by other member countries. The 1994 GATT negotiations—known as the Uruguay Round because they took place in the South American country of Uruguay—replaced the GATT with the WTO (World Trade Organization). (see *Free Trade* and *WTO*.)

Globalization—The name for an ongoing process in which trade, investment, people, and information travel across international borders faster and more easily. Globalization leads to greater worldwide instability since problems afflicting one country carry over to other countries, and corporations and capital investments are highly mobile, leaving a nation whenever they find better opportunities elsewhere.

Globalization as it is now happening is characterized by: production wherever it's the cheapest, trade with few barriers, and short-term investment wherever the return is highest. Current globalization is fueled by deregulation and advances in transportation and communication technology. While supporters say it will raise living standards around the world, globalization has created large-scale environmental damage, shifted power from people to corporations, and lowered living standards for many First and Third world residents.

Harmonize—To make consistent the trade standards used by all countries, in order to ease and accelerate the flow of trade. In practice, harmonization has meant lowering regulatory standards to those of the least restrictive countries.

IMF (International Monetary Fund)—The IMF was founded following the conclusion of the Second World War to stabilize currency exchange rates, and thus promote international trade. In the 1970s the IMF started providing loans to Third World nations and required them to carry out *structural adustment programs.* (see also *Neoliberalism* and *World Bank.*)

Intellectual Property Rights—Patents and copyrights. Many people favor intellectual property rights because they protect the rights of inventors to control the distribution of their discoveries. Others, including farmers and people in traditional societies, are concerned because corporations have been granted the exclusive rights to seeds, plants, and genetic codes depended upon for subsistence. In trade negotiations, the U.S. government has pushed countries to protect copyright and patent rights for much longer than the current laws in most countries. This makes it much more difficult for poor countries to authorize local production of generic medicines, like AIDS drugs in South Africa.

Investment—In the global economy, investment refers to direct investment in plants or services, indirect investment in stocks and bonds, real estate, and speculation. Investors are individuals, governments, and corporations who lend money to other individuals, governments, and corporations in the expectation of turning a profit. Although there are millions of small investors, a few very rich and powerful individuals and investment firms maintain significant control over the global economy.

MAI (Multilateral Agreement on Investment)—A trade and investment treaty negotiated in secret since 1995 at the OECD that would have extended the investor rights measures of the GATT/WTO. Among other things, the MAI would allow foreign corporations to sue governments. It would have made taxpayers pay for when environmental, labor, public health, and consumer protection laws limited corporate profits. The MAI was defeated by a grassroots campaign in 1998, but portions are in NAFTA and will likely reappear in other treaties including the FTAA.

Multilateral, Bilateral, and Unilateral—In theory, the WTO fosters negotiations among all of its members (multilaterally). In reality, many decisions are still made bilaterally (between two parties), principally between the United States and the European Union (EU). And the United States tends to impose trade sanctions on its own (unilaterally), although doing so is illegal under GATT.

NAFTA (North American Free Trade Agreement)—A trade agreement between the United States, Mexico, and Canada that removes tariffs on goods and services, deregulates investment, reduces travel restrictions for entrepreneurs and white-collar workers, and protects intellectual property rights. It passed Congress in 1993 despite opposition by unions, environmental groups, and farmers in all three countries. NAFTA has devastated U.S. manufacturing jobs and farmers and the environment in Mexico. It has not increased wages or working standards in any of the countries which are part of it. Its negative effects have been felt disproportionately by rural workers, women, the U.S. textile industry, and small farmers. NAFTA is seen as being a model of how free trade can work around the world and its investment chapter served as a blueprint for the MAI.

National Treatment—Global corporations and investors would like to see all businesses treated on equal terms because it would allow them to enter local markets, undercut local companies, employ cheaper labor, and avoid environmental regulation. Many new trade agreements say that governments may not favor local companies in any way. This could outlaw preferences for local, minority-owned, or women-owned businesses. Governments might not be able to build up their own local economies using taxpayer money. National treatment might outlaw campaigns like the antiapartheid movement in which states and cities refused to buy products from South Africa or invest in companies doing business there.

Neoliberalism—An economic ideology that calls for free markets and a minimal role for the government in the economy. In the United States, Reaganomics was a good example of neoliberalism. Free trade, privatization, cuts in social spending, antiunionism, and structural adjustment are all neoliberal policies.

NGOs (Non-Governmental Organizations)—Nonprofit organizations.

OECD (Organization for Economic Cooperation & Development)—Based in Paris, France, the OECD is an organization composed of the governments of twenty-nine advanced economies in North America, Europe, and the Pacific region. While the OECD primarily collects economic data and performs analyses, recently it negotiated the MAI, which would have been the organization's first success at developing enforceable binding rules for the global economy. (see *MAI*.)

Performance Requirements—Rules that a host government establishes on the performance of foreign investment to ensure that such investment benefits the local economy. A host government could require a foreign company to hire local people in management positions, to transfer technology, or to reinvest some profits in the local community. Performance requirements are prohibited under NAFTA.

Privatization—The sale of publicly owned goods and services to private companies.

Structural Adjustment—Economic policies based on neoliberal economics and strongly encouraged by the U.S. Treasury, IMF, and World Bank. Structural Adjustment Programs (SAPs) have resulted in protests, even riots, as a result of the social and economic hardship they have produced in many poor countries. SAPs create the type of fiscal climate and financial system transnational corporations prefer. They instruct governments to privatize, export more, spend less, deregulate, and reduce the government's role in the economy. In the United States, welfare reform and other policy changes made in the 1980s and 1990s have been likened to structural adjustment. Reaganomics was based on the same ideas as SAPs.

Takings (or expropriations)—Takings used to mean government seizure and nationalization of private property. However, in the context of the global economy, the meaning of takings has been expanded to include regulations and laws that cut into investor profits by requiring certain environmental, health and safety, labor, and other standards.

Third World Debt—The money many African, Asian, and Latin American countries owe to international financial institutions and private commercial banks forces them to implement policies that are ecologically and socially destructive. Third World countries became indebted in the 1970s as oil prices skyrocketed and exports lost value in relation to imports. In the early 1980s, interest rates quadrupled, making the debt unpayable. To keep from going bankrupt, countries had to accept *structural adjustment programs.* Between 1982 and 1990, Third World countries received $927 billion in aid, loans, grants, investment, and trade credits. At the same time, these countries were paying back $1.3 trillion in interest and principal. By 1990, Third World countries were sixty-one percent deeper in debt than before they started receiving large-scale assistance. A global grassroots campaign called Jubilee is calling for total cancellation of the poor countries' debt.

Trade—The movement of goods and services across national borders. Trade used to mean real goods like shoes. Now it covers services like consulting and financial services, or capital (money) that moves across borders for long-term investment like building a factory, short-term investment like buying stocks, or speclation in currency or stock futures. In the late 1990s, annual trade in real goods was $5 trillion, but the annual capital flows were $728 trillion—and about ninety percent of that was speculation.

Trade Barriers—For the last fifty years, trade negotiators have been trying to lower trade barriers—take away the taxes and restrictions that limit global trade. Most of that time was spent lowering trade barriers on real goods like shirts and shoes moving across borders. Now, however, more and more agreements are about services and capital flows (money), not real goods.

A trade barrier is anything that slows down the flow of real goods, services, or money across borders.

Tariffs are taxes on goods that cross borders. Because they increase the price of real goods like shirts or shoes, they cut down or slow down trade in those goods.

Quotas are limits on the amount of real goods coming into a country. The garment industry or unions might lobby for a shirt quota of two hundred thousand shirts a year to protect U.S. shirtmakers and jobs.

As trade agreements start covering areas like services and investment, they are attacking more nontariff barriers like:

Social standards like environmental regulations and labor laws to stop pollution or exploitation.

Process restrictions—rules about how products were made, like bans on products made with child labor, or tuna caught with nets that kill dolphins. Recent trade agreements say purchasers cannot discriminate between goods by how they were made, only how well they work.

Local content rules. A state government could say, "We're only going to buy cars made with at least fifty percent U.S. labor." Or "We're going to give preference to locally owned suppliers, or minority-owned or women-owned businesses."

Investment rules that say foreign investors can only buy a certain percentage of a local company (usually less than half).

Speed bumps that slow down money crossing borders. A government could say, "If you want to invest in our economy you have to keep your money here for six months." That limits fast-buck speculation, gives a country more control over its economy, and makes the global economy more stable.

Transnational Corporation (TNC)—Like multinational corporations, TNCs are corporations that operate in more than one country. Of the world's one hundred largest economies, fifty-one are transnational corporations and forty-nine are nations. TNCs are growing in size and number.

TRIPs—Trade-Related Intellectual Property Rights. The agreement under which intellectual property rights were brought into the GATT/WTO during the Uruguay Round.

U.S. Treasury—Though its official objective is to manage the finances of the U.S. government, the Treasury Department wields enormous influence over the global economy. It has a seventeen percent vote in the World Bank and IMF, which gives it veto power over their decisions. During the Asian financial crisis, then Deputy Treasury Secretary Lawrence Summers dictated the terms of the loan package which opened up South Korea to foreign ownership.

World Bank—Created in 1944 to rebuild Europe after World War II, the World Bank today funds development projects around the world. Forty percent of its loan portfolio is in oil and coal projects, effectively subsidizing the world's richest corporations as they perpetuate fossil fuel use and global warming. The Bank's own reports show that it is destroying forests and failing to decrease poverty. The World Bank Bond Boycott seeks to cut off the eighty percent of its funds which the Bank gets by selling bonds on the open market.

WTO (World Trade Organization)—The WTO was formed during the 1994 GATT negotiations. Its main purposes are to promote free trade and settle trade disputes. WTO member countries must make their national, state, and local laws conform with WTO rules, or face sanctions. In the WTO, decisions are reached behind closed doors and corporations have access that citizens do not enjoy.

Many thanks to the Tennessee Industrial Renewal Network and Dollars and Sense *magazine who wrote the original versions of this Glossary.*

Index

Note: *Italicized* page numbers refer to glossary terms.,

A

activism
  class diversity in, 150-151
  hip hop and, 67-68
  prison, 65-66, 67-69
  racial diversity in, 80-91, 96-97
  seeking diversity in, 86-100, 121-122
  shareholder, 28-30
  street theater, 152, 155-157
  student, 121-122, 191-198
  youth, 67-69
adjustment, structural, *313-314*
advocacy, development, resources on, 288
affinity groups, 166-168
  in Seattle WTO protest, 135-137
AFL-CIO. see also labor unions
  Central America and, 200, 201
  immigrants and, 60
agriculture. *see* farmers/farming
air pollution, monitoring, 37-40
alliances. *see* coalitions
Alternatives for the Americas, 309
Anglo. see whites
antiapartheid movement, 9, 234-239

antiracism, 90-91, 142-144. *see also* white supremacy, combating
  resources on, 284
  workshop, 98-100
antisweatshop movement, 189-190
arrests, preparing for, 278-279
Asia, women in, 42-44

B

The Bangor Clean Clothes Campaign, 209-217, 239
BC (Boise Cascade), protest against, 26-32
"bilateral," *312*
Billionaires for Bush (or Gore), 156-161
blacks, in activism, 145-149, 151. *see also* civil rights movement; diversity, in activism; whites
Boise Cascade, protest against, 26-32
borders. *see* cross-border organizing
Bretton Woods, *309*
Bucket Brigades, South Africa and, 37-42

C

campaigns, 4, 167
contributions to, 182-183, 185